Great Debates on
Convention on Human Rights

Palgrave Great Debates in Law

Series Editor
Jonathan Herring Professor of Law, University of Oxford

Company Law
Lorraine Talbot

Contract Law
Jonathan Morgan

Criminal Law
Jonathan Herring

Employment Law
Simon Honeyball

Equity and Trusts
Alastair Hudson

Family Law
Jonathan Herring, Rebecca Probert & Stephen Gilmore

Gender and Law
Rosemary Auchmuty (ed.)

Jurisprudence
Nicholas J McBride & Sandy Steel

Medical Law and Ethics
Imogen Goold & Jonathan Herring

Land Law
David Cowan, Lorna Fox O'Mahony & Neil Cobb

The European Convention on Human Rights
Fiona de Londras & Kanstantsin Dzehtsiarou

Palgrave Great Debates in Law

Great Debates on the European Convention on Human Rights

Fiona de Londras
Professor of Global Legal Studies,
University of Birmingham

Kanstantsin Dzehtsiarou
Senior Lecturer in Law,
University of Liverpool

First published 2018 by
PALGRAVE

Palgrave in the UK is an imprint of Macmillan Publishers Limited, registered in England, company number 785998, of 4 Crinan Street, London N1 9XW.

Palgrave® and Macmillan® are registered trademarks in the United States, the United Kingdom, Europe and other countries.

ISBN 978–1–137–60731–7

This book is printed on paper suitable for recycling and made from fully managed and sustained forest sources. Logging, pulping and manufacturing processes are expected to conform to the environmental regulations of the country of origin.

A catalogue record for this book is available from the British Library.

A catalog record for this book is available from the Library of Congress.

CONTENTS

PREFACE AND ACKNOWLEDGEMENTS

The European Convention on Human Rights (ECHR or Convention) is widely hailed as the most successful regional human rights instrument. The decisions of its European Court of Human Rights (ECtHR or Court) are cited all around the world, and every year tens of thousands of people turn to that very Court for relief and aid when they consider their human rights have been violated. In each of the 47 Contracting Parties to the Convention, the ECHR has an everyday impact, shaping law and public policy, being argued in domestic courts, and sometimes even becoming the locus for impassioned political and public debate on how the Convention works (or does not), and what rights it protects (or does not).

Law schools all over Europe feature courses on the Convention, at both undergraduate and postgraduate levels, as indeed do schools of political science, international relations and others. Much of the instruction on the Convention, at least in law schools, focuses on the case law of the Convention and approaches it on an article-by-article basis. This grounding in the Convention, the jurisprudence of the Court, and the emerging contestations around whether the Convention properly protects the rights of marginalised groups and those who might be said to be particularly vulnerable is a vital foundation for understanding the Convention. However, the law relating to the ECHR is voluminous, and in many courses there is limited space to do more than concentrate on a number of particular Articles, some of the most well-known case law and some topics of particular contention (such as LGBTQI rights, states of emergency and freedom of the press, for example).

Once an explorer of the ECHR has this grounding, a thematic approach to thinking, teaching and learning about the Convention becomes possible, and that is what we aim to facilitate with this book. Whilst there is, of course, a concentration at certain points on how the case law relating to a particular Article illustrates the debate we are considering, we do not purport to provide here a comprehensive account of the Convention, its case law, or the law and operation of any of its Articles. Instead, we aim to illuminate some debates by taking a wide lens on the ECHR, reaching across Articles to illustrate some points of contention, reaching across the tramlines between the national and international arenas for others, and reaching into the 'back' of the ECtHR—its organisation, working practices and Registry—for others still.

Through doing this we hope to spark debates and discussions, building on the solid grounding in the Convention that emerges from the necessary study of particular rights and lines of jurisprudence, and thereby to spark a deep and critical engagement with the Convention, the Court, and the European system for human rights protection.

We are indebted to Mima Markicevic and Magdalena Furgalska for research assistance and, in the latter case, for reading and commenting on the whole manuscript from a student's perspective.

We would like to thank Professor Jonathan Herring, Aléta Bezuidenhout and our anonymous readers from Palgrave.

ABBREVIATIONS

CDDH	Steering Committee for Human Rights	IMF	International Monetary Fund
CEDAW	UN Convention on the Elimination of all Forms of Discrimination Against Women	KFOR	NATO Kosovo Force
		LGBTQI	Lesbian, Gay, Bisexual, Transgender, Questioning and Intersex
CEO	Chief Executive Officer	NATO	North Atlantic Treaty Organization
ECB	European Central Bank		
ECHR	European Convention on Human Rights (Convention for the Protection of Human Rights and Fundamental Freedoms)	NGO	Nongovernmental Organisation
		PACE	Parliamentary Assembly of the Council of Europe
		SFIR	Stabilisation Force in Iraq
ECJ	European Court of Justice	TEU	Treaty on European Union
ECtHR	European Court of Human Rights	TRNC	Turkish Republic of Northern Cyprus
EU	European Union	UK	United Kingdom
HIV	Human Immunodeficiency Virus	UN	United Nations
		UN HRC	United Nations Human Rights Committee
ICRC	International Committee of the Red Cross	UNMIK	United Nations Mission in Kosovo
IHL	International Humanitarian Law	US	United States of America
ILC	International Law Commission	USSR	Union of Soviet Socialist Republics
ILO	International Labour Organisation	WTO	World Trade Organization

TABLE OF CASES

TABLE OF LEGISLATION

Introduction

When it was established, the European Convention on Human Rights (ECHR or Convention) was a pioneering document. It instituted a structure for the adjudication of rights claims that was genuinely ground-breaking. At the time, in the 1950s, Europe was a very different place to what it is now: it was a divided continent, ravaged by war and economically unstable, so concluding the Convention was no mean feat. This is all the more notable when one takes account of references in the Preamble to common values and heritage of the European states that were original signatories.[1]

These common values and heritage underpin the rights protected in the Convention, which can be broadly described as *primarily* civil and political, and divisible into absolute rights (no derogation, limitation or exception possible), qualified rights and limited rights. The rights themselves are found both in the core Convention document (i.e. the document as originally introduced) and in the protocols. Some protocols were introduced for reasons of institutional and procedural reform; others to introduce additional rights. All of them form part of the constant process of evolution of the Convention, its institutions, and its system of rights protection.

When originally introduced, the Convention outlined a set of rights to be applied across the Contracting Parties and by which those Contracting Parties would be held to account with, primarily vis-à-vis one another through inter-state claims. The number of Contracting Parties was small, and whilst there were some legal systemic differences between them (e.g. common vs. civil law, codified vs. uncodified constitutions, dualist vs. monist systems) there were also important commonalities such as commitment to the Rule of Law, democratic governance, judicial oversight of government activity, and rights protection at either legal or political levels in the domestic system. Whilst individual petitions (i.e. complaints against states by individuals) were contemplated, the mechanism by which they would take place was optional (i.e. states could opt in

---

[1] These were 'political traditions, ideals, freedoms and the rule of law'.

and accept the right of individual petition, and some did[2]) and the European Court of Human Rights (ECtHR or Court) as we know it now did not exist. Even acceptance of the jurisdiction of the Court was not mandatory, meaning that Contracting Parties could sign the Convention but not be supervised by the Court.[3] Indeed, the Court did not become permanent until 1998;[4] before then, adjudication was split between the Commission and the Court (not sitting permanently).

The Court becoming permanent was temporally aligned with significant changes in Europe: the Cold War was over, and Eastern Europe was undertaking a period of transition and transformation, including democratisation. By then the European Union had also changed significantly: there were 15 member states with plenty more waiting in the wings, the Union had developed a jurisprudence of fundamental rights protection as general constitutional principles of the European Union (EU),[5] talk of introducing an EU constitution was rife, and the courts of the Council of Europe (ECtHR) and the EU (Court of Justice) had developed a mutual recognition in terms of rights protection between the two legal systems upon which they adjudicated.[6]

These developments are significant for understanding the debates that we will canvas and consider throughout this book. They gave rise to a host of challenges: the number of people protected by the Convention expanded enormously to almost 800 million individuals, many of whom lived in states where there were multiple and systemic difficulties with rights protection not least because they were in the midst of post-Soviet transition. All of these people could have recourse to Strasbourg, and the workload – and backlog – increased enormously as a result. Furthermore, the common legal tradition and heritage mentioned in the Preamble to the Convention was no longer self-evident among the states – finding a common heritage between, for example, Ireland, Norway, Russia, Greece, Azerbaijan and Turkey is hardly a simple matter, and,

---

[2] Individual petition was accepted by Ireland, Denmark and Sweden whilst Belgium, France, Germany, Iceland, Italy, Luxembourg, the Netherlands, Norway, Turkey and the United Kingdom opted out: Bates, *The Evolution of the European Convention on Human Rights: From Its Inception to the Creation of a Permanent Court of Human Rights* (Oxford University Press, 2010), 101.

[3] The Court's jurisdiction was accepted by Ireland and Denmark, but rejected by Belgium, France, Germany, Iceland, Italy, Luxembourg, the Netherlands, Norway, Turkey, Sweden, and the United Kingdom: Ibid.

[4] Protocol 11, Article 19, ECHR.

[5] Case 26/62 *Van Gend en Loos v Nederlanse Administratie der Belastinge* [1963] ECR 1; Case 6/64 *Costa v Ente Nazionale Energia Elettrica (ENEL)* [1964] ECR 585; Case 11/70 *Internationale Handelgesellshaft mbH v Einfuhr- und Vorratsstelle für Getreide und Futtermittel* [1970] ECR 1125; Case 106/77 *Italian Minister of Finance v Simmenthal* [1978] ECR 629.

[6] *Bosphorus Hava Yolları Turizm ve Ticaret Anonim Şirketi v Ireland* [GC], no. 45036/98, ECHR 2005-VI; Costello, 'The Bosphorus Ruling of the European Court of Human Rights: Fundamental Rights and Blurred Boundaries in Europe' (2006) 6 *Human Rights Law Review* 87.

as will become clear throughout this book, it raises real challenges for the Court in achieving the difficult task of (a) developing a common minimum standard for rights protection, and (b) recognising diversity across the Council of Europe.

Throughout this book, we will consider the ways in which the Court and the Convention are challenged, and are successful (or not) in achieving these key tasks and aspirations which we take to be the key functions of the Convention, and thus a function of the Court that enforces it. The analysis will be framed primarily through the theory of 'legitimacy', which we understand as being capable of analysis by reference to consent, the moral purpose of human rights, methods of adjudication, subsidiarity and effectiveness.

CHAPTER 1

The Convention, the Court, and the Heart of the Matter

Throughout this book, we will consider specific debates about the European Convention on Human Rights (the Convention or ECHR), the rights it protects, and the ways in which states might be said to justifiably or legally infringe, or otherwise limit, those rights. All of these specific debates, however, connect with a larger question: *is the Convention legitimate?* This question is deceptively complicated, not least because of the complexity of legitimacy as an analytical category. That is what we start with in this chapter, which in turn acts as a gateway into key frameworks, concepts and actors that will help the reader to engage with the debates we outline in the chapters that follow. Having considered the different frameworks for understanding legitimacy vis-à-vis the ECHR and European Court of Human Rights (the Court or ECtHR), we go on to outline the institutional framework of the ECHR, including the judiciary and the Registry.

I. WHAT IS LEGITIMACY?

A good place to start with legitimacy is to understand it as being separable into four broad categories: input legitimacy, output legitimacy, outcome legitimacy and perceived legitimacy.

In simple terms *input legitimacy* relates to the processes by which decisions are made. In the context of the Convention and its enforcement this includes matters such as the mechanisms for the appointment of key actors (such as judges), the independence enjoyed by those actors, procedural regularity in the workings of the Court, mechanisms and processes of textual change (such as the agreement of new Protocols), and the like. *Output legitimacy*, on the other hand, relates to the quality of the outputs of the process itself, which, in this context, means the judgments of the Court. In that respect, any legitimacy analysis must look at both the methodological rigour and the quality of the reasoning employed. In this respect we can usefully consider not only whether justice was done in the particular case in question but also whether the case develops, applies or reinforces a right in a way that is sensible and effective for

1

the Convention system and rights enjoyment generally, and not only for the parties to the particular case in question. *Outcome legitimacy* is considered by reference to the outcome of the Convention and case law per se – what are the *outcomes* of the Convention's application in real terms? In other words, is the Convention *effective* by reference to both the Convention per se and the judgments of the Court enforcing and implementing that Convention? Does it lead to the rights violations identified by the Court being resolved, and to rights protection *generally* being improved across the Council of Europe member states?

Finally, *perceived legitimacy* is relevant – what are the perceptions of the stakeholders such as Contracting Parties or public at large? In this respect, the accuracy of those perceptions is not relevant. Rather, perceived legitimacy is an important analytical framework because an institution that starts with a legitimacy deficit (because, for example, it is not a democratic institution or because it is 'foreign') is likely to make decisions as to the extent to which it will exercise its powers (e.g. be innovative, evolve the Convention standards, wade into sensitive areas with enormous rights implications but which are politically sensitive, etc.) by reference to its understanding of its perceived legitimacy. In other words, perceptions of legitimacy are likely to impact on the Court's willingness to flex its muscles (or not to do so), especially in sensitive contexts. In terms of perceived legitimacy, the Court requires 'diffuse support', meaning support for the institution itself, even if a state disagrees with some of the decisions that it makes. Where a court enjoys diffuse support, stakeholders will perceive it as a credible decision maker whose decisions should attract compliance even when individual judgments might be subject to some criticism. That in turn requires them to see it as legitimate.

Sources of Legitimacy

The ECHR is an international treaty that is designed to impact, shape and restrict what states can do in respect of the people who are within their jurisdiction.[1] In other words, it has the capacity to reach into what was conventionally thought to be the most sovereign of spaces – the *domestic sphere* – and attempt to shape what happens there. Whilst that may seem to be a fairly standard feature of human rights law today (and it is), it was truly remarkable in the late 1940s and early 1950s when the Convention was introduced. Remember that the Universal Declaration on Human Rights was only adopted in 1948, and that core instruments of international human rights law such as the International Covenant on Civil and Political Rights and the International Covenant on Economic, Social and Cultural Rights were not introduced until 1966.

Thus, at the time of its coming into force, the ECHR was purporting to do something truly extraordinary: to make individuals the subjects of international

---

[1] Article 1, ECHR.

law, to shape the state's domestic activities, and to have a system of international adjudication to make states accountable should they fail to adhere domestically to the principles they had signed up to internationally. Given this context, and given the fact that many claims of *illegitimacy* that are currently made against the Court and Convention and which will be discussed throughout this book are thinly disguised claims of unjustified interference in the domestic sphere, the question of the source of the Convention's legitimacy is an important one. Here we canvass six possible sources that will be returned to – implicitly and explicitly – in the debates and discussions considered in this book.

a. Consent as a basis for legitimacy

As with all international treaties, one of the core sources for the legitimacy of the ECHR is the consent of states. International law is largely built on this core assumption that (a) all states can, and (b) all states do consent to the international rules to which they are bound. Of course, we now know that in many ways this 'consent' trope is a myth: for example, if a state wants to be a member of the European Union it must uphold human rights standards, which ordinarily means that it needs to ratify the ECHR. If that state is economically weak, politically unstable and democratically fragile it may well consider that it *needs* to join the European Union so much that it will simply do what the regulations require of it, including becoming a signatory to the ECHR. Here we might question the extent to which the state has truly *consented* the Convention, rather than being *coerced* into joining it. But from the perspective of orthodox international law this is somewhat irrelevant. It is assumed that all states enjoy sovereign equality; therefore, all states *consent* to be bound by the treaties to which they sign up, including the ECHR.

There are at least two reasons why consent alone is an inadequate account of how and why the Convention and its system enjoy legitimacy. The first relates to the costs of withdrawing consent. Denouncing the Convention and leaving the Council of Europe brings with it serious damage to reputation, which many states would not want to suffer, and some states might not be able to bear. In these circumstances a state may consider it less damaging to simply ignore an adverse judgment of the ECtHR, or half-heartedly engage in quasi-implementation, or routinely fall below the Convention standards for as long as possible than to actually leave the Convention. Thus, whilst consent is the most basic ground of legitimacy and may well keep the system together in formalistic terms, it is unable to ensure the effectiveness of the Convention system on its own.

The second reason why consent is an inadequate basis for legitimacy on its own is the distance between what a state might originally have consented to and what the Convention now means, largely through the innovations of the Court in its judgments. In order to keep the ECHR up to date, practical and effective, the ECtHR uses techniques such as evolutive interpretation (discussed in Chapter 4) to develop – some might say 'invent' – the meaning of the Convention, sometimes in directions that the signatories would never have envisaged at the time they originally consented to the Convention. Whilst one might argue that states consented both to the Convention 'as text' and the Convention 'as applied' by the Court, it is clear that it is some states' perception that the Convention now is drastically different in meaning, reach and intention than the Convention they signed up to. Accordingly, this calls into question how far 'consent' takes us as a source of legitimacy in respect of the Convention and, perhaps especially, of the Court.

b. Moral purpose as a basis for legitimacy

Most would agree that the protection and promotion of human rights is, in and of itself, a desirable or morally admirable 'end' so that actions done in pursuit of that enjoy at least a presumption of legitimacy. Recall the context in which the Convention was introduced: drafted, agreed upon and ratified in the immediate aftermath of a war that had 'shocked the conscience of mankind' and ravaged the continent of Europe, this new human rights regime was intended and designed to protect against the future emergence of any analogous forms of totalitarianism, barbarism and state-inflicted cruelty. Seen in this light, there is an argument that the protection of human rights through application of the Convention gives the Court and the Convention a certain moral purpose, character or nature.[2] The special purpose of human rights, and the commitment to their universal and equal protection, seen in this light, might be said to legitimate the Court's interference with decisions taken by sovereign states. Indeed, in many cases the Court has referred to the Convention's particular, rights-protecting character as underpinning its decision to take an evolutive, or otherwise, innovative approach to the development of Convention law.[3] Certainly, there are indications of such a view in the Preamble to the Convention itself, which states that fundamental freedoms are the foundation of justice and peace in the world. Of course, this is not to say that the mechanism by which the Convention protects human rights is necessarily either the morally preferable one or, even, morally defensible.

As will become clear throughout this book, there are issues about which there is profound moral disagreement across the Council of Europe, and which raise questions of the content and applicability of rights.[4] Abortion is, perhaps, an obvious example,[5] but so too are the putative right of people to marry a person of the same sex,[6] the use of assisted reproductive

---

[2] Letsas, *A Theory of Interpretation of the European Convention on Human Rights* (Oxford University Press, 2007).

[3] See, for example, *Soering v the United Kingdom*, 7 July 1989, Series A no. 161, para. 87.

[4] Waldron, *Law and Disagreement* (Oxford University Press, 1999).

[5] See, for example, *A, B and C v Ireland* [GC], no. 25579/05, ECHR 2010; *Vo v France* [GC], no. 53924/00, ECHR 2004-VIII; *Tysiąc v Poland*, no. 5410/03, ECHR 2007-I.

[6] See, for example, *Chapin and Charpentier v France*, no. 40183/07, ECHR 194; *Oliari and Others v Italy*, nos 18766/11 and 36030/11, 21 July 2015; *Schalk and Kopf v Austria*, no. 30141/04, ECHR 2010.

technologies,[7] the right to choose the time and means of one's death[8] and so on. These are questions where there are both deeply held but contrasting moral positions, and on which human rights law does not necessarily offer a simple, single, clear 'answer'. When the Court, then, is asked to adjudicate upon them – as it is, from time to time – it must tread through murky waters and make decisions which, for many, may be deeply immoral or perhaps even amoral. In such cases there are strong arguments for saying that the Convention and the Court have no prima facie morality-related legitimacy in asserting, applying and promoting a human rights position; instead, for many, such questions are ones on which democratically elected and accountable politicians ought to make *policy*, and translate that policy into law.

Quite apart from these cases in which there is no agreed moral position – or notion of what is 'right' or 'wrong' – there are further question marks about the extent to which the Convention and the Court enjoy some form of morality-based legitimacy. The Court primarily protects so-called civil and political rights, and pays remarkably little attention to socio-economic, cultural and group rights. Thus, whilst the Convention protects, for example, the right to a fair trial, to freedom of expression, and to a private life, it does not explicitly protect a right to health, a right to food, a right to an adequate standard of living or a right to be free from poverty. It does not expressly recognise group and cultural rights, and it is constructed on a decidedly individualistic basis. One might question whether such a charter can really protect human rights in a way that not only prevents the state from engaging in cruelty of various forms, but also in a way that enables people to truly flourish.[9] We will see in Chapter 7 that some of these apparent substantive shortcomings have been mitigated through both the jurisprudence of the Court and the development of the European Social Charter, but still one might argue that the ECHR simply reinforces socio-economic inequalities – or at least does nothing positively to address them – and thus approaches human rights within a problematic, unequal and statist paradigm. As a result, one might justifiably question whether the Convention's approach to rights protection really does endow it with sufficient moral purpose from which to derive legitimacy.

There are further accusations of exclusion or inadequacy that might be levied against the Convention. For example, there is a compelling argument to be made that the Convention, and its interpretation and application by the ECtHR, fail adequately to address the needs and rights of historically

---

[7] See, for example, *Parrillo v Italy* [GC], no. 46470/11, 27 August 2015; *Costa and Pavan v Italy*, no. 54270/10, 28 August 2012; *Evans v the United Kingdom* [GC], no. 6339/05, ECHR 2007-I.

[8] See, for example, *Koch v Germany*, no. 497/09, 19 July 2012; *Haas v Switzerland*, no. 31322/07, ECHR 2011; *Pretty v the United Kingdom*, no. 2346/02, ECHR 2002-III.

[9] See, for example, Egan, Thornton and Walsh, *The European Convention on Human Rights: A Socio-Economic Rights Charter?* (Bloomsbury, 2014); Baderin and McCorquodale, *Economic, Social, and Cultural Rights in Action* (Oxford University Press, 2007), 241–256.

marginalised and subjugated groups such as women, the Roma, disabled people and religious minorities.[10] If this is the case, one might argue that the ECHR cannot necessarily draw on the claim of moral purpose to legitimate its overall operation.

Thus, whilst the moral purpose of rights protection provides some basis for a claim of legitimacy on the part of the Convention and its application by the Court, there are sufficient question marks about the morality of the Court's positions, and the inadequacy or incompleteness of the Convention system, for this to be an insufficient source of legitimacy in itself.

c. Method as a basis for legitimacy
We have already noted that input legitimacy relates to the processes by which decisions are made, so that the methods by which the ECtHR comes to its decisions might also be a source of legitimacy for the Convention (as interpreted and applied by the Court) and for the Court itself. In this account, even an outcome on which there is, for example, profound moral disagreement might gain legitimacy from the process through which it has been reached. Thus, for the ECtHR ensuring consistency, coherence, legal certainty and predictability is key to making a claim for legitimacy based on the method of decision making that is used. This is not particular to the Strasbourg Court. Indeed, ensuring that there is a clear and well-reasoned basis for the decision reached by a Court, and ensuring consistency from one case to another, as well as applying a system of precedent (particularly in a common law system) are seen as elemental to judicial claims of legitimacy.[11]

Of course, the Court is not formally bound by any strict system or expectation of 'precedent' so to speak,[12] but it does tend to refer to its previous judgments in its case law, and it will depart from its existing position only in exceptional cases. Thus, even without a formal system of precedent, an informal

---

[10] See, for example, Anagnostou and Millns, 'Individuals from Minority and Marginalized Groups before the Strasbourg Court: Legal Norms and State Responses from a Comparative Perspective' (2010) 16 *European Public Law* 393; Martínez Guillem, 'European Identity: Across Which Lines? Defining Europe Through Public Discourses on the Roma' (2011) 4 *Journal of International and Intercultural Communication* 23; Peroni and Timmer, 'Vulnerable Groups: The Promise of an Emerging Concept in European Human Rights Convention Law' (2013) 11 *International Journal of Constitutional Law* 1056; Harvey, 'Protecting the Marginalised: The Role of European Convention on Human Rights' (2000) 51 *Northern Ireland Legal Quarterly* 445.

[11] These are the basic requirements of the procedural legitimacy. See Gribnau, 'Legitimacy of the Judiciary' (2002) 6 *Electronic Journal of Comparative Law,* Dzehtsiarou, 'Does Consensus Matter? Legitimacy of European Consensus in the Case Law of the European Court of Human Rights' (2011) *Public Law* 534, 539.

[12] In *Micallef v Malta* the Court stated that '[w]hile it is in the interests of legal certainty, foreseeability and equality before the law that the Court should not depart, without good reason, from precedents laid down in previous cases, a failure by the Court to maintain a dynamic and evolutive approach would risk rendering it a bar to reform or improvement' *Micallef v Malta* [GC], no. 17056/06, ECHR 2009, para. 81.

expectation that the ECtHR will follow its past jurisprudence operates. Indeed, as further discussed below, one of the ways in which a case can make its way to the Grand Chamber of the Court is where it does, or where it might, introduce an inconsistency or incoherence in the jurisprudence of the Court. Consistency and coherence in its case law is, then, something to which the Court gives close attention.

The method and quality of reasoning are also important to claims of input legitimacy in the ECtHR, just as for other courts. Thus, the Court provides the reasons for its decisions in a case, and, in doing so, tends to refer not only to its past judgments but also to the judgments of other courts and tribunals, to relevant reports, to states' practice, and, sometimes, to scholarly work.[13] Of course, like most courts, it is occasionally criticised for the quality of its judgments, just as it is sometimes praised, but it is worth noting that the sheer workload facing the Court almost certainly creates significant challenges in ensuring that a high quality of reasoning is expressed in writing for every case that is decided before the Court. The Court's resources are extremely limited: its budget (which covers all non-capital costs from judicial salaries to the Registry) for 2017, for example, was €71 million;[14] by contrast the budget for the US federal judiciary in 2015 was almost $7 billion.[15] This gives some indication of how stretched the resources in the Court are, and, thus, how limited the support for judgment writing must be in terms of both time (for judges and Registry lawyers) and research support, so that the crucial administrative task of finding an appropriate balance between the quality of reasoning and speed of operations is a difficult one indeed.

Furthermore, the Court has developed, and applies, particular approaches to reasoning in its case law, which have the effect (and potentially also the intention) of enhancing the legitimacy of its operations, its interpretation and application of the Convention, and the legitimacy of the entire ECHR system of rights protection. These techniques – such as European consensus, the margin of appreciation, and extensive use of comparative law – are important ways in which the Court not only shows that it reasons its decisions carefully and rigorously, and takes states' national dynamics into some account, but also that it is willing to exercise self-restraint, and that its decisions can be benchmarked against those of other courts. We return to these questions of method in Chapters 4 and 5.

Transparency is another feature of judicial method that can enhance the input legitimacy of a court. Unlike democratically elected institutions, courts are not accountable to the public, or at least not inasmuch as they can be voted out of office, for example. In many ways this is to ensure the independence and

---

[13] The examples are multiple. For analysis, see Dzehtsiarou, 'What Is Law For the European Court of Human Rights?' (2018) *Georgetown Journal of International Law* (forthcoming).
[14] ECHR Budget, available at http://www.echr.coe.int/Documents/Budget_ENG.pdf.
[15] Annual Report. Budget, available at http://www.uscourts.gov/statistics-reports/fundingbudget-annual-report-2015.

impartiality of judges. This lack of accountability can be compensated for by transparency in the adjudicatory process. Although deliberations of the judges are held behind closed doors, the hearings, when held, are open. In almost all cases the procedure is written; oral hearings are only organised for cases that are being heard in the Grand Chamber and a very small number of Chamber cases. The hearings are webcast on the Court's website. Almost all documents submitted by the parties and third parties are accessible by the public. Only internal judicial documents are confidential.

d. Subsidiarity as a basis for legitimacy

The ECtHR is a subsidiary international court. This means that disputes about compliance with the Convention should first be dealt with in national courts, and only come to Strasbourg once domestic remedies have been exhausted (we return to this in Chapter 3). This is an important principle in the Convention: the Court is not an appellate court and it is not a substitute for national legal systems. Furthermore, its subsidiary character is a key driver behind the Court recognising that Contracting Parties may enjoy some variation in their practices, and to decide some matters of policy not clearly regulated by the Convention for themselves provided minimum standards of rights protection are complied with (we discuss this further in Chapter 5). Adhering to its character as a subsidiary court is an important source of the Court's, and thus the Convention's, legitimacy. Indeed, so important is this that Protocol 15 will add explicit mentions of subsidiarity and the margin of appreciation to the Preamble when it comes into effect.

Of course, the principle of subsidiarity can be used to underpin claims that the Court should leave states to do as they wish; that it should apply less scrutiny to states' human rights protection than it sometimes does. This same concern has been expressed by the former President of the ECtHR, Dean Spielmann, who said, 'I sometimes detect, a sense that subsidiarity is code for something else, for less scrutiny from Strasbourg. That it means taking the "self" out of judicial self-restraint.'[16] This points to the concern of some that states' expectations of 'subsidiarity' might be that the Court would simply 'stay out' of sensitive domestic matters; a position that is, of course, quite at odds with the basic idea of the Court applying the Convention, and the Convention being an effective protection of individual rights. This indicates some of the difficulties with pointing to subsidiarity as a source of legitimacy: it means different things, and creates different expectations, in different stakeholders.

Subsidiarity can be both procedural and substantive. Procedurally, we know that subsidiarity means the Court can only consider a case once domestic remedies have been exhausted. This rule, contained in Article 35 and considered in Chapter 3, means that the national institutions have the opportunity to resolve a Convention incompatibility without the need for international supervision,

---

16 Spielmann, 'Whither Judicial Dialogue?', available at http://www.echr.coe.int/Documents/Speech_20151012_Spielmann_Sir_Thomas_More_Lecture.pdf, 10.

and that the Convention is applied domestically and thus becomes embedded in domestic law through practice. Controversy sometimes arises when the Court allows an applicant to bypass this rule because it establishes that there are no effective remedies to protect the applicant's rights in the domestic system.[17] This exception cannot undermine the fact that as a rule admissibility gives effect to procedural expectations of subsidiarity.

Understood as a substantive concept, subsidiarity might be said to mean that the Court should not only follow the national system in procedural and chronological terms but also take into account the substance and process of decisions made on the national level in reaching its own judgment. Although this does not mean that the Court must blindly follow the national decision makers, what it does likely mean is that the Court is expected to recognise national decision makers as having a high level of knowledge of the domestic situation, law, politics and risks and, thus, to grant at least some deference to those national decisions. Indeed, as we will see in Chapter 5 in particular, that is frequently the case.

e. Effectiveness as a basis for legitimacy

We have already mentioned that output legitimacy is considered by reference to the outcome of the Convention and case law per se, i.e. it concerns whether or not the Convention actually 'works'. Where a system and instrument are effective, this adds to their legitimacy, particularly among stakeholders who might be highly reliant on the institution and system in question. Thus, effectiveness is a key indicator and source of legitimacy for the Convention and its system of enforcement.[18] However, in order to understand whether something is effective we have to know what its purposes and objectives are and, in relation to the Convention, this is something about which there is some disagreement. For some, the Convention exists now for the same reasons as it existed when it was first introduced: to act as a 'beacon to those at the moment in totalitarian darkness [...] [to] give them a hope of return to freedom'.[19] On this reading, the Convention is a safeguard in the most extreme of circumstances and not, necessarily, a set of human rights standards that can and do reach into every part of the state's domestic and, sometimes, overseas activities. However, that vision of the Convention's purpose reflects a limited and, arguably, outmoded concept of what human rights instruments are and are

---

[17] See, for example, *O'Keeffe v Ireland* [GC], no. 35810/09, ECHR 2014. For discussion on exhaustion of domestic remedies in this case see O'Mahony, 'Subsidiarity of ECHR in O'Keeffe v. Ireland: A Response to Hardiman', *Constitutional Project @ UCC*, 5 September 2014, available at http://constitutionproject.ie/?p=353.

[18] Dothan, *Reputation and Judicial Tactics: A Theory of National and International Courts* (Cambridge University Press, 2015).

[19] Speech of Sir David Maxwell-Fyfe on the occasion of signing the European Convention on Human Rights, 4 November 1950. As quoted in Bates, *The Evolution of the European Convention on Human Rights: From Its Inception to the Creation of a Permanent Court of Human Rights* (Oxford University Press, 2010), 5.

for. It also recognises only a certain kind of systemic oppression as needing or justifying the intervention of international standards.

We might say that there are still people in Europe who live in a kind of totalitarian darkness, for whom the Convention truly is a beacon of light: LGBTQI people in parts of the Continent who are routinely persecuted for as much as daring to hold hands in the street; Roma who are not permitted to educate their children in a culturally appropriate manner; Muslim women who are criminalised for their decision to dress in what they consider to be religiously appropriate ways; asylum seekers who are held in sub-standard detention centres; victims of trafficking and sexual exploitation; women for whom exercising reproductive autonomy is a criminal offence; suspected terrorists who are detained, questioned and deported without trial. Our continent of Europe is rife with smaller and larger instances of oppression, abuse, detention and rights violation. For many the ECHR is not only a pathway to justice but, in fact, their only hope of it.

Seen this way, effectiveness is not only about ensuring that there is no widespread totalitarianism in Europe, but also that people can and do rely on the Convention (in domestic law, in their everyday interactions with the state, and ultimately in litigation in Strasbourg) to help them to challenge and, ultimately, repress these forms of abusive state power. Whether or not the Convention, and its application by the ECtHR, 'works' is both in the eye of the beholder and a key source of perceived legitimacy.

II. How Does the Court Operate?

Establishment of the ECtHR in Strasbourg was a revolutionary event in international law, which changed the dynamic and the relations between individuals and states. Never before could individuals bring a complaint to an international body and demand that state authorities provide justifications for interfering with their human rights. This presented both opportunities and challenges to the Court. When states agreed to the jurisdiction of the Court, it was clear that they were consenting to some external judicial oversight with a resultant reduction in their right to simply rebut any criticisms of their treatment of their own people with claims of 'sovereignty', but the extent to which the Court would develop its jurisprudence, and the reach of the Convention into states' internal affairs, could not have been predicted. The ECtHR has become an incredibly important judicial institution, not only for the Council of Europe's member states, but also internationally, and its judgments have major repercussions in domestic law and politics quite beyond what appears to have been contemplated at the time of its establishment.[20] Now, quite contrary to what might

---

[20] Keller and Stone Sweet, *A Europe of Rights: The Impact of the ECHR on National Legal Systems* (Oxford University Press, 2008); Motoc and Ziemele, *The Impact of the ECHR on Democratic Change in Central and Eastern Europe: Judicial Perspectives* (Cambridge University Press, 2016).

have been expected,[21] the Court is permanent, inter-state cases are very rare, and individual complaints are plentiful. There is a sense among some member states that what they signed up for and what the Court has become are vastly different propositions. As we will see throughout the book, this is arguably the crux of some of the major tensions between, for example, the UK and the Court. But how did this state of affairs come about? And how does the ECtHR actually work?

History and Development of the Convention

As first designed, the ECHR system comprised three main organs supervising compliance with the ECHR in Strasbourg. First, there was the European Commission of Human Rights. When an applicant wanted to lodge a complaint he or she would first submit it to the Commission, which would consider it and lodge it before the Court only if it deemed it to be well-founded. It outlined its reasons for these decisions in written opinions. Where that happened, the case would be considered by the ECtHR, which was not a permanent body but met a number of times a year in Strasbourg. Just as now, the judgments of the Court were legally binding on the respondent party or parties to the case. The third institution was the Committee of Ministers, made up of representatives of each of the member states of the Council of Europe. The Committee of Ministers had some competence to resolve cases politically, but its main role was to supervise the implementation of decisions of the ECtHR.[22]

- *Protocols 11 and 14*

Throughout its history, the Strasbourg system of human rights protection has been reformed many times. Significant reforms are done through the adoption of Protocols, which can be substantive or procedural. Substantive protocols add human rights (for example, Protocol 1 added the right to private property (Article 1), the right to education (Article 2) and the right to free elections (Article 3) into the Convention) or substantive guarantees (for example, Protocol 6 prohibited the death penalty). Procedural protocols amend the structure and the working methods of the Court. In institutional terms, what was probably the most fundamental reform of the Convention was brought about by Protocol 11, which came into force in 1998. It created the Strasbourg

---

[21] Lord McNair: 'it is tolerable that her Majesty's Government, having signed and ratified the European Convention of 1950, should adopt the attitude that our laws and our administration of justice are so perfect and so superior to those of our fellow signatories that it is unnecessary for the machinery of the Convention to apply to the United Kingdom' as quoted in Bates, *The Evolution of the European Convention on Human Rights* (above, n. 19), 186. See also Schabas, *The European Convention on Human Rights: A Commentary* (Oxford University Press, 2015).

[22] Protocol 11, Article 46, ECHR.

system of human rights protection as we know it today, and was introduced in response to the dramatic geopolitical changes in Europe and the expansion in members of the Council of Europe.

The key change introduced in Protocol 11 was abolition of the Commission. This meant that applicants could bring their complaints directly to the Court, rather than going through this 'filtering' system. Accordingly, the Court became a permanent institution[23] with full-time judges.[24] The right of individual petition and the jurisdiction of the Court became mandatory, meaning that, from that point on, all states ratifying the Convention had to accept the jurisdiction of the ECtHR, and all those within the jurisdiction of those states could make individual petitions to it. Jurisdiction of the Court and the right of individual petition had to be specifically agreed to by the states before Protocol 11 came into force.

Following on from this institutional reform and the expansion of the membership of the Council of Europe, the number of individual petitions to the Court sky-rocketed. By 2011–2012 there were more than 150,000 pending applications to the Court,[25] and, in 2013, 65,900[26] new applications were lodged. The Court was suffocating under this workload. For some, the Court was simply a victim of its own success; since its establishment it had become well known to people across Europe and was seen as the route to justice by people whose domestic legal system had, in their view, failed them.[27] Others were of the opinion that the number of pending applications reflected the failure of Contracting Parties to give proper effect to the Convention and the Court's judgments in their domestic legal systems, particularly given the high number of repetitive (or 'clone') cases coming before the Court.[28] These were cases relating to a question of legal interpretation that had already been established in the Court's jurisprudence, but either the state in question had failed to resolve the issue, or other Contracting Parties had not adjusted their legal systems to take account of the Convention principles laid down in judgments of the Court in respect of which they were not respondents.

---

[23] Ibid., Article 19.

[24] Ibid., Article 21(3).

[25] 'The ECHR in Facts and Figures' (2011), available at http://www.echr.coe.int/Documents/Facts_Figures_2011_ENG.pdf.

[26] 'The ECHR in Facts and Figures' (2013), available at http://www.echr.coe.int/Documents/Facts_Figures_2013_ENG.pdf.

[27] See, for example, Leach, *Taking a Case to the European Court of Human Rights* (3rd edn, Oxford University Press, 2011), and Buyse and Hamilton (eds), *Transitional Jurisprudence and the ECHR: Justice, Politics and Rights* (Cambridge University Press, 2011).

[28] See, for example, de Londras, 'Dual Functionality and the Persistent Frailty of the European Court of Human Rights' [2013] *European Human Rights Law Review* 38, and Dzehtsiarou and Greene, 'Restructuring the European Court of Human Rights: Preserving the Right of Individual Petition and Promoting Constitutionalism' [2013] *Public Law* 710.

Whatever the cause (and failure to give effect to the Convention in domestic law is something we return to in Chapter 2), all of this meant that the Court was in crisis: it simply did not have the capacity to deal with this volume of applications. The response was Protocol 14, which was opened for ratification in 2004. This allowed for procedural changes, including single-judge adjudication[29] for the speedy rejection of clearly inadmissible applications.[30] The drafters of this Protocol asked the Contracting Parties to ratify it urgently; the system was creaking under the pressure of huge numbers of cases and needed reform. However, it required ratification by all Contracting Parties before it could come into effect, and Russia, in particular, dragged its heels.[31] Indeed, the final ratification (from Russia) did not come until 2010, at which point Protocol 14 came into force.

The changes introduced in 2010 were far less radical than had been brought about by Protocol 11. It allowed single judges to reject clearly inadmissible applications, where before that required a committee of three judges.[32] Three-judge committees were then given a new competence to decide on repetitive or 'clone cases' on the basis of well-established case law.[33] Overall, then, Protocol 14 was primarily concerned with streamlining, whereas Protocol 11 had effectively retooled the entire Strasbourg machinery.

- *The Rules of Court*

Although Protocols are the means of treaty change within the Convention system, they are not the only way in which the working methods of the Strasbourg institutions can be reformed. Often the Court itself spearheads important reforms through changing its working methods and, particularly, its Rules of Court. The Rules of Court lay down the procedural workings of the Court and are not ratified by the Contracting Parties. Whilst the fact that these Rules come from the Court itself might be said to endow them with somewhat less legitimacy than the Convention and its Protocols, they have a considerable advantage over formal Treaty change because they can be both flexibly applied and speedily amended. They can also assist the Court in developing and applying methods for the prompt handling of cases and, indeed, the reduction of the Court's backlog. Stricter or looser application of the Rules can reduce or increase the number of pending applications, as illustrated by the working of Rule 47.

---

[29] Protocol 14, Article 26, ECHR.
[30] Ibid., Article 12.
[31] See, for example, Bowring, 'Russia and Human Rights: Incompatible Opposites?' (2009) 1 *Gottingen Journal of International Law* 257.
[32] Protocol 14, Article 27, ECHR.
[33] Ibid., Article 28.

This Rule simply lays down the format in which an application to the Court is to be made and makes clear what pieces of information must be included. However, for a very long time the Rule was not strictly applied, so that applications which did not conform with Rule 47 were still registered with the Court. Since 2014 this has changed. Now the Court has begun to apply this Rule more rigorously and has stopped registering applications that do not comply with it.[34] This has had a dramatic effect on a number of applications registered by the Court. Non-registration very often means that the Court will never have to deal with that application again as the applicant often cannot resend the application in the correct format within the time limit of six months. Although one cannot prove an exact link between the strict application of Rule 47 and the number of registered applications to the Court, the statistics do show a temporal correlation between the two. In 2013 65,800 applications were registered with the Court. In 2014 it was 56,200 (a reduction of 15 per cent) and in 2015 it was 40,650.

Reform of working methods, as well as decisions about the strategic direction of the Court, are carried out within the Court's own internal structures: the Plenary Court, the Bureau, and the Presidency. The Plenary Court consists of all current Judges of the Court. It elects the President and other senior judges from its membership.[35] It also elects the Registrar and Deputy Registrar of the Court,[36] and adopts the Rules of Court and other significant changes in the Court's procedure. The Bureau consists of the most senior Judges of the Court[37] and seems to be one of the most important institutions of the Court, determining its everyday administration. According to the Rules of Court, the President directs the work and administration of the Court. The President also represents the Court and is responsible for its relations with the authorities of the Council of Europe. These internal structures play a vital role in the operation of the Court and the conduct of its judges. For example, voted on by the Plenary Court, the Resolution on Judicial Ethics allows the President to determine its application in individual cases, and he or she can consult the Bureau.

Changes in institutional form and working methods have certainly helped the Court to tackle its backlog. From a high of 99,900 in 2013, it has been reduced to 64,850 in 2015. However, further reform seems to still be required. For this, Protocol 15 has been drafted and opened for ratification. Whilst not yet in force at the time of writing, it receives detailed attention in Chapter 3.

---

[34] See, for example, Wagner, 'Don't Mess Up Your European Court of Human Rights Application … A New Rule' (*UK Human Rights Law*, 11 Dec. 2013), available at https://ukhumanrightsblog.com/2013/12/11/dont-mess-up-your-european-court-of-human-rights-application-a-new-rule, and Buyse, 'Stricter Rules for Lodging Complaints at the European Court' (*ECHR Blog*, 12 Dec. 2013), available at http://echrblog.blogspot.co.uk/2013/12/stricter-rules-for-lodging-complaints.html.
[35] Rule 8, 'Rules of Court', ECHR.
[36] Ibid., Rules 15–16.
[37] Ibid., Rule 9A.

Structure and Procedure

The judiciary of the ECtHR comprises 47 judges (one from each Contracting Party) who are resident in Strasbourg and work full-time in the Court. As a consequence of Protocol 14, the Court can sit in four different formations: single judge, Committees of three judges, Chambers of seven judges, and a Grand Chamber of 17 judges. The formation of the Court that considers an application depends largely on (a) whether it is admissible and how complex the admissibility decision is, and (b) the complexity of the merits of the case. The admissibility decision is essentially a question of whether the case complies with a formal set of criteria established by the Convention. Some of these are quite technical (for example, every applicant should be a 'victim' of the alleged rights violation[38]), whereas others seem more substantive (for example, that an application is not manifestly ill-founded[39]). In contrast with judgments on the merits, decisions of inadmissibility are rarely published and often scarcely reasoned.

In practice, a Registry lawyer usually decides the formation of the Court to which a case is initially assigned. So, where the preliminary Registry decision is that the application is clearly inadmissible it is assigned to a single judge formation. A judge should not receive any such application from the state of which she is a member, and so judges who are sitting in single-judge formations are assigned particular states. The obligations of a single judge rotate among the members of the Court. This points to an important issue, and one which we return to in Chapter 3: in practice, it is a Registry lawyer who is deciding on admissibility in these cases, with the formal decision then taken by the Court sitting in a single-judge formation. Certainly, if that single judge does not agree with the Registry determination she can refer it to a larger formation of the Court, but this shows that seemingly administrative decisions in the Registry can carry serious weight in the Court per se and effectively determine the fate of an application. More complex questions as to admissibility are decided by a Committee, Chamber or Grand Chamber.

Administratively the Court is further divided into five Sections, two with 10 judges and three with nine. Sections are established for three-year periods, should be balanced in terms of gender and geographic representation, and should reflect the different legal systems among the Contracting Parties.[40] Each Section has a President who oversees case management within the Section, and each country is assigned to a particular Section.

---

[38] Article 35(3)(b), ECHR. See also Vogiatzis, 'The Admissibility Criteria under Article 35(3)(b) ECHR: A "Significant Disadvantage" to Human Rights Protection?' (2016) 65 *International and Comparative Law Quarterly* 185.

[39] Article 35(3)(a), ECHR. See also Gerards, 'Inadmissibility Decisions of the European Court of Human Rights: A Critique of the Lack of Reasoning' (2014) 14 *Human Rights Law Review* 148.

[40] Rule 25(2), 'Rules of Court' (above, n. 35).

For a variety of reasons some cases end up in the Grand Chamber, which with its 17 judges is the most authoritative formation of the Court. Not only is the Grand Chamber the largest formation, but it also always contains its most senior judges: the President, the Vice-Presidents of the Court, and the Presidents of the Sections. The Grand Chamber hears a very small number of cases per year when one considers the workload of the Court overall. Ordinarily, it only hands down no more than 30 judgments every year, although there is no strict limit on the number of cases it can hear. There are only two routes, though, by which an individual complaint can end up in the Grand Chamber.

The first is that a party to the case makes an application (known as a referral) under Article 43 of the Convention within three months of a Chamber judgment. A panel of five judges will then decide on whether the case raises a serious question as to the interpretation or application of the Convention, or a serious issue of general importance; if so it refers the case to the Grand Chamber for new consideration. Very few referral applications under Article 43 are successful. The second route to the Grand Chamber is by 'relinquishment' under Article 30. This happens when the Chamber dealing with the case decides that the Grand Chamber should determine it instead of the Chamber itself. According to Article 30, this should happen where the case raises a serious question of interpretation of the Convention or where the resolution of a question might be inconsistent with a judgment previously decided by the Court, but relinquishment is only possible where the parties to the case consent to it. Where that happens, all judges sitting in the Chamber case will form a part of the Grand Chamber in this case.[41] Once introduced, Protocol 15 will remove the parties' right to object to a decision to relinquish a case to the Grand Chamber.

III. How Are Judges Appointed?

It is sometimes said that the Judges of the ECtHR are nothing more than unelected bureaucrats.[42] However, the reality is quite different. These judges are all experienced lawyers (some as practitioners, some as judges in their home jurisdictions, some as professors) who are nominated by their home state and then voted into office by the Parliamentary Assembly of the Council of Europe (PACE). The Contracting Party is required to draw up a shortlist of three nominees following a rigorous national procedure, after which the Committee on the Election of Judges to the ECtHR – a 20-person committee of the PACE – prepares a report on each candidate for the full PACE, which includes its recommendations. The PACE then votes on the nominated judges.

---

[41] Ibid., Rule 24(2)(c).
[42] Doughty, 'Human rights court "is a threat to democracy": Ex-Lord Chief Justice blasts unelected Strasbourg judges' *The Daily Mail*, 1 October 2014, available at http://www.dailymail.co.uk/news/article-2775796/Human-rights-court-threat-democracy-Ex-Lord-Chief-Justice-blasts-unelected-Strasbourg-judges.html.

The Convention itself does not elaborate much on the qualifications of potential Judges of the Court, beyond noting in Article 21 that they must be of high moral character and must either possess the qualification required for appointment to high judicial office or be Jurisconsults of recognised competence. These criteria are, of course, somewhat vague, and there is no guarantee that their inclusion in the Convention will ensure that only highly qualified lawyers with expertise in human rights will actually end up serving as judges of the ECtHR, but in spite of this it is true that they are not remarkably different to the kinds of qualifications for appointment as a judge that are found in many domestic jurisdictions, including the UK.[43]

Appointment of Judges

That is not to say that the methods and processes for appointing judges to the Court are not worthy of review and consideration. Indeed, over the past decade judicial appointment and independence have been prominent concerns in debates surrounding the Court, even to the extent that election of judges was the subject of a special report from the PACE in 2011.[44] As is the case in many judicial systems, the process by which judges are selected is key to ensuring quality (including diversity) and independence on the bench. Thus, the process for election of judges to the ECtHR is worthy of some consideration here.

The Convention states that the PACE – the deliberative organ of the Council of Europe made up of members of the national parliaments of each member state – should elect a judge from a list of three candidates nominated by the Contracting Party.[45] It was previously the case that the states would send a list of three candidates in the order of their preference (rather than alphabetically) and the preferred candidate would normally be elected. In this system the combination of politically motivated nominee selection at national level and lack of rigour at PACE level meant that Judges of the Court were not always as well qualified or competent as they ought to have been.[46] However, the PACE now takes a much more active role in screening candidates and assessing their suitability and qualification for the Court, including demanding more rigorous national processes.

Of course, the national selection of three nominees is the most important stage in appointing competent and independent judges to serve in Strasbourg. The national government is required to issue a public call for applications, and to select the three final nominees in a fair and transparent manner, but

---

[43] Constitutional Reform Act 2005.

[44] 'Ad hoc judges at the European Court of Human Rights: an overview', Committee on Legal Affairs and Human Rights, AS/Jur (2011), available at https://goo.gl/rs4gM7, 36.

[45] Article 22, ECHR.

[46] See, for example, Louciades, 'Reflections of a Former European Court of Human Rights Judge on his Experiences as a Judge' (2010), available at http://www.errc.org/article/roma-rights-1-2010-implementation-of-judgments/3613/8.

the European institutions in question have limited means of ensuring that this is done properly. Instead, the European system necessarily, and perhaps inevitably, relies on the rigour, independence and effectiveness of the national selection procedures to filter a large field down into a list of the three most qualified judges able and willing to serve on the Court.

The concept of qualification here requires some nuancing; there are some elements of the role that are not usually required in national judges. In many ways these are practical: the candidates should be able and willing to move to Strasbourg for the duration of their time on the Court, and they should be able to speak and work in both French and English. This is in addition to being substantively qualified and meeting the criteria of Article 21 as already mentioned. In addition, single-sex lists of nominees from states will only be considered by the PACE if the sex in question currently makes up under 40 per cent of the judges on the Court or if there are exceptional circumstances that justify derogating from the general rule, which is that single-sex lists are prohibited.[47] As well as these basic rules, a further check on the list of nominees that goes to the PACE is the fact that the candidates are required to present their qualifications in a standard CV format (to facilitate comparison between them), and these CVs are initially sent to an Advisory Panel – mostly consisting of former judges of the ECtHR – which can express a view to the state that some or all of the candidates they propose are unqualified for the post. The state is not required to follow this advice, but it is made available to the PACE.

After the list of three candidates is transferred to the PACE the special Committee on the Election of Judges to the ECtHR interviews the candidates. As a result of these interviews the PACE can return the list to the national government and suggest submitting a different list. Although this sounds like a somewhat drastic measure, it is not entirely unusual as, for example, interviews can reveal that a candidate's spoken French or English is not sufficiently developed for them to serve effectively on the Court. On the other hand, once the Committee is satisfied with the list of three candidates it communicates its views to the PACE, including an indication of the Committee's preferred choice. This information is made publicly available (as are the candidates' CVs) and the PACE votes according to the recommendations of the Committee in many cases.

This multi-layered process of selection makes for a sometimes slow and somewhat cumbersome process of judicial appointment to the ECtHR, but it is designed to increase the likelihood that only qualified candidates will end up serving in the Court. It cannot, of course, entirely guard against governments nominating, and the PACE electing, 'governmental agents', but it does reduce the likelihood that bad faith nominations will result in under-qualified judges that act in a partisan manner in favour of their own states.

---

[47] Resolution 1366 (2004) of the PACE, as amended by Resolution 1426 (2005) and Resolution 1627 (2008).

The Principle of National Representation

Every Contracting Party has a judge on the Court through the so-called principle of national representation. This is intended to ensure that in every case there is always someone with expertise in the national legal systems that are being examined, and as a result the judge from the respondent state is always a member of the Chamber or Grand Chamber in which a case is being considered.[48] Thus, if a case is brought against Iceland the Icelandic judge will be a member of the Chamber, and if the case is referred to the Grand Chamber he will sit in the Grand Chamber again in the same case. The rationale is that this national judge will be able to inform his colleagues about the particularities of the national system, but this could be done by a non-voting judge in the case, or even by a qualified Registry lawyer preparing briefs in respect of the system in question. It does not necessarily require a voting national judge on the panel. We make this point because the principle of national representation has some potentially undesirable implications for judicial independence, whether actual or perceived, in the Court.

First, the knowledge that the national judge will always sit in a case against the Contracting Party may create some perverse incentives for the state in question to nominate 'loyal' judges to the Strasbourg Court. The processes described above are designed to guard against that, but they cannot absolutely prevent it. Second, the national judge can hear the same case twice where, as in our example above, it is heard in the Chamber and then successfully referred to the Grand Chamber. If this were to happen in a national court there would be a strong case that it violated the right to a fair trial (a right which is, itself, protected by Article 6 of the Convention). As a result, some judges prefer to recuse themselves from sitting in the Grand Chamber and an ad hoc judge is nominated from the Contracting Party to sit as the 'national' judge in the case in question. Where this happens it can effectively resolve the potential conflict identified here, but judges are under no obligation to take this route. This brings us to the third concern with the principle of national representation: it has resulted in a system of ad hoc judges who serve where the national judge cannot sit on the case. This might be for reasons of principle as noted above or, for example, because the case is one in which the judge was involved (as advocate or judge) in the national system before being appointed to Strasbourg. Whilst on the face of it the system of ad hoc judges is perfectly reasonable, if not sensible, it was the cause of considerable controversy for some time. It has been argued that sometimes governments would appoint a particular judge for a particular case; the pool was not stable and instead a government would be asked for an ad hoc judge for a specific case. Often this ad hoc judge would be drawn from sitting judges in the national system, and it is not unusual that a government would be aware of the personal views of its more senior judges in relation to particular issues or controversial areas of law. The concern was that this kind of informal knowledge influenced the selection of ad hoc judges, in relation to whom the procedural safeguards in the PACE that

---

[48] Article 26(4), ECHR.

apply to the appointment of permanent judges to Strasbourg do not operate. Now, however, some precautions have been taken against this. Contracting Parties must submit a list of three potential ad hoc judges, one of whom is to be selected by the President of the Section to sit on the case in question (or, in the case of the Grand Chamber, by the President of the Court).[49] Whilst this addresses concerns it does not, of course, resolve them, as there are no required procedures for selection of the shortlist of three that goes to the Court. Some states have gone further than this and choose to invite an existing judge of the Court, who was nominated by another state, to act as its ad hoc judge when the situation arises. This has been done by Luxembourg and Hungary, for example, but the practice is not at all widespread.[50]

Length and Conditions of Tenure

In the Strasbourg system, as elsewhere, conditions of tenure are key to helping maintain and guarantee judicial independence. Article 23 of the Convention lays down the fact that judges can be appointed for one, non-renewable nine-year term only (previously, renewable six-year terms[51]) and that Judges of the Court must retire at 70. However, it was not always the case that the judges on the Court had particularly well-developed conditions of tenure. There is no clear and guaranteed pathway back to work following a term of office in Strasbourg. The judges cannot normally keep their positions at the national level during their time in Strasbourg; so, when it is time to retire from the ECtHR some judges would have no further career at the national level. There is no guarantee of employment for the judges and there is some chance that they might be more prone to influence at the end of their tenure in the Court in order to secure some chances of getting into the highest judicial offices back home. This issue calls for some meaningful resolution by the Council of Europe and the Contracting Parties, but has not yet been effectively addressed.

IV. The Other Relevant Bodies

The Registry of the Court

Although the judges are the primary decision makers, the Registry of the Court contains its institutional memory, and much of its intellectual and organisational capacity. It also exercises considerable influence over the Court, even making prima facie decisions about whether cases are clearly inadmissible or not. In spite of this, the Convention itself describes the Registry very briefly. Article 24 provides that the Court shall have a Registry, the functions and organisation of

---

[49] Rule 29, 'Rules of Court' (above, n. 35).

[50] List of ad hoc judges for the year 2017, ECtHR. Available at http://www.echr.coe.int/Documents/List_adhoc_judges_BIL.pdf.

[51] Mowbray, 'Protocol 14 to the European Convention on Human Rights and Recent Strasbourg Cases' (2004) 4 *Human Rights Law Review* 331, 335–336.

which shall be laid down in the Rules of Court. However, the Rules are also not comprehensive in this respect. The Registry consists of lawyers from across the Contracting Parties. Ordinarily these would be drawn from most, if not all, Contracting Parties and would normally deal with the applications coming from their countries of origin. The Registrar and Deputy Registrar are at the heads of the Registry and they are responsible for its organisation and activities.

Although the Registry is somewhat in the shadows, its work is crucial. Given the very large workload of the Court, a number of tasks that we tend to associate with judges are actually carried out by members of the Registry. In this the ECtHR is hardly alone, but it is nevertheless noteworthy. For example, it is not unusual for a Registry lawyer to prepare a first draft of a judgment. Of course, the judges can suggest amendments and redraft certain parts but very often the Registry first proposes the reasoning.

Registry lawyers often determine the destiny of applications to the Court. This is demonstrated by just three examples. First, they decide whether the application complies with the formalities for application so that it is processed at all. Second, they decide whether it is clearly inadmissible, in which case it goes to a single judge. Thirdly, there may be cases in which the deciding judge(s) does not have competence in the language in which the application is submitted, in which case she must rely on the note summarising the application that has been submitted by the member of the Registry.[52] Although Registry lawyers have a significant role in the operation of the Court, much of what the Registry does is not subject to public accountability mechanisms such as the media scrutiny to which the judges on the Court are subjected. Thus, it is crucial for the operation of the entire Convention system that the integrity and independence of the Registry is guaranteed. Strangely, however, the Registry is rarely considered in depth in other academic treatments of the Court.

Protecting and guaranteeing the independence of the Registry means, as a first step, ensuring the independence of the lawyers who work there, and that, in turn, requires some understanding of the institutional structure in question. The Registry has a pyramid structure with the Registrar and Deputy Registrar on the top and temporarily employed lawyers on the bottom of the pyramid. The Court has a very unusual employment strategy for these temporary lawyers (so-called B-lawyers). They are employed on four-year contracts that cannot be extended and which do not have any pathways for internal promotion.[53] As with any short-term contractual employment this is sub-optimal.[54] Fixed-term employees have fewer incentives to develop institutional loyalty than permanent employees, and perhaps this is even more the case since they cannot, by the terms of their contract, be promoted in that institution.[55] Furthermore,

---

[52] Rule 18A, 'Rules of Court' (above, n. 35).

[53] Dzehtsiarou, 'One of the Keys to the ECHR Problems', *Human Rights in Ireland*, 11 September 2012, available at http://humanrights.ie/announcements/one-of-the-keys-to-the-ecthr-problems/#more-16311.

[54] Ibid.

[55] Ibid.

four years is a relatively short cycle in circumstances in which one is learning the (somewhat idiosyncratic) ropes of the institution at the start and seeking new employment (by necessity) at the end.[56] In spite of this, however, it is B-lawyers who are often entrusted with the crucial task of first screening and filtering the incoming applications. Clearly, ensuring the independence and job security of B-lawyers is vital, but it is to date largely unaddressed by the Court.

Within the Registry there are a number of 'departments'. The Office of Jurisconsult is of particular interest here. Rule 18B of the Rules of Court provides that the Court shall be assisted by a Jurisconsult for the purposes of ensuring the quality and consistency of its case law. He or she provides opinions and information to the judicial formations and members of the Court. This is a significant task; for example, a Jurisconsult might suggest that by adopting a particular judgment the Court would create a conflict within its case law, which may indicate a need for the Chamber to relinquish the case to the Grand Chamber. Although the judges are free to disagree with the opinion of the Jurisconsult, they are taken seriously. As might be expected, however, the Jurisconsult's notes are confidential so it is difficult to assess the impact of this office in real terms. The Jurisconsult is chosen by the Bureau of the Court after a public competition. The Secretary General of the Council of Europe makes the formal appointment.

Another department of the Registry that is worth mentioning is the Research and Library Division. As well as managing the library, this department is entrusted with the important task of preparing comparative research reports for some Chamber and nearly all Grand Chamber cases. These reports are requested where a Judge Rapporteur determines that the case is complex and that it is important to know how the matter at hand is dealt with in the other member states to the Convention. This report can also provide information about the Court's own case law, international legal norms, EU law, and other comparative jurisdictions on the issue under consideration. Where they are prepared, these comparative law reports are available to the judges sitting in the case but they are not open to the general public. Arguably, these reports make the reasoning and judgments of the Court more informed and enhance the legitimacy and persuasiveness of the Court's rulings, and they can be influential when the Court is determining the presence or absence of European consensus (which we discuss further in Chapter 4).

What this short overview of the Registry illustrates is that this important part of the Court is critical to its operation and has the capacity to exert significant influence over its work. This makes it all the more surprising that it is so infrequently considered in the literature, so opaque in its operations, and so apparently inattentive to the independence and job security of many of its members.

---

[56] Ibid.

The Committee of Ministers

The Court's legitimacy and effectiveness to a large extent depend on how well its judgments are implemented by the Contracting Parties to the Convention. The Court's reputation grows when the Contracting Parties routinely execute the judgments and consider the ECtHR as a proper forum for deciding complex questions of human rights protection. When the Court's judgments are criticised and not executed, the reputation of the Court suffers. Therefore, it is important to ensure that the judgments of the ECtHR are taken seriously.

According to Article 46 of the ECHR, the judgments of the ECtHR are legally binding and the Committee of Ministers is entrusted with the task of supervising their execution by the Contracting Parties. The Committee of Ministers is made up of the Ministers for Foreign Affairs of Member States of the Council of Europe or their representatives. It meets four times a year to discuss the execution of judgments. Out of all of the judgments handed down by the Court, very few receive detailed considerations in these meetings; usually they discuss no more than five judgments per country.

Having discussed a case, the Committee of Ministers adopts a decision that explains what needs to be done by the government of the respondent state in order to execute the judgment.[57] If the State is persistent over time in its non-execution the Committee of Ministers might adopt an interim resolution that shows its serious concern regarding the issue. Among other means of diplomatic pressure the Head of the Committee of Ministers can send a letter to the government concerned with a request to execute the judgment or, in exceptional cases, determine that the progress of implementation should be scrutinised during regular weekly meetings of the Committee of Ministers. The Committee of Ministers can also send the judgment back to the Court for infringement procedures under Article 46(4) of the ECHR. This can happen if two-thirds of the Committee of Ministers agree to initiate the infringement procedures. Then the Grand Chamber of the ECtHR will have a chance to confirm that the case has not been executed, although it cannot impose any further or punitive sanctions for the failure to execute. The ultimate sanction for non-execution is the suspension of the representation of the state in the Committee of Ministers and the PACE, and the suspension of the membership of the Council of Europe with subsequent potential withdrawal.[58] These measures are extraordinary and are almost never used.

When the state has taken all necessary measures to execute the judgment of the ECtHR the Committee of Ministers adopts the final resolution and closes its supervision. Whilst the Committee of Ministers is responsible for supervising the execution of judgments, much of the day-to-day monitoring is actually done by the Department for the Execution of Judgments of the Court, many of whose members would have previous experience of working in the

---

[57] Article 46(2), ECHR.
[58] Article 8, Statute of the Council of Europe.

Registry. The Department assists both the Contracting Parties in implementing judgments and the Committee of Ministers in supervising implementation.
Lawyers in the Department draft the decisions of the Committee of Ministers
and prepare files for the meetings. We discuss execution further in Chapter 8.

The Human Rights Commissioner

The final part of the institutional infrastructure to be considered at this point is
the Human Rights Commissioner. This office was established in 1999,[59] and is
tasked with promoting education in, awareness of and respect for human rights
as embedded in the human rights instruments of the Council of Europe.[60] The
Commissioner is elected by the PACE by a majority of votes cast from a list
of three candidates drawn up by the Committee of Ministers,[61] and engages
in extensive country monitoring visits and the preparation of thematic reports
with the themes determined by the Commissioner himself. Thematic reports so
far prepared range across areas as diverse as children's rights, counter-terrorism,
economic rights, LGBTQI rights, and migration.

   The Human Rights Commissioner is mentioned in the ECHR only once:
in Article 36. This Article deals with third-party interventions. These interventions can be submitted by the Contracting Parties, non-governmental organisations, and even groups of academics in order to inform the Court about
legal arguments relevant to the case concerned. The Human Rights Commissioner is specifically mentioned as an organ that may submit written comments
and take part in hearings in the Chamber or Grand Chamber. The value of the
Commissioner's right to intervene is not clear, given that the Court already
refers to the Commissioner's reports in cases where no intervention is made.
Indeed, the Commissioner has intervened only 13 times since 1999, and all of
these interventions have been based on country and thematic reports that are
already in the public domain.[62]

CONCLUSION

This chapter sets out the general framework against which the debates we consider in this book are assessed, as well as familiarising the reader with key institutions that will be relevant to these debates. The Strasbourg system of human
rights protection needs to be well balanced and effectively structured in order
to work, and in order to be able to make reasonable claims to legitimacy. The
Court and its judges should be independent and competent so as to ensure
input legitimacy; other bodies of the Council of Europe must work with the

---

[59] Resolution (99) 50, Council of Europe.
[60] Ibid., Article 3.
[61] Ibid., Article 9.
[62] Council of Europe, 'Third-party Interventions by the Commissioner for Human Rights',
available at http://www.coe.int/en/web/commissioner/third-party-interventions.

Contracting Parties to enhance the effectiveness of the ECtHR's judgments to improve the output legitimacy of the judgments. Combined with the perceived moral legitimacy of pursuing rights protection, these structures contribute to the perceived legitimacy of the Court, and thus to the workings of the Convention system for the protection of human rights.

Further Reading

Bates, *The Evolution of the European Convention on Human Rights: From Its Inception to the Creation of a Permanent Court of Human Rights* (Oxford University Press, 2010), Chapter 1.

Dothan, *Reputation and Judicial Tactics* (Cambridge University Press, 2015), Chapters 2–4.

Dzehtsiarou and Coffey, 'Legitimacy and Independence of International Tribunals: An Analysis of the European Court of Human Rights' (2014) 37 *Hastings International and Comparative Law Review* 271.

Glas, *The Theory, Potential and Practice of Procedural Dialogue in the European Convention on Human Rights* (Intersentia, 2016), Chapter 2.

Lemmens, 'Criticising the European Court of Human Rights or Misunderstanding the Dynamics of Human Rights Protection' in Popelier, Lambrecht and Lemmens (eds), *Criticism of the European Court of Human Rights* (Intersentia, 2016), 23–40.

Letsas, *A Theory of Interpretation of the European Convention on Human Rights* (Oxford University Press, 2007), Chapter 1.

Sovereignty and Authority

The European Convention on Human Rights (ECHR or Convention) does not operate in a vacuum: it is only one source of law with which states must comply at any given time, and which must somehow be harmonised if states are to meet all of their legal obligations. This raises challenging questions that arise in different ways in different circumstances: first, a 'contest' can emerge between the Convention as interpreted and applied by the European Court of Human Rights (ECtHR or Court) and domestic law, including often domestic constitutional law. In these situations concerns and claims as to national sovereignty add a particular dimension to the debates about authority, which we consider in Debate 1. A second set of questions arises when it comes to the relationship between the Convention and other bodies of international law, such as European Union (EU) law and Resolutions of the UN Security Council. States need to comply with multiple legal obligations at the same time. For reasons of practicality, these obligations must be reconcilable. In these circumstances, the ECtHR may be required to determine how all of these obligations can apply in harmony, and in a manner that effectively protects human rights. We consider the relationship between the EU and the ECHR in Debates 2 and 3, and between the Convention and other sources of international law in Debate 4.

Debate 1

Who has the final word in human rights cases: the Court or the contracting parties?

This part of this chapter is about the distribution of power between the Contracting Parties and the ECtHR: who is the ultimate policy maker in the area of human rights standards? This is a question that leads to major tensions. It is almost inevitable that at some point a respondent party to a case will be unhappy with the judgment of the Court. It was created to supervise Contracting Parties' compliance with the Convention and can, thus, make legally binding findings[1] that a state has violated the Convention, limiting the

---

[1] Article 46, ECHR.

sovereign privilege of the Contracting States to set their own human rights agenda without reference to international standards.

It is entirely to be expected that Contracting Parties may sometimes be unhappy with and criticise judgments of the Court, but in some extreme cases this criticism can lead to a 'standoff' and that is the kind of situation with which we are primarily concerned here. When constructively put, states' negative reactions to the Court's decisions may encourage the Court to find a more nuanced position, engage in judicial dialogue, and carefully navigate the boundaries of its competence. The implications of standoff can be far more detrimental to the Convention, potentially even resulting in crisis.

The exchange of rulings between the ECtHR and the UK Supreme Court in the *Al-Khawaja/Horncastle* cases is a good illustration of constructive collaboration between the Court and Contracting Parties.[2] These cases concerned the legal rule, which allows hearsay evidence (any statement of fact other than one made, of his own knowledge, by a witness in the course of oral testimony)[3] to be admitted in certain circumstances. It was claimed that this violated the Court's 'sole and decisive test', which means that if the testimony of an absent witness is the sole and decisive reason for conviction then a violation of Article 6 of the ECHR will be almost automatically established.[4] There is, thus, a tension between the hearsay rule of evidence in the UK and the ECtHR-established case law on the right to a fair trial, and this is precisely the tension that arose in *Al-Khawaja and Tahery v the United Kingdom*.[5]

Al-Khawaja had been convicted for indecent assault on the basis of statements from a victim who died before she could be cross-examined in court. These statements were the only direct evidence in the case. The Chamber of the ECtHR found a violation of the Convention because the judgment of the national court relied solely on the hearsay evidence. Given the extent to which such a finding would disrupt the settled laws of evidence in the UK, it was referred to the Grand Chamber.

However, before the Grand Chamber case could be heard, the UK Supreme Court had an opportunity to present its legal position on the same issue in the case of *R. v Horncastle*.[6] The Supreme Court expressed the view that the 'sole and decisive test' that was developed by the ECtHR is too rigid and inflexible to be practicable and does not take into account various safeguards provided by national law in the common law criminal system. In other words, the Supreme Court expressed the view that the ECtHR had misunderstood the safeguards attendant to the hearsay rule and thus had acted in error in finding that it violated Article 6.

The Supreme Court's reaction to *Al-Khawaja and Tahery* turned out to be influential in the Grand Chamber's later consideration of the case. Building

---

[2] *Al-Khawaja and Tahery v the United Kingdom* [GC], nos 26766/05 and 22228/06, ECHR 2011 and *R. v Horncastle* [2009] UKSC 14, [2010] 2 AC 373.

[3] *R. v Horncastle* (above, n. 2).

[4] *Al-Khawaja and Tahery v United Kingdom* (above, n. 2).

[5] Ibid.

[6] *R. v Horncastle* (above, n. 2).

on the Supreme Court's judgment, the Grand Chamber found no violation of Article 6 in relation to Mr Al-Khawaja. In doing so, it reassessed the 'sole and decisive test' and made it more flexible in order to reflect the safeguards provided in the UK. Judge Bratza, in his concurring opinion, called this exchange of legal opinions 'a good example of the judicial dialogue'.[7] In reality it is rather unusual for a national court to have the opportunity to intervene more or less directly in this way: the period of time between the Chamber and Grand Chamber decision is usually relatively short, and an appropriate case does not always arise in the domestic courts. That does not mean, however, that no other opportunities for judicial dialogue arise. The judges of the ECtHR and national authorities have multiple opportunities for formal and informal dialogue, through conferences, personal interactions, extra curial speeches and writings, and quasi-social events such as the beginning of the judicial year in the ECtHR.

Of course, there are instances in which dialogue fails and the Court and the Contracting Parties face a deadlock in their relations: the Contracting Party refuses to execute the Court's judgment, and the Court refuses to revisit its position. Such a situation is thankfully rare, but clearly damaging to the whole system of human rights protection. The well-known standoff over prisoners' right to vote illustrates this well.

In the 2005 case of *Hirst v the United Kingdom (no. 2)* the ECtHR found that the UK law prohibiting prisoners from voting violated the right to free elections as protected by Article 3 of Protocol 1.[8] Whilst a state could impose a ban on some prisoners voting, a blanket ban breached the Convention and thus, in the view of the Court, required reform. The political reaction in the UK was negative; an overwhelming majority of Parliament voted to maintain the law as it was, with many claiming that it was Parliament, not the ECtHR, that should make this decision. The Government expressed a similar sentiment, and so the judgment went unexecuted.

Popular reaction was largely in agreement with this, perhaps to some extent because Mr Hirst himself was an 'unsympathetic character'. Not only had he been convicted of manslaughter, but in winning this case he had, it was sometimes said, opened the door for 'murderers and rapists' to vote, against the will of the sovereign Parliament. The fact that the Court had not held that Mr Hirst had to be allowed to vote,[9] but rather that a *blanket* ban could not be maintained, did not seem to placate this criticism. Quite the contrary, to some extent. The Court claimed that the right to free elections requires that whether or not someone can vote in any given election must be determined by reference to a Convention compatible rule or law, where exclusions are proportionate and limited. On this reading, the finding in *Hirst (no. 2)* simply requires that such a rule or law be introduced. However, for others, *Hirst (no. 2)* effectively created a right to vote.

---

[7] *Al-Khawaja and Tahery v United Kingdom* (above, n. 2). Concurring opinion of Judge Bratza.

[8] *Hirst v the United Kingdom (no. 2)* [GC], no. 74025/01, ECHR 2005-IX.

[9] Ibid., para. 84.

Article 3 of Protocol 1 is unusual for the Convention system; it does not explicitly provide for an individual right. It clearly creates an obligation to hold elections at reasonable intervals by secret ballot to ensure the free expression of the will of the people. In *Hirst (no. 2)* the Court interpreted this as including a right to vote. Whilst the importance of voting rights is undeniable, the variety of forms in which these rights can be provided is notable. As the Court acknowledged, at the time a number of European states had a blanket ban on prisoners voting and there was no common practice across the Council of Europe. Thus, one might have expected states to be given a wide margin of appreciation in deciding on voting rights.[10] Instead, the Court both developed a right to vote *and* prohibited blanket bans on prisoner votes, thus giving states a limited margin of appreciation on this matter. For many who opposed *Hirst (no. 2)*, the problem was not only with prisoners voting, but also with how the Court went about reaching its decision.

The judgment in *Hirst (no. 2)* was just the beginning of a long saga that is far from over. In a number of judgments following *Hirst (no. 2)* the Court started to specify which restrictions on prisoner voting would comply with the Convention. As has already been pointed out, the Court in *Hirst (no. 2)* did not require all prisoners in a given country to have a right to vote, but it did not explain precisely what would be Convention-compliant.[11] In *Frodl v Austria*, the Chamber of the Court held that the decision to disenfranchise a prisoner should be taken by the judge and only when the nature of the offence justifies restricting the political participation of the offender.[12] Austria requested referral of the judgment to the Grand Chamber but this was rejected. The Chamber judgment became final and was implemented by Austria.[13] In 2008 the Court delivered a judgment in the case of *Calmanovici v Romania*, condemning a blanket ban on prisoner voting, but again did not specify which system of prisoner disenfranchisement would conform to the ECHR.[14] This judgment was implemented and most prisoners can now vote in Romania.

In 2010, five years after *Hirst (no. 2)* became final, the Court delivered a pilot judgment in the case of *Greens and M.T. v United Kingdom*.[15] This did not add much clarity as to what exactly should be done by the Contracting Party in order to satisfy the standard developed in *Hirst (no. 2)*. The Court merely reiterated its decision from that case and gave the United Kingdom six months to comply. This judgment has still not been executed.

In 2012, the Grand Chamber decided another case concerning prisoner voting rights – *Scoppola v Italy (no. 3)*.[16] The UK government submitted a

---

[10] The Court acknowledged that there was no uniform practice on prisoner voting across the Contracting Parties.

[11] *Hirst v United Kingdom (no. 2)* [GC], (above, n. 8), para. 84.

[12] *Frodl v Austria*, no. 20201/04, 8 April 2010, para. 34.

[13] Bates, 'Analysing the Prisoner Voting Saga and the British Challenge to Strasbourg' (2014) 14 *Human Rights Law Review* 503, 509–510.

[14] *Calmanovici v Romania*, no. 42250/02, 1 July 2008.

[15] *Greens and M.T. v the United Kingdom*, nos 60041/08 and 60054/08, ECHR 2010.

[16] *Scoppola v Italy* (no. 3) [GC], no. 126/05, 22 May 2012.

third party intervention arguing that the Court had misinterpreted the Convention in *Hirst (no. 2)*,[17] but in spite of this the Court reiterated the principle laid down in that case, although it was more precise as to what this actually means. Whilst not overruling *Hirst (no. 2)* the Court nevertheless overruled *Frodl* by stating that '[w]hile the intervention of a judge is in principle likely to guarantee the proportionality of restrictions on prisoners' voting rights, such restrictions will not necessarily be automatic, general and indiscriminate simply because they were not ordered by a judge'.[18] The Court established that in Italy disenfranchisement applies only to those prisoners who are convicted for crimes that can be punished by imprisonment for longer than three years.[19] This system was sufficient for the Court to declare that the ban was not automatic or blanket and it consequently found no violation of the Convention.

The next stage of the prisoner voting saga occurred in Russia. In 2013 the Court delivered a judgment in *Anchugov and Gladkov v Russia*.[20] The facts of the case are nearly identical to those in *Hirst (no. 2)*, the only significant difference being that automatic disenfranchisement is enshrined in the Constitution of Russia, in its entrenched part which can only be amended by adoption of a new Constitution.[21] The Russian government argued that this was a significant consideration, which should affect the scope of the margin of appreciation afforded to the government,[22] a claim to which the Court did not accede, finding the Russian law in violation of the Convention.

In Russia, the judgment in *Anchugov* led to a significant backlash against the ECtHR. The Court suggested that the Russian Constitutional Court should interpret the Constitution in a way that would comply with the reading of the Convention adopted by the ECtHR. This has not happened. In its judgment of 14 July 2015, the Russian Constitutional Court declared that Russia can depart from its international obligations if compliance with them would violate the Russian Constitution.[23] When ruling on this issue one of

---

[17] Ibid., para. 78.

[18] Ibid., para. 99.

[19] Ibid., para. 106.

[20] *Anchugov and Gladkov v Russia*, nos 11157/04 and 15162/05, 4 July 2013.

[21] Article 135 of the Constitution of the Russian Federation, available at http://www.constitution.ru/en/10003000-10.htm.

[22] *Anchugov and Gladkov v Russia* (above, n. 20), paras 85–87.

[23] Decision of the Constitutional Court of the Russian Federation from 14 July 2015 N 21-П 'in the case of verification of constitutionality of Article 1 of the Federal Law "On Ratification of the Convention For the Protection of Human Rights and Fundamental Freedoms and Its Protocols", sections 1 and 2 of Article 32 of the Federal Law "On International Treaties of the Russian Federation", sections 1 and 4 of Article 11, subsection 4 of section 4 of Article 392 of the Civil Procedural Code of the Russian Federation, Sections 1 and 4 of Article 13, subsection 4 of section 3 of Article 311 of the Arbitration Procedural Code of the Russian Federation, sections 1 and 4 of Article 15, subsection 4 of section 1 of Article 350 of the Administrative Court Proceedings Code of the Russian Federation, and subsection 2 of Section 4 of Article 413 of the Criminal Procedural Code of the Russian Federation in relation to the request of the group of the members of state Duma (parliament)', available at http://rg.ru/2015/07/27/ks-dok.html (in Russian).

the judgments that the Russian Constitutional Court clearly had in mind was *Anchugov and Gladkov v Russia*. Also, the Russian Parliament – the State Duma – has adopted amendments to the law of the Constitutional Court allowing it to declare judgments of the ECtHR to be unenforceable in so far as they contradict the foundational norms of the Constitution.[24] Unsurprisingly, the first case that the Constitutional Court was asked to consider under this new procedure was the case of *Anchugov and Gladkov* and it ruled that the Russian Constitution does not allow prisoners to vote and that this determined the matter, rather than the Convention.[25] As a result, both Russia and the ECtHR reached a dead end – the Court's judgment cannot be executed without adoption of a new Constitution in Russia which is a difficult and risky affair.

After *Anchugov and Gladkov* the ECtHR decided another prisoner voting case, *Söyler v Turkey*. In Turkey, the voting ban is applicable only to those who committed intentional crimes.[26] Starting from 2001, prisoners who were convicted for involuntary offences have been allowed to vote.[27] The Court, however, was not satisfied with this regime because in relation to intentional crimes the Turkish system was even harsher than the one in Russia, Italy or the United Kingdom. For instance, even those former prisoners who are conditionally released could not recover their voting rights until their sentence was over.[28] In addition, the Court pointed out that the ban in Turkey is indiscriminate in nature as it does not take into account the gravity of the crime committed or the length of imprisonment.[29] This judgment, therefore, adds some confusion as to the standard that the Contracting Parties should apply in this field: avoiding an absolute and indiscriminate ban is no longer the only requirement. Some other requirements are relevant too. The ban in Turkey was clearly not absolute – those in prison for involuntary crimes could continue enjoying their right to vote – but the measures against those who were imprisoned for intentional crimes appeared to be disproportionately harsh. Although this uncertainty leaves the Court with some flexibility when deciding future cases, it still coveys an impression of ad hoc decision making. The meaning of 'absolute and indiscriminate' seems to change over time, depending on the circumstances.

As in the UK and Russia, the Turkish authorities were not particularly impressed by this judgment, and it has not yet been executed. The Turkish government has informed the Committee of Ministers that the Supreme Electoral

---

[24] The Amendments to the Federal Constitutional Law on the Constitutional Court of the Russian Federation of 14 December 2015 N 7-ФКЗ, available at http://docs.cntd.ru/document/420322320.

[25] The Judgment of the Russian Constitutional Court as to the Possibility of Execution of the Judgment of the ECtHR in the case of *Anchugov and Gladkov v Russia*. Press release of the judgment is available at http://www.ksrf.ru/ru/News/Pages/ViewItem.aspx?ParamId=3281b (in Russian).

[26] *Söyler v Turkey*, no. 29411/07, 17 September 2013, para. 26.

[27] Ibid., para. 30.

[28] Ibid., para. 38.

[29] Ibid., para. 41.

Council in Turkey can lift the voting ban in individual cases.[30] However, the Committee of Ministers is not satisfied with these measures and has claimed that '[t]hese decisions [...] concern the elections for which they were issued and do not constitute a general remedy for the violation found by the Court'.[31]

Yet another judgment with similar facts was delivered by the ECtHR in July 2016 in a case of *Kulinski and Sabev v Bulgaria*.[32] As in Russia, in Bulgaria a prisoner voting ban is enshrined in the Constitution. In its very concise judgment the Court merely reiterated the principles adopted in *Anchugov and Gladkov* without any further elaboration. It is too early to say but there is a very high chance that this will be another unimplemented judgment of the Court.

Thus, the prisoner voting debate is a good illustration of a power struggle between the Court and the Contracting Parties; a struggle that is deeply rooted in notions of sovereignty and authority. It raises questions such as: 'Why should the Court have the last word in this debate?' and 'Why should judges have the authority to determine the policy question of whether prisoners should vote or not?'

We might ask why it is that this question has generated so much controversy. As already noted, one can criticise the reasoning of the Court in these cases, but there is more to it than that. Three key conditions are present for this to cause such a standoff. First, because voting rights are usually determined by legislation, national parliaments can block the execution of the Court's judgment. Second, the judgment concerns unpopular minorities, easily vilified in the media and among the voting public. Third, parliamentarians may perceive this to be a question in which the ECtHR should not get involved. In some countries, this may be because the question is perceived as 'political'. In others, it may be a microcosm of broader Euroscepticism. In others, such as Russia and the UK,[33] it may be a mixture of both.

The accumulation of these three conditions may explain why decisions as to prisoner voting cause standoff in some countries, but not in others. Thus, in Austria, the judgment in *Frodl v Austria*[34] was executed without any major issues,[35] and in Ireland the national parliament initiated appropriate reforms

---

[30] Action Plan of Turkey of execution of the ECtHR judgment in the case of *Söyler v Turkey*, available at https://rm.coe.int/CoERMPublicCommonSearchServices/DisplayDCTMContent?documentId=09000016804a2814.

[31] Execution of the case *Söyler v Turkey*, available at http://www.coe.int/t/dghl/monitoring/execution/Reports/pendingCases_en.asp?CaseTitleOrNumber=soyler&StateCode=&SectionCode=.

[32] *Kulinski and Sabev v Bulgaria*, no. 63849/09, 21 July 2016.

[33] Backbenchers' debate on the question of prisoner voting ban 2011: Hansard Report, available at http://www.publications.parliament.uk/pa/cm201011/cmhansrd/cm110210/debtext/110210-0002.htm.

[34] *Frodl v Austria* (above, n. 12).

[35] Federal law amending the Federal Constitutional Law, the National Elections Regulation 1992, the Federal President Election Law 1971, the European Elections Act, the Voter Evidence Law 1973, the European Voter Evidence Law, the Law on Referendums 1972, the Law on Popular Petitions 1989, the Law on National Surveys 1973 and the Code of Criminal Procedure 1975, available at https://www.ris.bka.gv.at/Dokumente/BgblAuth/BGBLA_2011_I_43/BGBLA_2011_I_43.pdf (in German).

without there having been any specific ECtHR judgment against them.[36] Yet in Russia, Turkey, the UK, and potentially in Bulgaria – all states with growing levels of Euroscepticism – the prisoner voting issue is a major bone of contention.

Undoubtedly, the Court should not avoid dealing with important social issues even if they concern a challenging topic on which the national parliament might have something to say. To do so would undermine the *raison d'être* of the Court, namely the protection of minorities and other unpopular groups who cannot be protected through normal democratic processes. But the ECtHR still needs to take account of the possible backlash to its decisions and be prepared to confront it.

With the prisoner voting saga, one might say that the ECtHR dragged itself into a legitimacy trap. Even now, more than 10 years after the judgment in *Hirst (no. 2)*, this trap continues to give the Court's critics its critics a fertile ground on which to question its authority. The Court needs to navigate within a very narrow corridor between doing too much and not doing enough, between ensuring its authority and respecting sovereignty of the Contracting Parties. The Court needs to have the Contracting Parties on board because implementation of the judgments is almost entirely voluntary despite some diplomatic pressure from the Committee of Ministers. If states systematically ignore the judgments of the Court, they will lose its authority and influence. At the same time if the Court is too deferential to the Contracting Parties it will also gradually lose its authority because it will be ineffective in its key mission of protecting human rights. It seems that in the prisoner voting case law the Court got it wrong and overstepped its legitimacy wall – an imaginary boundary beyond which it could not go. Perhaps Europe was not ready to abandon prisoner-voting bans; perhaps the Court needed to wait for consensus to crystallise before developing Article 3 of Protocol 1 in this way. As we will see in Chapter 4, incrementalism of this kind can well be a way to avoid such a standoff.

Debate 2

What is the relationship between the EU and the ECHR?

Twenty-eight of the 47 Contracting Parties to the Convention are also member states of the European Union and, thus, under obligations to comply with both the ECHR and EU law. On the face of it, this might be a difficult task. At least in the earlier decades of its operation, the European Union (as it now is) was not a human rights organisation. Rather, its primary purpose was to pursue its four freedoms: free movement of goods, free movement of workers, free movement of capital, and freedom to provide services. All of these were fundamental to the effective establishment of the common market and its smooth operation, so that they were the key focus for the authorities and institutions in Brussels and Luxembourg.

---

[36] Electoral (Amendment) Act 2006, *Number 33 of 2006.*

However, as EU law developed, EU citizens began to challenge it on the grounds, among other things, that it violated their human rights. The difficulty for these applicants in earlier cases was that human rights were not explicitly protected in EU law. Of course, these people had rights under the ECHR, but the EU was not a party to the Convention (and so one could not make a complaint directly against the EU in Strasbourg). Therefore, the application had to be directed to the individual Contracting Parties to the ECHR, which were legally bound to implement EU laws. Some of these laws (particularly Regulations) have direct effect, i.e. they become domestic law by virtue of becoming EU law and without the intervention of the national state in the meantime.[37] Others (such as Directives) do require implementing measures by the state, so that there is a piece of domestic law that might be challenged rather than needing to directly challenge the EU law itself.

Thus, figuring out the ways in which a person who resided in a member state of the EU could enjoy her rights under the ECHR even when the laws of the EU are being implemented was a difficult task.

Interestingly, it was the European Court of Justice (as it was then called), rather than the ECtHR, that took the first major steps in ensuring that EU law does not breach human rights norms. This is what happened in the case of *Internationale Handelsgesellschaft* decided in 1979.[38] Although the applicant was not successful in that case, the Court made the following important finding:

> [...] respect for fundamental rights forms an integral part of the general principles of law protected by the Court of Justice. The protection of such rights, whilst inspired by the constitutional traditions common to the Member States, must be ensured within the framework of the structure and objectives of the [Union].[39]

Of course, it is one thing to find that rights must be protected within EU law, but identifying which rights those are is a great challenge especially when, as was then the case, the law of the EU itself did not include express fundamental rights protections. The European Court of Justice in *Internationale Handelsgesellschaft* referred to 'the constitutional traditions common to the Member States' when referring to the rights that might be protected in EU law, but having in mind the diversity in constitutional traditions it is almost impossible to list the rights that EU law should comply with. In the later case of *Nold*,[40] however, the European Court of Justice moved a step further. Again, it mentioned these common constitutional traditions across the EU, but it also referred to international human rights treaties.[41] In Chapter 1 we noted the

---

[37] *Costa v Ente Nazionale Energia Elettrica* (ENEL) [1964] ECR 585.
[38] *Internationale Handelsgesellschaft mbH v Einfuhr- und Vorratsstelle für Getreide und Futtermittel*, 1970 ECR 1125.
[39] Ibid., para. 4.
[40] *Nold v Commission* [1974] EUECJ C-4/73, C-4/73.
[41] Ibid., para. 13.

Preamble to the ECHR, which refers to 'common values' of the original signatory states – a phrase that bears some similarity to that used by the European Court of Justice. Indeed, in the later case of *Rutili* the ECHR received specific mention.[42] All of this means that, through its case law, the European Court of Justice effectively established (a) that protection and enjoyment of fundamental rights is a general principle of EU law, (b) that these rights are those that are shared between the member states' common constitutional traditions, and (c) that they are broadly reflected in the rights protected by the ECHR.

Whilst these were important developments for EU law in particular, they did not address the question of how the ECHR conceived of the relationship between EU law and the Convention. This was most extensively addressed by the Court in the case of *Bosphorus Hava Yolları Turizm ve Ticaret Anonim Şirketi v Ireland* (*Bosphorus*).[43] This case neatly illustrates how states may be required to comply with different international obligations at the same time. The case concerned an aircraft, leased by *Bosphorus Airways* from a Yugoslavian owner, which had been impounded by Ireland. In impounding the aircraft, Ireland had been implementing a piece of EU law (Council Regulation 990/93), which in turn had been introduced to give effect to sanctions against what was then the Federal Republic of Yugoslavia, imposed by the UN Security Council, as part of its reaction to the Yugoslav war. *Bosphorus* claimed that this interfered with its right to property under Article 1 of Protocol 1 of the ECHR. Interestingly, it had first claimed a breach of rights in the European Court of Justice but failed in that case because the Court held any interference that existed was proportionate.[44] Thus, having failed in the ECJ, Bosphorus attempted to establish a violation of the ECHR in Strasbourg.

In rejecting this claim, the ECtHR reflected on the relationship between international law (including EU law) and the Convention. In so doing, it laid down what has become known as the *Bosphorus* presumption:

> In the Court's view, State action taken in compliance with such legal obligations is justified as long as the relevant organisation is considered to protect fundamental rights, as regards both the substantive guarantees offered and the mechanisms controlling their observance, in a manner which can be considered at least equivalent to that for which the Convention provides [...]. By 'equivalent' the Court means 'comparable'; any requirement that the organisation's protection be 'identical' could run counter to the interest of international cooperation pursued [...]. However, any such finding of equivalence could not be final and would be susceptible to review in the light of any relevant change in fundamental rights protection.

---

[42] *Rutili v Ministre De L'Interieur* [1975] ECR 1219.
[43] *Bosphorus Hava Yolları Turizm ve Ticaret Anonim Şirketi v Ireland* [GC], no. 45036/98, ECHR 2005-VI.
[44] *Bosphorus Hava Yollari Turizm ve Ticaretas v Minister for Transport, Energy and Communications and Others* [1996] EUECJ C-84/95.

If such equivalent protection is considered to be provided by the organisation, the presumption will be that a State has not departed from the requirements of the Convention when it does no more than implement legal obligations flowing from its membership of the organisation.

However, any such presumption can be rebutted if, in the circumstances of a particular case, it is considered that the protection of Convention rights was manifestly deficient.[45]

Following on from this, and given that the protection of rights is a general principle of EU law (as outlined above), the EU was identified as an international organisation that enjoyed this presumption. What this means, in effect, is that where a state is implementing EU law it is assumed that the EU law itself respects the ECHR unless a manifest deficiency in rights protection is established in respect of the particular law in question. The ECtHR was prepared to be more deferential to legal rules that originated in the EU than those emanating from national legal orders.

This presumption is not without controversy. There are at least two bases upon which one might be sceptical of it. The first is the additional burden that it might be said to place on anyone who is trying to assert their Convention rights in respect of the implementation of EU law. For these applicants, there is a starting assumption that the law in question is Convention-compliant *simply because* it comes from the EU, an organisation that is not itself a Contracting Party to the Convention (something we consider further below). Although the burden of establishing a violation *always* falls on the person asserting a breach of rights, in these cases that burden seems somewhat heavier simply because the state is implementing EU law. In other words, the standard of scrutiny is effectively lowered because the state is implementing an international obligation. The second question that arises here is why the EU should enjoy such a presumption in the first place. On balance, it seems likely that it should: fundamental rights are legally protected within the EU, EU measures can be annulled for failure to respect rights, and the Court of Justice of the European Union has repeatedly shown itself to be willing to do this. On the other hand, there is no shortage of examples of EU measures that have been found to not comply with human rights (for example on mass surveillance,[46] or terrorist blacklisting[47]). In other words, just as states can sometimes take a misstep and introduce law that violates human rights, so too can the EU. Bearing this in mind, one might question if it is justifiable that the EU is endowed with this presumption of compliance with a human rights treaty to which it is not a signatory.

In spite of these questions, however, the *Bosphorus* presumption continues to apply. This was made clear in the recent case of *Avotiņš v Latvia*.[48] The facts

---

[45] Ibid., paras 155–156.

[46] Joined cases C 293/12 and C 594/12 *Digital Rights Ireland* [2014] OJ C 175.

[47] Joined cases C 402/05 and C-415/05P *Kadi and another v European Union Council* [2008] OJ C 36.

[48] *Avotiņš v Latvia*, no. 17502/07, 25 February 2014.

of this case are complex, but for our purposes we need only note that there was a debt-related judgment against *Avotiņš* from a Cypriot court, which his creditors attempted to enforce in Latvia where he resided. *Avotiņš* challenged the Latvian court's order, which had been issued under a piece of EU law known as the Brussels I Regulation. This allows for mutual recognition of civil judgments across the domestic courts of the member states of the EU. This Regulation provides that in enforcing such judgments, domestic courts in the country where enforcement is sought 'may under no circumstances [review] its substance', rather they must accept it. This is in line with the EU's principle of mutual recognition; that all states in the EU have rights protections and are parties to the ECHR and thus it can be assumed that their procedures and processes are human rights compliant. Here the applicant claimed that the Cypriot judgment had been given in violation of his right to defence, and thus that Latvia breached his right to due process under Article 6 of the Convention by enforcing it.

The ECtHR held that the *Bosphorus* presumption could be applied here: in the field of mutual recognition EU law required rights compliance in a manner that could be considered at least equivalent to that demanded by the ECHR. But of course this is not the end of the story: a violation of the Convention could still be found if *Avotiņš* established that the protection of rights in the EU in the field of mutual recognition was 'manifestly deficient'.

This judgment made clear that 'manifestly deficient' is a difficult standard to meet. The ECtHR was highly critical of the fact that EU law requires courts to recognise and enforce the judgments of other courts without being able to enquire as to its substance. However, it seems that this was still not enough to rebut the *Bosphorus* presumption. The Court held:

> the Court must satisfy itself [...] that the mutual recognition mechanisms do not leave any gap or particular situation which would render the protection of the human rights guaranteed by the Convention manifestly deficient [...] [W]here the courts of a State which is both a Contracting Party to the Convention and a Member State of the European Union are called upon to apply a mutual recognition mechanism established by EU law, they must give full effect to that mechanism where the protection of Convention rights cannot be considered manifestly deficient. However, if a serious and substantiated complaint is raised before them to the effect that the protection of a Convention right has been manifestly deficient and that this situation cannot be remedied by European Union law, they cannot refrain from examining that complaint on the sole ground that they are applying EU law.[49]

Note the final sentence here: not only must someone raise a 'serious and substantiated' claim that EU law was 'manifestly deficient' in protecting his Convention rights, but so too must he establish 'that this situation cannot be

---

[49] Ibid., para. 116.

remedied by European Union law'. Only if all of these conditions are fulfilled will the *Bosphorus* presumption be rebutted.[50]

The upshot of all of this, then, is that EU and ECHR law have both developed to build a 'mosaic' of rights protection in Europe.[51] On the one hand, the EU has developed fundamental rights as a general principle of EU law and, indeed, following the Treaty of Lisbon there is now a Charter of Fundamental Rights of the European Union, which has constitutional status in the EU and uses the ECHR as a key interpretive guide.[52] Meanwhile, the ECtHR has developed a legal presumption in *Bosphorus* that is designed to ensure that ECHR Contracting Parties can implement EU law in a practicable and effective way, but which may have sacrificed effective rights protection on the altar of efficiency by making it almost impossibly difficult to rebut that presumption in any given case. Undoubtedly, this is at least partially because the EU itself cannot be directly challenged in the ECtHR. This leads us to the next debate: should the EU accede to the ECHR?

Debate 3

Should the EU accede to the ECHR?

The EU has not yet acceded to the ECHR.[53] This is, in some ways, curious as EU accession to the Convention has long been on the cards and the Lisbon Treaty introduced the commitment that the EU 'shall' accede to the ECHR.[54] Moreover, Protocol 14 that entered into force in 2010 amended the Convention to allow the EU to accede. Indeed, the plans for accession have accelerated in recent years, to the extent that a draft accession agreement has been agreed.[55]

This draft accession agreement was sent to the Court of Justice of the European Union for its assessment of its legality and, quite to the surprise of many, it found that as designed the draft agreement was not lawful.[56] There were a number of reasons for this, and full accounts are provided elsewhere,[57] but of

---

[50] See also *Michaud v France*, no. 12323/11, ECHR 2012.

[51] See Douglas-Scott, 'Europe's Constitutional Mosaic: Human Rights in the European Legal Space' in Shaw, Tierney and Walker (eds), *Europe's Constitutional Mosaic* (Hart Publishing, 2011); See also Douglas-Scott, 'A Tale of Two Courts: Luxembourg, Strasbourg and the Growing European Human Rights Acquis' (2006) 43 *Common Market Law Review* 629.

[52] Article 6, TEU.

[53] For some time it was thought that the EU did not have the legal competence to accede to the Convention: *Opinion 2/94* [1996] ECR I-1759.

[54] Article 6(3), TEU.

[55] Draft revised agreement on the accession of the European Union to the Convention for the Protection of Human Rights and Fundamental Freedoms (47+1(2013)008rev2).

[56] Opinion 2/13 *Accession of the European Union to the European Convention for the Protection of Human Rights and Fundamental Freedoms* ECLI:EU:C:2014:2454.

[57] See, for example, Larik, 'The Accession of the European Union to the European Convention on Human Rights' (2014) 51 *Common Market Law Review* 1542; Lock, 'The Future of EU Accession to the ECHR after Opinion 2/13: Is It Still Possible and Is It Still Desirable?' (2015) 11 *European Constitutional Law Review* 239.

particular interest for our purposes is the role of the autonomy of EU law in the Court's reasoning.

As Douglas-Scott has noted, '[t]he autonomy of EU law, and its specific, *sui generis* nature, has been a running theme throughout its legal history'.[58] Among other things this principle means that the Court of Justice – and *only* the Court of Justice – determines the meaning of EU law. Whilst this was originally designed to ensure that national courts could not propagate alternative interpretations of EU law and thus undermine the unity of EU law, here it was also presented as a key reason to reject an arrangement in which the ECtHR has the capacity to call into question the Court of Justice's findings as to EU law. This has been heavily criticised by EU lawyers[59] and raises important broader questions about the role and identity of the Court of Justice, but for our purposes it highlights a key tension that might arise should the EU accede to the Convention.

It is one thing to say that the two courts might develop a system of mutual respect and presumed compliance, and even that together they have developed an impressive system of European public law, but it is quite another to suggest that the EU might be *bound* by the Convention as interpreted and applied by the ECtHR. The latter was, it seems, beyond the pale for the Court of Justice, raising a question as to whether the Court of Justice is contesting the authority of the ECtHR in an analogous fashion to that seen in Debate 1 of this chapter. Finding a way around this seems difficult, to say the least, and causes one to wonder whether the EU should accede at all. These questions go far beyond the (serious) doubt that now exists as to whether it would be *possible* to draft an accession agreement that would comply with EU law as interpreted by the Court of Justice. This raises the question of whether accession is necessary for the purposes of rights protection.

On the one hand, EU accession to the Convention would allow for further streamlining of the ECHR and EU fundamental rights law, thus further developing what we may term 'European public law', as well as ensuring that all areas of EU activity were subject to judicial review of some kind in some court. These are not insignificant or undesirable aims. However, on the other hand there is a strong argument that accession to the ECHR is simply unnecessary. This is worth exploring further. We have already seen that as early as 1970 the Court of Justice made it clear that fundamental rights were protected by EU law, and it soon became established that a violation of rights could be the basis for annulling a piece of EU law. Now there is a Charter of Fundamental Rights which gives further effect to that principle. The Charter's Preamble states that it aims 'to strengthen the protection of fundamental rights in the light of changes in society, social progress and scientific and technological developments by making

---

[58] Douglas-Scott, 'Autonomy and Fundamental Rights: The ECJ's Opinion 2/13 on Accession of the EU to the ECHR' (2016) *Europarättslig Tidskrift (Swedish European Law Journal)* special edition, 31.

[59] Lock, 'The Future of EU Accession' (above, n. 57).

those rights more visible in a Charter', and it applies to the EU at all times and to member states when they are applying EU law. Indeed, the Charter arguably goes beyond the ECHR by protecting various social rights, including the right to work (Article 15), rights of the elderly (Article 25), right of access to a free placement service for job seekers (Article 29), and a right of access to health-care (Article 35). Where a right in the Charter is also in the Convention, the Charter right is to be understood by reference to how the corresponding Convention right is understood, so that the ECHR acts as a 'floor' of protection with the Court of Justice free to interpret the Charter as giving more protection to rights than the Convention, but never as giving less.[60]

Given all of this, it is not entirely clear what 'added value *for rights protection*' would come from accession, particularly given the complexity and difficulty of accession following the Court of Justice *Opinion 2/13*. Lock acknowledges that so many concessions would have to be made to satisfy the requirements laid down in *Opinion 2/13* that accession may have the effect of reducing, rather than increasing, rights protection in real terms.[61] Were this to be the case, it is difficult to see what is to be gained from accession in real terms.

However, there are at least three creditable arguments that accession should still be pursued. First, having two regional courts, both of which are developing a human rights jurisprudence, might create multiple and perhaps conflicting standards of human rights protection. Even though, as already noted, rights protected in the EU's Charter of Fundamental Rights and the ECHR must be interpreted by the Court of Justice using the Convention as a 'floor', this does not entirely preclude the possibility that European human rights law will become (further) fragmented. Whilst fragmentation can lead to higher standards of rights protection, this is not inevitably the case, meaning that for some – including the CDDH[62] – the possibility of fragmentation is a cause for concern so that a failure of accession 'might in the long term cause serious damage to the credibility, authority and long-term future of the Convention mechanism'.[63] Second, if we were to accept that the protection of rights by the Court of Justice of the European Union, referring to the Convention as the Charter requires it to, meant that accession is not necessary, it would be difficult to see why the same argument should not be made by states wishing to leave the ECHR and whose domestic legal systems also protect rights. Nothing about the Court of Justice of the European Union makes it so clearly distinguishable from, for example, domestic constitutional or supreme courts as to say that this argument can be applied *only* to it. Third, accession would mean that the EU would be held accountable for complying with the Convention,

---

[60] Article 52(3), Charter of Fundamental Rights of the European Union.

[61] Lock, 'The Future of EU Accession' (above, n. 57).

[62] Steering Committee for Human Rights – a Council of Europe body that among other competences can propose further reforms of the ECtHR.

[63] CDDH, *Report on the Longer Term Future of the European Convention on Human Rights CDDH* (2015) R84 Addendum I, 65.

thus plugging the accountability gap that arises from the application of the *Bosphorus* presumption to Contracting Parties' application of ever-expanding EU law.[64]

Debate 4

What is the relationship between the ECHR and other sources of international law?

Of course, not all Contracting Parties to the ECHR are also member states of the EU, but all do have a range of international legal obligations that they must abide by. There are other potential clashes. What happens, for example, where a state is engaged in an armed conflict? Are their obligations under the Convention set aside, or do they continue to operate? We consider issues related to armed conflict in Chapter 6, but for now we can concentrate on the specific question of how (and if) the Convention applies when states are giving effect to their other international legal obligations.

This question arises most sharply when states are implementing Chapter VII resolutions of the UN Security Council. These are resolutions passed for the purposes of international peace and security, and which are binding on all member states of the United Nations (UN) by virtue of the Charter of the UN. Article 103 of that same Charter further provides:

> In the event of a conflict between the obligations of the Members of the United Nations under the present Charter and their obligations under any other international agreement, their obligations under the present Charter shall prevail.

This raises a serious question, and a difficult one: if a UN Security Council Resolution requires a Contracting Party to the ECHR to act in a manner that violates Convention rights, can a violation be found, or does Article 103 of the UN Charter effectively compel states to act in such a way? This is by no means an insignificant query. If the answer is that states must comply with the Convention at all times, then they may be placed in an almost impossible situation of irreconcilable international obligations. However, if Article 103 of the UN Charter means that states are required to subordinate their Convention obligations to their other international obligations where they are in conflict, the whole concept of Convention rights as legal protections is called into question, not least because the UN Security Council itself is not obliged to have regard to the ECHR when formulating its Chapter VII resolutions.

In the joined cases of *Behrami v France* and *Saramati v France, Germany and Norway*, the Grand Chamber was asked to consider whether Contracting Parties to the ECHR could be held liable for breaches of the Convention in respect of acts done when they were acting as part of NATO's Kosovo

---

[64] See, for example, Lock, 'The Future of EU Accession' (above, n. 57).

peacekeeping forces (KFOR) and the United Nations Mission in Kosovo (UNMIK).[65] These forces were UN-led, multinational forces acting under Security Council Resolution 1244 (1999). Rather than determine the question put to it per se, the Court held that the actions of member states in these circumstances were attributable to the UN (which is not a Contracting Party to the ECHR) not to the Contracting Parties themselves. Thus, no assessment of Convention-compatibility could be undertaken: these actions simply did not 'count' as actions of the ECHR Contracting Parties.[66]

In many ways, this approach seems like 'avoidance'; rather than have to determine the impact of Article 103 of the UN Charter on Convention obligations, the Court simply side-stepped the issue through its attribution decision. What *Behrami* suggests is that *when acting as part of a UN mission* established by resolution of the UN Security Council, Contracting Parties to the ECHR will not be subjected to Convention analysis.[67] From a rights protection perspective this is deeply problematic, especially as the Court has also found that there is no breach of the right of access to a court under Article 6 where a domestic court affords the UN immunity[68] from claims, even where the actions were done within the Council of Europe and with the involvement of European states.[69]

In sum, this means that where there is a UN mission *neither* the ECHR Contracting Parties involved in the mission nor the UN are likely to be held accountable under the Convention. There is, rather, a substantial accountability gap here which the ECtHR has not found a way to plug and has, arguably, exacerbated by its decision in *Behrami*. This raises serious questions about the effectiveness of the Convention and its system: if Contracting Parties are not accountable for violations of the Convention when they act under the auspices of the UN, and if the UN enjoys immunity which is recognised by the ECHR system, surely there is reason to wonder at the ability of the Convention to properly protect rights. The fact that the operations in question often involve military intervention and high-risk times of armed conflict adds a further dimension of risk to rights, which is discussed in full in Chapter 6 (on the Convention in times of insecurity, including war).

The Court has taken a somewhat more Convention-promoting path in respect of situations where Contracting Parties are *implementing* UN Security Council resolutions through their domestic laws or actions. This has been a

---

[65] *Behrami v France* and *Saramati v France, Germany and Norway* (dec.), nos 71412/01 and 78166/01, 2 May 2007.

[66] Ibid., para. 44.

[67] See also *Banković and Others v Belgium and Others* (dec.) [GC], no. 52207/99, ECHR 2001-XII which is discussed in full on Chapter 6 (where Contracting Parties operated as part of a NATO mission).

[68] Article 105, Charter of the United Nations.

[69] *Stichting Mothers of Srebrenica and Others v the Netherlands* (dec.), no. 65542/12, ECHR 2013.

particularly difficult question for the Court in recent years, as individuals have challenged the ways in which member states have implemented UN Security Council requirements to disrupt the financial affairs of people, organisations and states for the purposes of, for example, disrupting terrorist financing and sanctioning states.[70]

The most recent case in this line is *Al-Dulimi and Montana Management Inc. v Switzerland*,[71] decided in June 2016. This case concerned UN Security Council Resolution 1483 (2003), through which all UN member states had been required to freeze all funds and assets of the former government of Iraq, of Saddam Hussein, and of senior members of the former Iraqi regimes and their immediate family members or legal entities. The frozen and seized assets would then be transferred to the Development Fund for Iraq. The persons and entities to whom the sanctions regime would apply were identified by a Sanctions Committee established by the Security Council, and both of the applicants had been placed on the list by this Committee, following which Switzerland had begun proceedings to appropriate their assets in Swiss banks.

The applicants claimed that the methods by which they were put on the list violated their rights under Articles 6 and 13 of the Convention because there was no channel by which listing could be disputed through judicial review. This posed a quandary for the Court: it cannot directly review the actions of the Sanctions Committee because the UN is not a Contracting Party to the Convention. However, it can – and did – consider whether, in implementing Resolution 1483, Switzerland had complied with its obligations under the ECHR. In this respect it found a breach of the Convention because Switzerland did not allow for judicial review of the applicants' listing in its domestic courts. Switzerland argued that it was obliged to implement Resolution 1483 and that, in any case, Article 103 of the UN Charter made it clear that its obligations under that Charter prevailed over its obligations under the Convention.

The question of whether there was a conflict between the requirements of Resolution 1483 and those under the Convention was key to the decision in the case: after all, Article 103 only applies '[i]n the event of a conflict between the obligations of the Members of the United Nations under the present Charter and their obligations under any other international agreement'. Switzerland argued that there was clearly a norm conflict between Resolution 1483 and the Convention so that it was bound to apply the Resolution and freeze these assets. However, for eight of the judges on the Grand Chamber there was no necessary conflict. In earlier cases on similar sanction regimes the Court had introduced a presumption that Security Council resolutions were intended to comply with human rights law,[72] so that they would be taken to do so unless

---

[70] See especially *Al-Jedda v the United Kingdom* [GC], no. 27021/08, ECHR 2011; *Nada v Switzerland* [GC], no. 10593/08, ECHR 2012.

[71] *Al-Dulimi and Montana Management Inc. v Switzerland* [GC], no. 5809/08, ECHR 2016.

[72] *Al-Jedda v the United Kingdom* (above, n. 70); *Nada v Switzerland* (above, n. 70).

they explicitly said otherwise.[73] On this reasoning, when a provision in a Resolution is unclear, it is to be interpreted harmoniously with the ECHR and a presumption of compliance (similar to the *Bosphorus* presumption) is to be applied.

The finding that no conflict with the Convention will be found to arise unless it is explicitly constructed by the wording of a Resolution is a deft way to step around the logical implications of Article 103 being engaged (which would be that a Contracting Party is not obliged to comply with the Convention where it conflicts with the Resolution). However, there is a question mark over how helpful this is in real terms. In *Al-Dulimi*, as in similar cases, the state remains obliged to apply the Resolution to those persons and entities listed by the relevant Sanctions Committee of the UN. Domestic courts cannot serve as a forum for review of the UN Security Council: they do not have the authority to overrule a decision of the Security Council, which is not subject to their jurisdiction. Indeed, in *Al-Dulimi* the Court accepted as much, holding:

> Turning to the precise obligations imposed by the Convention on Switzerland in the present case, the Court accepts that the Federal Court was unable to rule on the merits or appropriateness of the measures entailed by the listing of the applicants. [...] However, before taking the above-mentioned measures, the Swiss authorities had a duty to ensure that the listing was not arbitrary.[74]

The Court thus required the state in question to obtain sufficient information to allow its courts to be able to scrutinise the listing, but one wonders what kind of order a court that found the listing to have been arbitrary could possibly make. Does the ECtHR seriously contemplate a domestic court ordering a government to refuse to implement a UN Security Council Resolution in any particular case? Might it be ordered to make representations for delisting to the Sanctions Committee? How should a domestic court deal with situations where the information provided to ground the listing is highly sensitive and cannot be revealed to the listed person or entity? Or with situations where the grounding information cannot be shared with the court but is instead summarised in a statement from the government? The Court held that Article 6 would be violated if listed persons and entities could not submit information to the domestic court, or if relevant information was not sought from the Sanctions Committee (even under a confidential procedure), but there is little clarity about how the rights violation could be effectively remedied in such cases.

There is similarly little clarity on how the harmonious interpretation is to be implemented in practice. This likely depends on the extent to which the Court holds a Contracting Party has a 'scope of discretion' in applying the Resolution in any particular case. Security Council Resolutions are applied by

---

[73] In *Nada v Switzerland* the presumption of compliance was rebutted by the clear wording of the Resolution, Ibid.

[74] *Al-Dulimi and Montana Management Inc. v Switzerland* (above, n. 71), para. 150.

states *within their domestic legal systems*; in other words, the means to achieving the end of compliance can vary across different legal systems. In principle, this suggests that a Contracting Party to the Convention might design a means of implementing a Security Council Resolution in domestic law that complies with the Convention. However, one wonders whether this is realistic in the case of sanctions regimes: states are legally obliged to freeze the assets of persons and entities included on the list drawn up by the Sanctions Committee so that, in practice, there is very little discretion to be exercised. In spite of this, both the ECtHR and, in similar litigation, the Court of Justice of the European Union[75] have held that such discretion *does* exist, and that rights must be respected when exercising this discretion unless the Resolution explicitly provides otherwise.

At first blush, this appears somewhat futile: it does very little in real terms to truly resolve the question of authority that arises for a state when it appears to be bound to comply with two sets of international obligations that are difficult to reconcile. It may well be that the real value of decisions such as *Al-Dulimi* is that they shape how ECHR member states are likely to make representations to the UN Security Council when sanctions and similar regimes are being designed, so that they can try to ensure fair(er) procedures are built into the extensive regimes of financial disruption that have been introduced to deal with terrorism and insecurity.[76] Beyond that, however, it is difficult to see how cases such as *Al-Dulimi* – admirable in principle – are effective in practice.

CONCLUSION

The ECtHR operates within a complex system of multiple international obligations that the national governments are required to implement. Moreover, the national governments also enjoy significant authority in deciding how these obligations are implemented. Since the interrelations between national and international obligations, and between various levels of international obligation themselves, are not clearly hierarchal, obligations can sometimes seem to conflict with one another. When one of those sets of obligations originates in the ECHR this creates significant challenges for the effectiveness of the Convention, and requires delicate handling by the Court. As we have seen in this chapter, in trying to address these difficult questions, the Court has largely attempted to engage productively with both national authorities and international standards, finding ways to make them work together, to integrate them, and to respond to the operation of national legal systems. That said, the

---

[75] *Kadi and another v European Union Council* (above, n. 47).
[76] For a similar argument in respect of the *Kadi* decision see de Londras and Kingston, 'Rights, Security and Conflicting International Obligations: Exploring Inter-Jurisdictional Judicial Dialogues in Europe' (2010) 58 *American Journal of Comparative Law* 359.

Court's judgments are binding, and the obligation to execute (i.e. give effect to) these judgments exists whether the national authorities agree with them or not. We return to this latter point in far more detail in Chapter 8.

Further Reading

Bates, 'Analysing the Prisoner Voting Saga and the British Challenge to Strasbourg' (2014) 14 *Human Rights Law Review* 503.

Douglas-Scott, 'Europe's Constitutional Mosaic: Human Rights in the European Legal Space' in Shaw, Tierney and Walker (eds), *Europe's Constitutional Mosaic* (Hart Publishing, 2011).

Lock, 'The Future of EU Accession to the ECHR after Opinion 2/13: Is It Still Possible and Is It Still Desirable?' (2015) 11 *European Constitutional Law Review* 239.

Tzevelekos, 'When Elephants Fight it is the Grass that Suffers: "Hegemonic Struggle" in Europe and the Side-Effects for International Law' in Dzehtsiarou et al. (eds), *Human Rights Law in Europe* (Routledge, 2014).

CHAPTER 3

Admissibility

Although rarely covered in much detail in the academic literature, admissibility is extremely important. More than 90 per cent of all applications are declared inadmissible,[1] meaning that the substantive claims of rights violation in the vast majority of complaints submitted to the Court are never considered by the judges there. Articles 34 and 35 of the European Convention on Human Rights (ECHR or Convention) outline the criteria for admissibility that any application submitted to the European Court of Human Rights (ECtHR or Court) must comply with in order to be considered on the merits. According to Article 34:

> The Court may receive applications from any person, non-governmental organisation or group of individuals claiming to be the victim of a violation by one of the High Contracting Parties of the rights set forth in the Convention or the Protocols thereto.

Article 35 establishes the admissibility criteria:

1. The Court may only deal with the matter after all domestic remedies have been exhausted, according to the generally recognised rules of international law, and within a period of six months from the date on which the final decision was taken.
2. The Court shall not deal with any application submitted under Article 34 that
   (a) is anonymous; or
   (b) is substantially the same as a matter that has already been examined by the Court or has already been submitted to another procedure of international investigation or settlement and contains no relevant new information.

---

[1] That 90 per cent of applications are inadmissible is the Court's own assessment. For instance, the Court's own report on admissibility mentions this figure. *The Admissibility of an Application*, available at www.echr.coe.int/Documents/COURtalks_Inad_Talk_ENG.PDF, 1.

3. The Court shall declare inadmissible any individual application submitted under Article 34 if it considers that:

(a) the application is incompatible with the provisions of the Convention or the Protocols thereto, manifestly ill-founded, or an abuse of the right of individual application; or

(b) the applicant has not suffered a significant disadvantage, unless respect for human rights as defined in the Convention and the Protocols thereto requires an examination of the application on the merits and provided that no case may be rejected on this ground which has not been duly considered by a domestic tribunal.

Admissibility rules are a key mechanism for managing the Court's workload and, to some extent, for maintaining its institutional identity as a subsidiary regional court. Admissibility rules are also, however, a barrier to individuals all across the Council of Europe from accessing substantive adjudication in Strasbourg. Thus, both the substance and the practice of admissibility-related decision making in the ECtHR matter greatly not just for the everyday work of the Court but for any serious engagement with questions of effectiveness and legitimacy which, as we have already seen in Chapter 1, motivate much of our enquiry throughout this book. In Debate 1 of this chapter we consider the relationship between admissibility and the legitimacy of the ECtHR. In some ways this is related to the question of who can make an application to the Court – who counts as a 'victim' of an alleged Convention violation? And how serious should an alleged violation be for the ECtHR to consider it? We discuss these issues in Debates 2 and 3.

At first glance, it may appear that admissibility criteria are 'simple' rules, capable of technical and technocratic application. Whilst admissibility decisions do often involve a high degree of technocratic and bureaucratic decision making, often by the Registry, it will become clear throughout this chapter that the Court retains much discretion. The rules and their application are such that the Court can often find a way to deem admissible a case that it considers warrants substantive adjudication even if it seems to violate the admissibility criteria. This cuts the other way too, of course, so that the criteria can be applied with particular stringency if there is a caseload backlog that needs to be addressed. Thus, admissibility mechanisms available to the Court enable it to choose the most important applications and consider them, even if they are not, strictly speaking, admissible. This is certainly not an uncontroversial approach to admissibility, and raises questions about how much discretion the ECtHR should have in deciding on admissibility; questions we consider in Debate 4.

In Debate 5 we consider how the Court can negotiate two competing objectives: being an effective constitutional tribunal that can shape European Public Order and reviewing each and every application that has been submitted to the Court. The Court's application of the rules of admissibility is crucial here. If admissibility is narrowly defined then few applications will filter through the system and the Court will have more time to deal with 'important' applications. Having said that, this approach is not without drawbacks: it can reduce individual applicants' faith in the system.

Debate 1
How do admissibility criteria affect the Court's legitimacy?

In Chapter 1 we argued that subsidiarity, effectiveness and judicial methodology are important bases of the ECtHR's legitimacy. Two admissibility criteria are directly linked to these: exhaustion of domestic remedies, and the six-month time limit for lodging an application.

Exhaustion of domestic remedies under Article 35 is a reflection of procedural subsidiarity. It requires that domestic mechanisms be 'exhausted' before the ECtHR is asked to consider an alleged violation, so that the national mechanisms have the opportunity first to assess and, where appropriate, redress the violation. The six-month rule ensures that the Court's decisions are predictable and do not disrupt the domestic legal order any more than is necessary by placing some temporal certainty on whether the domestic resolution of an alleged rights violation is likely to be contested at the European level. Both of these criteria seem fairly straightforward and capable of relatively easy assessment, and routine and formal application. However, as with any rules, the extent to which they might be rigidly or flexibly applied can have implications for the extent to which the entity applying them (here the ECtHR) is perceived to be acting legitimately in doing so. So, should a potentially extremely grave violation be deemed inadmissible, and thus not considered, because it was received one hour after the time limit had expired? And if not – if there is a case for a more flexible application of the rule – how can consistency in application be achieved so that the Court does not appear arbitrary or capricious in its admissibility decisions?

Let us consider this first in relation to the six-month rule; perhaps one of the most straightforward and strictly applied admissibility criteria. Thousands of applications are declared inadmissible because they were not submitted on time. After Protocol 15 comes into force the time limit will be further reduced to four months, potentially increasing the occurrence of out-of-time applications, at least in the short term. The Court does not normally allow extension of the six-month period, although it used to allow for the time limit to be met through a fairly minimal engagement by the applicant with the Court. Only around 10 years ago, an applicant or her lawyer could send a letter briefly explaining the facts of the case and, if that letter arrived within the six-month period, it would stop the time successfully and the full application could be submitted on a later date. Sometimes this would be months or even years later, and the Court would reject the subsequent application only if too much time had elapsed between the introduction of the initial letter and the full application form. This system was very beneficial to the applicants but of course raised challenges for the Strasbourg system of human rights protection as so many files remained open, often for years, before any substantive decision on them could be taken. Thus, the ECtHR decided to stop this practice and now the six-month time limit can only be interrupted by a fully completed application form. Save for some special circumstances (like continuing violations or multiple violations) the Court appears, thus, to have prioritised legal certainty and predictability in its application of the six-month rule.[2]

The Court has much broader discretionary powers when assessing whether domestic remedies have been exhausted. First, the Court must decide whether the available remedy in domestic law is effective, so that an applicant would be required to exhaust it before going to Strasbourg. Of course, this involves the Court in making substantive decisions as to the quality of remedies provided in domestic law, but this ensures that states cannot evade supervision by the ECtHR simply by introducing formal and ineffective remedies. This leads inevitably to the application of discretion in admissibility decision making. What does it mean for a remedy to be effective?

The Court normally states that an effective remedy is capable of acknowledging a violation and offering *restitutio in integrum* or adequate compensation if restitution is not possible.[3] Remedies that cannot directly address and rectify alleged violations (like determinations of ombudspersons)[4] or which cannot immediately prevent deterioration of the applicant's situation are considered ineffective. In extradition cases, for example, applicants are not required to exhaust any domestic remedies that would be incapable of suspending the proposed extradition if granted.[5] The Court reserves considerable discretion in deciding whether a remedy is *in principle* effective or not. If a remedy that is considered effective in principle is not exhausted then the application will be declared inadmissible as premature, but if someone exhausts a remedy that is considered ineffective in principle she might miss the six-month time period so that her application to Strasbourg would be inadmissible. Just because a remedy is ineffective in principle does not mean that it might not be effective in a particular case, but such a case would not change its nature in the eyes of the ECtHR, and future complainants would not be required to exhaust it. To illustrate: a potential applicant might apply to an ombudsperson who might manage to resolve this particular case, so that the applicant would not be a 'victim' from the perspective of the ECtHR, but this would not mean that every potential future applicant would have to engage with an ombudsperson whose powers

---

[2] See, for example, *Idalov v Russia* [GC], no. 5826/03, 22 May 2012, paras 127–133 for multiple violations; *McDaid and Others v the United Kingdom* (dec. European Commission), nos 34822/97 and five others, 9 April 1996 for continuing violations; and Rule 47(6)a that provides that only a full application form can now interrupt the six-month term.

[3] See, for example, *Lukenda v Slovenia*, no. 23032/02, ECHR 2005-X, para. 44; *Demopoulos and Others v Turkey* (dec.) [GC], nos 46113/99 and seven others, ECHR 2010, para. 114.

[4] See *Egmez v Cyprus*, no. 30873/96, ECHR 2000-XII, para. 67.

[5] See, for example, *De Souza Ribeiro v France* [GC], no. 22689/07, ECHR 2012.

are considered too limited for this process generally to be deemed an effective remedy under the Convention.

Changes in the means of its application and operation can shift the status of a remedy from 'ineffective in principle' to 'effective in principle', or vice versa. This of course reflects the fact that the effectiveness of a remedy will often very much depend on the context in which it is made and received, and the enforcement infrastructure that surrounds it. Thus, the Court first assesses the effectiveness of the remedy per se when it is introduced on the national level, and then considers its effectiveness in practice, sometimes changing its assessment by reference to how the remedy works 'in the real world'. This can be illustrated by reference to the Italian 'Pinto Law': an attempt to remedy undue delays in criminal proceedings which the Court has frequently found to violate Article 6 of the Convention.[6]

Responding to these repeated findings of violation, the Italian authorities introduced the 'Pinto Law' in 2001. This provided for special judicial review of the length of proceedings and some compensation where undue delay was considered to have occurred. Initially, the Court deemed this remedy effective.[7] However, its optimism about the remedy soon dissipated as Italian national courts began applying the 'Pinto Law' in practice. In *Scordino v Italy* the ECtHR determined that the amount of compensation that is awarded by Italian courts under the 'Pinto Law' is incompatible with the Court's practice, meaning that the remedy was ineffective and therefore did not need to be exhausted.[8] The remedy was, thus, in principle ineffective.

From the point of view of the state authorities, this approach might be seen as an assault on the principle of procedural subsidiarity because the 'Pinto Law' may have been effective in at least some cases. However, the legitimacy of the ECtHR would be undermined if an applicant had to wait for a long time on the national level for an ineffective remedy simply because the ECtHR is reluctant to make determinations of 'in principle' ineffectiveness. Here, as in all cases of establishing whether a remedy is effective or not, the Court must balance the applicants' interests against the systemic interest in maintaining procedural subsidiarity and be prepared to intervene if applicants' rights are not properly protected. This allows for the Court to balance its interest in procedural subsidiarity, the Contracting Parties' interest in being subjected to international supervision only where the national system has inadequately tried to attend to rights violations, and individuals' interest in the protection of their human rights. The connections between all of these interests and, indeed, the difficult task of balancing them, on the one hand, and the development and maintenance of legitimacy, on the other, is clear.

---

[6] See, for example, *Capuano v Italy*, 25 June 1987, Series A no. 119 and *Di Mauro v Italy* [GC], no. 34256/96, ECHR 1999-V.
[7] See, for example, *Daddi v Italy* (dec.), no. 15476/09, 2 June 2009.
[8] *Scordino v Italy* (dec.), no. 36813/97, ECHR 2003-IV.

Debate 2

Who can apply to the Court?

Article 34 states that the Court can receive applications from any person, non-governmental organisation or group of individuals claiming to be the 'victim' of a violation. The concept of 'victim' is, thus, important here. The Court cannot accept applications that would require it to consider laws *in abstracto* (i.e. applications asking the Court to undertake an abstract review of the compatibility of a legal provision with the ECHR[9]) but must instead deal with concrete situations of alleged violation. This partly reflects the institutional limitations of the Council of Europe. Where a domestic constitutional court undertakes an abstract review that results in a finding with potentially far-reaching impacts, the other organs of the state (such as the parliament) can attempt to mitigate that, perhaps by proposing a constitutional change in a corrective referendum or similar. In other words, the judicial power is usually counter-weighted within the infrastructure of the state. This is not as clearly the case in the Council of Europe, where no such counter-weight can easily be identified. Perhaps even more importantly, abstract review allows for very wide judicial intervention in governance of a scale and nature that is not clearly appropriate to a supranational court. National governments, parliaments and the judiciary have the primary responsibility for the administration of the state; as the ECtHR is subsidiary its findings should intrude on the domestic sphere only inasmuch as required by the application of the Convention to concrete factual circumstances. This is precisely why the Court needs to be able to identify a victim: so that a concrete scenario can clearly be sketched and the assessment and judgment made in relation to that.

Having said that, there are more complex cases, such as in relation to covert surveillance discussed below, in which the applicant simply cannot prove that she is a direct victim of a violation. On a strict application of the rules, the Court should declare such an application inadmissible, even if it means that apparent violations of the Convention go un-dealt-with by the Court. In reality, the Court exercises some flexibility and discretion here; if there is absolutely no other way to bring the potential violation before it, the ECtHR may deem the application admissible. Otherwise, it will strike it out and await a complaint in which the victim requirement has been fulfilled.

Although the victim requirement seems straightforward on the face of it, of course there are some situations where a direct victim cannot easily be identified. The Court will occasionally elect to allow those applications to be considered on the merits, prioritising the effective protection of rights over the legal

---

[9] Some national constitutional courts can review constitutionality of a law disconnected with its application in a particular case. For example, abstract review is allowed in Germany, Italy, Spain, Moldova, Serbia, Montenegro and many other countries. See Sadurski, *Rights Before Courts* (2nd edn, Springer, 2008).

certainty that would come with a strict and uncompromising application of this admissibility rule. We identify four areas in which the ECtHR, whilst not resorting to abstract ruling, significantly departed from a strict construction of the victim requirement.

Victims of Covert Activities

In some cases the Court will receive an application about covert activities undertaken by the state. Here, the applicant cannot of course strictly establish victim status, as the covert nature of the activities in question means that nobody can tell for certain whether they were subject to them or not unless this becomes evident in the subsequent criminal proceedings. Here, the Court should, strictly speaking, deem the application inadmissible, but doing so would mean that the covert nature of the activity would be enough to insulate it from the ECtHR's supervision: a clearly undesirable situation. The Court can, thus, consider the victim requirement to be satisfied under certain circumstances. This is well illustrated by the recent Grand Chamber judgment in the case of *Roman Zakharov v Russia* in which the applicant challenged secret surveillance of telephone communications in Russia under Article 8.

Here, the applicant could not establish that his telephone communications had been surveilled; the surveillance was, after all, *secret*. However, rather than deem the application inadmissible because victim status could not conclusively be established, the Court prioritised the effectiveness of human rights protection and considered the probability that the applicant's phone conversations were actually interfered with to assess whether the victim requirement was satisfied. The Court stated that it

> accepts that an applicant can claim to be the victim of a violation occasioned by the mere existence of secret surveillance measures, or legislation permitting secret surveillance measures, if the following conditions are satisfied. Firstly, the Court will take into account the scope of the legislation permitting secret surveillance measures by examining whether the applicant can possibly be affected by it, either because he or she belongs to a group of persons targeted by the contested legislation or because the legislation directly affects all users of communication services by instituting a system where any person can have his or her communications intercepted. Secondly, the Court will take into account the availability of remedies at the national level and will adjust the degree of scrutiny depending on the effectiveness of such remedies.[10]

In other words, if the applicant is a member of a group that may be affected and there is no remedy on the national level that would protect his interests then the Court will find this application admissible, even if individual victimhood cannot conclusively be established.

---

[10] *Roman Zakharov v Russia* [GC], no. 47143/06, ECHR 2015, para. 171.

Unidentifiable Victims

The same dilemma between legal certainty and effectiveness is evident when it is hard to identify a particular victim from a group of potential victims. Here, the ECtHR cannot be sure that each and every applicant is a victim of a violation but nevertheless deems their applications admissible. In *Finogenov and Others v Russia*[11] the Court was asked to consider whether the use of gas against terrorists during the Moscow theatre siege in October 2002 was compatible with the ECHR. In this case, the government argued that the deaths of 125 hostages were not caused by the gas used during the rescue operation, but were due to pre-existing illnesses exacerbated by the siege. The Court was reasonably sceptical about the fact that 125 persons of different age and physical conditions could die simultaneously at the same place from various pre-existing health conditions.[12] At the same time, the Court could not rule out that none of the deaths had been thus caused. The question was whether the likelihood that some of the deceased were not victims should mean that all of the applications were struck out. The Court thought not:

> As transpires from the Government's submissions, and as the events of the case clearly show, the gas was, at best, potentially dangerous for an ordinary person, and potentially fatal for a weakened person. It is possible that some people were affected more than others on account of their physical condition. Moreover, it is even possible that one or two deaths amongst the applicants' relatives were natural accidents and were not related to the gas at all. Nevertheless, it is safe to conclude that the gas remained a primary cause of the death of a large number of the victims.[13]

If legal certainty had been prioritised in this case (so that the possibility that the applicants had not been victims resulted in the case being deemed inadmissible) the extent to which the Russian government had violated (or complied with) the Convention in planning and executing this operation could not have been considered at all by the ECtHR.

Deceased Victims

Another context in which the Court prioritises effectiveness over legal certainty is when nobody but a specialised NGO can bring a complaint on behalf of a deceased applicant. For a long time it has been the Court's practice that if an applicant is dead her case can be continued only by her relatives. If such relatives are not known, are absent, or do not have an interest in the case then it is to be discontinued. This rule was reconsidered by the ECtHR in *Centre for Legal Resources on behalf of Valentin Câmpeanu v Romania*. The victim in this

---

[11] *Finogenov and Others v Russia*, nos 18299/03 and 27311/03, ECHR 2011.
[12] Ibid., para. 201.
[13] Ibid., para. 202.

case had severe mental disabilities and was HIV positive. His mother had abandoned him at birth, and he died in grossly inadequate conditions in the care of the state. The Court described these conditions thus:

> On 20 February 2004 a team of monitors [...] noticed Mr Câmpeanu's condition [...] Mr Câmpeanu was alone in an isolated room, unheated and locked, which contained only a bed without any bedding. He was dressed only in a pyjama top. At the time he could not eat or use the toilet without assistance. However, the staff at the [hospital] refused to help him, allegedly for fear that they would contract HIV. Consequently, the only nutrition provided to Mr Câmpeanu was glucose, through a drip. The report concluded that the hospital had failed to provide him with the most basic treatment and care services.[14]

In this case, there were no relatives who could bring the case to the Court on behalf of the deceased. The ECtHR had to consider whether a nongovernmental organisation, the Centre for Legal Recourses (CLR), could apply on his behalf. The CLR was neither the direct nor indirect victim of this violation, and had no power of attorney from the deceased. A strict application of the rules would suggest that the application ought to have been deemed inadmissible. The Court, however, came to a different conclusion by stating that

> in the exceptional circumstances of this case and bearing in mind the serious nature of the allegations, it should be open to the CLR to act as a representative of Mr Câmpeanu, notwithstanding the fact that it had no power of attorney to act on his behalf and that he died before the application was lodged under the Convention. To find otherwise would amount to preventing such serious allegations of a violation of the Convention from being examined at an international level, with the risk that the respondent State might escape accountability under the Convention as a result of its own failure to appoint a legal representative to act on his behalf as it was required to do under national law. Allowing the respondent State to escape accountability in this manner would not be consistent with the general spirit of the Convention, nor with the High Contracting Parties' obligation under Article 34 of the Convention not to hinder in any way the effective exercise of the right to bring an application before the Court.[15]

Here, the CLR was clearly not the victim but the Court decided that in the interest of fairness and effective rights protection the application warranted assessment on its merits. It thus made it clear that in exceptional cases NGOs could continue an application on behalf of a deceased victim. This exception to the victim rule has since been used in at least two other cases: *Kondrulin v*

---

[14] *Centre for Legal Resources on behalf of Valentin Câmpeanu v Romania* [GC], no. 47848/08, ECHR 2014, para. 23.

[15] Ibid., 112.

Russia[16] and *Association for the Defence of Human Rights in Romania –Helsinki Committee on behalf of Ionel Garcea v Romania.*[17]

Corporate Victims

As legal persons, corporations can make applications to the ECtHR; the question is who can take the application on their behalf. Normally, that would be the head of the corporate body such as the CEO or director. However, if the corporation is in the process of liquidation this question becomes more challenging. Whilst a state-appointed liquidator should ordinarily represent the company, in certain circumstances the shareholders might lodge an application with the Court. In the case of *Agrotexim and Others v Greece* the Court held that this would only be permitted where 'it is clearly established that it is impossible for the company to apply to the Convention institutions through the organs set up under its Articles of incorporation or – in the event of liquidation – through its liquidators'.[18] Whilst this is a very high standard, it does not absolutely preclude a shareholder-initiated application to the Court where it is necessary because the ordinary organs of the company, for whatever reason, cannot act in this way on its behalf. In the case of *Capital Bank AD v Bulgaria* the ECtHR explained that allowing a state-appointed liquidator to represent a particular company in the ECtHR will in some cases lead to undermining 'the very essence of the right of individual applications by legal persons, as it would encourage governments to deprive such entities of the possibility to pursue an application lodged at a time when they enjoyed legal personality'.[19] That would in turn mean that the rights enjoyed by legal entities under the Convention became illusory. In *OAO Neftyanaya Kompaniya Yukos v Russia* the Court once again used its discretion at the admissibility stage. The applicant company was effectively bankrupted and sold by the Russian authorities, meaning that it had ceased to exist before the Court had a chance to consider the case.[20] Strictly speaking, then, no victim existed and the application should have been deemed inadmissible. The ECtHR declared this application admissible because otherwise it would encourage authorities to liquidate companies in order to avoid international responsibility for violation of their rights.

These four examples illustrate a few important principles. First, the Court takes the victim requirement seriously, usually applying it strictly to ensure an appropriate level of legal certainty. Second, if it is impossible to prove victim status or an application cannot be made by the victim directly the Court may prioritise the effectiveness of human rights protection over strict application of the victim rule, and allow the application in order to ensure the complaint

---

[16] *Kondrulin v Russia*, no. 12987/15, 20 September 2016.

[17] *Association for the Defence of Human Rights in Romania – Helsinki Committee on behalf of Ionel Garcea v Romania*, no. 2959/11, 24 March 2015.

[18] *Agrotexim and Others v Greece*, 24 October 1995, Series A no. 330-A, para. 66.

[19] *Capital Bank AD v Bulgaria*, no. 49429/99, ECHR 2005-XII, para. 80.

[20] *OAO Neftyanaya Kompaniya Yukos v Russia* (dec.), no. 14902/04, 29 January 2009.

can be adjudicated upon. The Court thus attempts to strike a balance between strict application of the rules and effectiveness-oriented discretion, illustrating that even the most straightforward-looking admissibility criteria involve some degree of *judgement* in their application.

Debate 3

How significant must disadvantage be?

In 2010 Protocol 14 introduced a new admissibility criterion focusing on the significance of the alleged violation. Following that adjustment, Article 35(3)(b) now reads:

> The Court shall declare inadmissible any individual application submitted under Article 34 if it considers that:
>
> [...]
>
> (b) the applicant has not suffered a significant disadvantage, unless respect for human rights as defined in the Convention and the Protocols thereto requires an examination of the application on the merits and provided that no case may be rejected on this ground which has not been duly considered by a domestic tribunal.[21]

After Protocol 15 enters into force, the application of this admissibility criterion will be broadened by removal of the requirement that it is only applicable if the case has been duly considered by a domestic tribunal.

This criterion adds considerable discretion at the stage of assessing admissibility. It also calls into question the extent to which the Court may have to balance broader, systemic interests (in prioritising the 'most important' cases) and the principle of individual complaint and individual justice in the ECtHR.

> On the face of it, 'no significant disadvantage' appears to be a criterion that is intended to allow the Court to be more selective by filtering out less important cases (with importance being determined by using significance of disadvantage as a proxy), thus allowing the ECtHR to focus on cases that might be said to have more potential for development of the Convention.[22]

The former Prime Minister of the United Kingdom David Cameron famously called the ECtHR a 'small claims court' and it seems this amendment of the

---

[21] The Brighton Declaration proposes amendment of this Article to remove the phrase 'and provided that no case ... tribunal'; Brighton Declaration, para. 15.

[22] de Londras and Dzehtsiarou, 'Managing Judicial Innovation in the European Court of Human Rights' (2015) 15 *Human Rights Law Review* 523, 531. The history of the introduction of this new criterion points to its attempt to achieve all of these things: Buyse, 'Significantly Insignificant? The Life in the Margins of the Admissibility Criterion in Article 35 § 3 (b) ECHR' in McGonigle et al. (eds), *The Realization of Human Rights: When Theory Meets Practice. Studies in Honour of Leo Zwaak* (Intersentia, 2013).

Convention was a response to such criticism.[23] Whenever the question of significant disadvantage is considered by the Court[24] as a matter of admissibility, an underlying claim is being made that reflects the tension between the Court as a constitutionalist actor and the Court as simple adjudicator of individual complaints.

> The implicit claim is either (i) that the disadvantage suffered is so significant that a refusal to hear the case when it is otherwise inadmissible would be unjustifiable on constitutionalist grounds, even if its resolution requires judicial innovation and (ii) that the disadvantage suffered is so insignificant (thus the case does not raise 'real' constitutionalist questions) that even compliance with the other admissibility grounds ought not to be sufficient for the Court – overburdened and in need of rationalising its workload as it is – to agree to hear it.[25]

Under no circumstances could it be suggested that this analysis is simple or automatic or that it requires no discretion.

The Court has made it clear that determining whether the disadvantage suffered by the applicant was significant requires consideration of both '[t]he applicant's *subjective* feeling about the impact of the alleged violations has to be justifiable on *objective* grounds'.[26] This means that the Court will consider what is at stake (the objective element) and the impact of this potential damage on the applicant (the subjective element). Of course, both require a good deal of judgement in order to assess them, even as a matter of admissibility.

The criterion also raises questions about the extent to which the Convention is beginning to shift from a principle of individual justice and universality of rights protection. It is of the essence of human rights as protected by contemporary law that they are available to all, and that all breaches are subject to mechanisms to ensure that they are remedied. The 'no significant disadvantage' admissibility criterion seems to undermine this, suggesting that the ECtHR will only step into ensure protection of human rights if the alleged violation caused significant discomfort. This is of course justifiable from a purely instrumental point of view: the Court does not have unlimited resources, it cannot replace national systems of human rights protection, and dealing with minor claims can potentially delay its involvement with larger-scale issues. One might argue that the 'no significant disadvantage' requirement is a proper compromise between the ideal of universality and the reality of limited resources. On the one hand, the Convention allows small claims to be rejected; but on the other hand, the Convention puts an obligation on the Court to consider

---

[23] Watt, 'David Cameron Calls for Reform of European Court of Human Rights', *The Guardian,* 25 January 2012, available at www.theguardian.com/law/2012/jan/25/david-cameron-reform-european-court.

[24] This new admissibility criterion can be raised by a respondent government or by the Court on its own motion, see *Ionescu v Romania* (dec.), no. 36659/04, 1 June 2010.

[25] de Londras and Dzehtsiarou, 'Managing Judicial Innovation' (above, n. 22), 531.

[26] *Korolev v Russia* (dec.), no. 25551/05, ECHR 2010 (emphasis added).

the consequences for the constitutionalist development of the Convention of declaring the case inadmissible due to there being no significant disadvantage. Pursuant to Article 35 the ECtHR should not deploy this admissibility criterion if 'respect for human rights' requires examination of the case. Thus, it seems that if the issue is of prima facie constitutionalist importance, lack of significant disadvantage becomes irrelevant. Due to the fact that neither 'significant disadvantage' nor 'respect for human rights' can be exactingly defined, it may well be that the ECtHR will be free to use wide discretion in application of this criterion so that it might be relaxed in order to do justice, as we have seen that many of the other admissibility criteria are.

Debate 4

How much discretion should the Court have in deciding admissibility?

In Debates 2 and 3 we have already established that admissibility criteria leave the Court with a considerable amount of discretion, even in what seems at first glance to be a 'merely' technical assessment of admissibility. This may seem confounding. As Tickell has observed:

> Determination of the admissibility of applications is conceived as the self-evident administration of clear rules, operating without flexibility and without discretion. Case 'filtering' under the Convention's admissibility criteria is envisaged as a solid 'iron cage' of weary but dogged administration, its clear rules gating the legally, politically and ethically laden work of adjudication which admissible, 'meritorious' cases are subjected to. This distinction is neatly captured by the official terminology. The admissibility of an application is determined by a 'decision', while the merits of a case are assessed in a 'judgment'. Admissibility decision-making is not a 'judgment' in institutional terms, but in the orthodox understanding, it is also assumed to involve no judgment on the part of judges and Registry lawyers.[27]

However, in truth there are *no* admissibility criteria that would exclude discretionary decision making. Indeed, so extensive is the discretion in practice that what is passed off as an admissibility decision might often seem much more like a judgment on the merits, even though strictly speaking a judgment on merits should have a greater level of reasoning that can be analysed than is usually the case with decisions on admissibility. Most admissibility decisions are not published, but they are final and cannot be appealed. Moreover, the judges usually decide inadmissibility on the basis of a short note prepared by the lawyers of the Registry who are often from the respondent state against which the application

---

[27] Tickell, 'Dismantling the Iron-Cage: the Discursive Persistence and Legal Failure of a "Bureaucratic Rational" Construction of the Admissibility Decision-Making of the European Court of Human Rights' (2011) 12 *German Law Journal* 1786, 1789.

was brought. These notes explain the basic facts of the case and (very) briefly the reasons for declaring it inadmissible. Lists of putatively inadmissible cases

> transmitted electronically to the single judges contain only one or two sentence summaries of each matter recommended for dismissal, identifying the right being invoked; the judges do not see the applications and a few have complained of feeling that they are expected to 'rubber-stamp' the decisions of the Registry.[28]

Although these notes from the Registry are checked and re-checked by more experienced lawyers, the original 'filtering' is often done by a relatively inexperienced B lawyer (as discussed in Chapter 1). This initial screening is crucial for the fate of the case. Of course, a reasonable amount of trust should be an integral part of a judicial system, but some key safeguards need also to be maintained. With the enormous number of inadmissible applications that the Court rejects every year, it is reasonable to imagine that some really important issues may slip through this system. Although this shadow decision making is very effective and quick in tackling the Court's backlog, it begs a lot of questions in terms of procedural legitimacy. In 2017 it was announced that the Court will start informing the applicants of which criteria of admissibility a particular application failed to comply with. This new approach may enhance the transparency of admissibility decision making. However, not even that change will resolve the fact that the criteria themselves allow for (sometimes quite significant) discretion.

The requirements that there would be no abuse of the right of individual petition and that the application ought not to be manifestly ill-founded both allow for very significant discretion. The Court used abuse of petition to reject 'petty' applications even before Protocol 14 introduced the 'no significant disadvantage' admissibility criterion discussed in Debate 3.[29] Abuse of petition can mean anything from providing false documents[30] or identity[31] or failing to update the Court about important developments in the case on the national level to use of offensive language[32] or disclosure of the terms of friendly settlements. Undoubtedly, decisions about apparent abuse of the right of petition are complex. They require an understanding of the national legal system and national language, and often call for an assessment of an applicant's aim in making an application. Although some instances declaring an application to be an abuse of right of individual petition can be rather straightforward, in others it is anything but.

The same is true of manifestly ill-founded claims, which are those that treat the ECtHR as a court of fourth instance, applications with a clear absence

---

[28] Shelton, 'Significantly Disadvantaged? Shrinking Access to the European Court of Human Rights' (2016) 16 *Human Rights Law Review* 303, 309.

[29] See *Bock v Germany* (dec.), no. 22051/07, 19 January 2010 and *Dudek v Germany* (dec.), no. 12977/09, 23 November 2010.

[30] *Poznanski and Others v Germany* (dec.), no. 25101/05, 3 July 2007.

[31] *Drijfhout v Netherlands* (dec.), no. 51721/09, 22 February 2011.

[32] *Kolosovskiy v Latvia* (dec.), no. 50183/99, 29 January 2007.

of a violation, unsubstantiated applications and the like. In these cases, the line between an admissibility decision (manifestly ill-founded) and a merits decision (no violation) seems very thin indeed, and the Court appears to use substantial discretion in categorising the outcome as one or the other. Let us illustrate this by reference to situations where there is a clear or apparent lack of violation. In *Mentzen v Latvia* the applicant complained that the Latvian authorities had changed her surname according to Latvian spelling rules.[33] Although the ECtHR has established that there was an interference with the rights protected by the Convention and discussed the proportionality of the interference, the result was that the application was deemed manifestly ill-founded instead of the Court making a finding of no violation. Although legally speaking the outcome is almost the same, there is a procedural difference (where there is no violation a case can be referred to the Grand Chamber) and a symbolic difference for the applicant.

In some instances those cases that are declared manifestly ill-founded by the ECtHR are not only accepted by other international tribunals but result in violations being found there. In *Singh v France*[34] the ECtHR considered whether the French requirement to appear bareheaded on official photographs is compatible with the freedom of religion of the followers of the Sikh religion who are obliged to wear a turban. The ECtHR decided that religious rights can be limited in the interests of public safety, and declared the application manifestly ill-founded. The same applicant brought a complaint about the same matter to the Human Rights Committee (UN HRC) – the UN body that supervises implementation of the International Covenant of Civil and Political Rights. Article 18 of the Covenant protects the freedom to manifest religion similar to that which Article 9 of the ECHR provides. The UN HRC declared this application admissible and found a violation of the Covenant in this case. It is quite normal that different international tribunals weigh different aspects of the proportionality test differently. The situation here is more troubling, though, as by finding the case to be manifestly ill-founded, the ECtHR denied the opportunity for the applicants to be heard on the merits, whilst another tribunal considered this case and found violation.[35]

Steven Greer has written:

> It is naïve [...] to regard the manifestly ill-founded criterion as an objective test. Determining if an application is, or is not, manifestly ill-founded requires the exercise of judgment and the interpretation of conduct, facts, and norms; it is, therefore, inescapably discretionary. Some commentators maintain that many complaints are rejected on this basis simply because the Court does not have the resources to consider them properly.[36]

---

[33] *Mentzen v Latvia* (dec.), no. 71074/01, ECHR 2004-XII.
[34] *Singh v France* (dec.), no. 4479/07, 13 November 2008.
[35] *Singh v France*, HRC, 26/09/2013, CCPR/C/108/D/1928/2010.
[36] Greer, 'What's Wrong with the European Convention on Human Rights' (2008) 30 *Human Rights Quarterly* 680, 686.

The authors of Harris, O'Boyle and Warbrick Law of the European Convention on Human Rights also confess that manifestly ill-founded decisions lead to the rejection of complaints that are not manifestly deficient on their merits. However, they offer at least two reasons why this practice should be continued nonetheless:

> First, in single judge and Committee formations, it allows the Court summarily to declare cases inadmissible, thus freeing judicial time for more deserving cases. Second, it allows Chambers of the Court to dispose of cases where, even though the issues may be quite complex, nothing useful is to be gained from communicating the case and obtaining the views of the respondent government: so called '*de plano* inadmissibility' decisions.[37]

For these authors, then, manifestly ill-founded decisions may well involve the exercise of a great deal of discretion in the context of deciding on admissibility, but this can be justified by the need to keep an overburdened and under-resourced court operating effectively. This is yet another illustration of the Court having to negotiate competing grounds of its legitimacy. On the one hand the Court has to deliver judgments in a timely manner; on the other it should avoid allowing procedural simplifications to create so much discretion that equally meritorious cases may have utterly divergent outcomes.

Whilst the requirement that applications must not be 'manifestly ill-founded' gives the Court very extensive discretion, significant discretion can also be exercised in relation to other criteria. Let us take, for example, what happens when a victim loses her victim status because 'the national authorities have acknowledged, either expressly or in substance, and then afforded redress for, the breach of the Convention'.[38] Even if these conditions are satisfied the ECtHR might consider whether there are any reasons related to European Public Order that would justify continuation of the proceedings.[39] The Court has also reserved some discretion in deciding whether the redress provided by the Contracting Party is sufficient to justify discontinuation of a case. In *Ciorap v Moldova (no. 2)*, for example, the Moldovan Supreme Court explicitly acknowledged that denial of medical treatment combined with the conditions of detention amounted to inhuman treatment of the applicant and awarded him a compensation of €600 for non-pecuniary damage. The ECtHR might have considered the applicant's victim status to have been resolved through this award, but instead declared the case admissible because the compensation was grossly inadequate.[40]

The ECtHR cannot accept an application if it has been adjudicated by or is pending at another international tribunal. Although rare, the decision of

---

[37] Harris et al., *Harris, O'Boyle and Warbrick Law of the European Convention on Human Rights* (3rd edn, Oxford University Press, 2014), 78–79.

[38] *Amuur v France*, 25 June 1996, Reports of Judgments and Decisions 1996-III, para. 36.

[39] *Paez v Sweden*, 30 October 1997, Reports of Judgments and Decisions 1997-VII, para. 30.

[40] *Ciorap v Moldova (no. 2)*, no. 7481/06, 20 July 2010.

admissibility in such cases involves assessment of the parties in the respective proceedings, the relevant legal provisions relied on by them, the scope of their claims, and the types of the redress sought in order to assess whether they are properly regarded as the same complaints. This is not always straightforward. In *Folgerø and Others v Norway*, the Court considered whether the refusal of the Norwegian authorities to grant the applicants a full exemption from religious classes in public schools violated their rights under Articles 9 ECHR and 2 of Protocol 1. A very similar complaint was submitted by another complainant to the UN HRC. Moreover, the complaint was brought to the UN HRC after the same national proceedings to which both groups of applicants were parties.[41] To all intents and purposes, then, these were very similar if not effectively the same complaint, but the ECtHR declared the application admissible, formally focusing on the fact that the applicants in the UN HRC and ECtHR were not the same people as the applicants in the case before it. In contrast, we can consider *POA and Others v the United Kingdom*. This concerned the blanket ban on industrial action by prison officers. The applicants – the prison officers' trade union and two of its officials – argued that the ban was incompatible with Article 11 ECHR. The complaint had been also raised before the International Labour Organisation (ILO) Committee on Freedom of Association, and according to the Court the complaints to the ILO and ECtHR were virtually identical, although not all the applicants were the same.[42] Some of the applicants to the ECtHR were individual persons, not the trade union as such, and they were not and could not be the claimants in the ILO as it only accepts collective applications. However, the Court declared this application inadmissible because 'applicants must be seen as being closely associated with the proceedings and the complaints before the Committee on Freedom of Association, by virtue of their status as officials of the POA'.[43] It is difficult to see what can have made the difference between *Folgerø and Others* and *POA and Others*, but one was deemed inadmissible and the other not, both under the same principle. Here the effects of the Court's discretion were clearly felt.

Even the very narrowest of admissibility criteria allow for some discretion. Take, for example, the rule against anonymous applications. This requires that the applicant be identified in applications, and when a case is communicated to the respondent government the name of the applicant will be revealed. The rationale behind this is fairly simple: the respondent government needs to know who the applicant is if it is to be able to prove that alleged human rights violation did not happen. The Court normally informs the Contracting Parties about the name of the applicant even if she is afraid that such disclosure will put her at risk of ill-treatment. Whilst the applicant can be anonymised in such a case, this only means that the public at large will not know her name; the respondent state still will. Even in respect of this – seemingly unambiguous –

---

[41] *Folgerø and Others v Norway* [GC], no. 15472/02, ECHR 2007-III.

[42] *POA and Others v the United Kingdom* (dec.), no. 59253/11, 21 May 2013, para. 28.

[43] Ibid., para. 28.

rule, however, the Court exercises discretion. In *Shamayev and Others v Georgia and Russia* the applicants were of Chechen origin and were awaiting extradition from Georgia to Russia. The events complained of took place during the war in Chechnya and the applicants were wanted in Russia on suspicion of terrorism. Some of the applicants submitted pseudonyms instead of their real names in their initial applications to the Court (they later disclosed their true identities). The Russian government argued that the application was anonymous and should be declared inadmissible, but the ECtHR disagreed, stating that 'the Court does not question the fact that, behind the tactics of concealing true identities for reasons that can be understood, there are persons who are real, concrete and identifiable by a sufficient number of indicia, other than their names'.[44] This can be contrasted with '*Blonje' v the Netherlands* in which the applicant also used a pseudonym but the Court declared the case inadmissible.[45] There are very few published decisions of the Court dealing with anonymity as it seems that the majority of such cases are dealt with by a single judge and never pronounced publicly. Although the *Shamayev* judgment is exceptional it underpins the argument that we are making here, namely that admissibility is far from being free from judicial discretion and the process of admissibility needs to be closely scrutinised.

Debate 5
How does admissibility relate to effectiveness?

It seems that the Court derives at least some of its legitimacy in the eyes of individuals from the fact that it accepts applications from each and every person who is under the jurisdiction of one of 47 Contracting Parties to the Convention. Of course, inadmissible applications can and perhaps should be rejected, and we have already seen that the criteria of admissibility have plenty of discretion built into them. As a result, the outcome of an application is not always easily predictable. This lack of predictability has allowed some commentators to argue that the Court picks and chooses which applications it deems important enough to assess on their merits through admissibility decisions.[46] The suggestion is that the Court is really making decisions about importance, prioritising cases of potential constitutionalist significance, but continuing to perform the 'dual functions' of individual and constitutional justice.

This allegation is perhaps given fuel by the fact that admissibility decisions are lacking in transparency; there is not usually a written and reasoned judgment

---

[44] *Shamayev and Others v Georgia and Russia* (dec.), no. 36378/02, 12 April 2005.
[45] '*Blonje' v the Netherlands* (dec.), no. 7245/09, 15 September 2009.
[46] Paper by Greer and Wildhaber, 'Revisiting the Debate about "Constitutionalising" the European Court of Human Rights' (2012) 12 *Human Rights Law Review* 655; de Londras, 'Dual Functionality and the Persistent Frailty of the European Court of Human Rights' (2013) *European Human Rights Law Review* 38.

explaining the admissibility decision. The Court justifies this by reference to the limited resources available and the practical difficulties of providing reasons in every inadmissibility decision. The truth is that in most cases unsuccessful applicants do not even know which admissibility criterion they failed to fulfil.[47] Given this, the argument goes that the Court may well be moving away from a vision of individual justice and instead embracing the framework of constitutional justice within which it only needs to focus on vaguely defined strategic cases that can improve the system of human rights as a whole.

This conclusion can also be corroborated by references to the Court's official priority policy,[48] which was introduced in 2009 to ensure important cases would be dealt with in a timely manner. Before 2009, all cases were dealt with in chronological order, which meant that some crucial issues that needed prompt resolution could be stuck in the Court's docket for years. Pragmatically, the introduction of this priority policy strengthens the constitutionalist capacity of the ECtHR, meaning that the applications raising questions capable of having an impact on the effectiveness of the Convention system in a general sense have priority even over the applications related to the right to life, the prohibition of torture and the prohibition of slavery. This at least suggests that the Court is prioritising its resources in order to concentrate on its general impact on the development of human rights standards, rather than focusing them on remedying individual human rights violations *for the sake of ensuring they are remedied*.

This not only has an impact on the Court's ability to develop its constitutional role, which some consider would increase its overall effectiveness, but also on the likelihood of the Contracting Parties being the subjects of adverse decisions. As it stands, over 80 per cent of admissible cases result in a finding of violation of the ECHR[49] so that, as Shelton has commented, '[l]imiting admissibility means limiting condemnation'.[50] Of course, the proponents of limited admissibility argue that the Court is simply unable to deal with all applications that are submitted to it and loses its impact on shaping European Public Order when it tries to do so.[51] However, there are at least two counter-arguments to that.

First, the Court derives at least some of its moral legitimacy from the fact that every person under the jurisdiction of the 47 Contracting Parties can bring

---

[47] The Court has recently announced that it will inform the applicants about the ground of inadmissibility. However, it seems unlikely that the Court will offer any reasons why a particular ground should be applied in a case at hand. See 'European Court Launches New System For Single Judge Decisions', *Human Rights Europe*, 1 June 2017, available at www.humanrightseurope.org/2017/06/european-court-launches-new-system-for-single-judge-decisions/.

[48] 'The Court's Priority Policy', available at www.echr.coe.int/documents/priority_policy_eng.pdf.

[49] In 2016 the Court delivered 993 judgments; in 828 judgments (83 per cent) the Court found at least one violation of the Convention (HUDOC database search).

[50] Shelton, 'Significantly Disadvantaged?' (above, n. 28), 306.

[51] See de Londras, 'Dual Functionality' (above, n. 46).

a complaint and this complaint will be dealt with. This rule is egalitarian and non-arbitrary (at least on the face of it). Here two clear sources of the Court's legitimacy might be in tension with one another: its effectiveness and its moral purpose of universal rights protection. Can the Court sacrifice some less important applications (irrespective of how this might be defined in practice) in order to achieve more impact in particular problematic areas? Of course, the answer to this question will be a matter of degree, depending on how much positive impact the Court can make and how many applications should be sacrificed in order to achieve that. If it takes the Court decades to come to an important application because it has to deal with hundreds of low importance or inadmissible applications, then its effectiveness will be very low. On the contrary, if the Court concentrates on a handful of 'important' cases, ignoring all other potentially meritorious applications, then the ECtHR might lose its role as an effective adjudicator and applications may simply not make their way to the Court at all. Taken from this perspective, the argument goes that the ECtHR needs to strike a very delicate balance between assessing the importance of the issues it deals with and maintaining the right of individual petition. Indeed, this is effectively what the Court already attempts to do.

Second, in order to have a positive impact on rights in at least some Contracting Parties the Court cannot easily avoid repetitive cases. This is because it has become clear that countries in respect of which repetitive cases are brought are either unwilling or unable to adopt effective solutions to systemic and recurring human rights violations (such as detention conditions or delays in criminal proceedings) and that the Court offers (and should offer) some satisfaction to the aggrieved applicants.[52] One might wonder whether this is the proper role of an international tribunal, but on the other hand it may create sufficient pressure on Contracting Parties to introduce reforms to avoid constant embarrassment on the international level that there would eventually be a positive rights-enhancing outcome.[53]

We must not forget that we still live in a Europe where many millions of people cannot receive redress in their domestic legal systems, where human rights abuses are daily and serious, and where for many the ECtHR truly is the only hope of protecting rights and effecting change. In these circumstances, it is difficult to avoid the argument that the Court ought to continue to take individual applications, even where they might not seem serious enough for the level of resource that will be applied to addressing them, because people frankly *need* it to do so. However, what we have seen in this chapter is that through application of the admissibility criteria in ways that display significant discretion this is not necessarily happening, or at least not consistently enough to sustain

---

[52] Dzehtsiarou and Greene, 'Restructuring the European Court of Human Rights: Preserving the Right of Individual Petition and Promoting Constitutionalism' (2013) *Public Law* 710.

[53] The reform of the system of enforcement of final national judgments in civil cases in Russia was at least partially a result of a major number of applications adjudicated by the ECtHR; see *Burdov v Russia* (no. 2), no. 33509/04, ECHR 2009.

this argument. Neither is the Court clearly abandoning this approach and embracing a constitutionalist approach. For some, it is precisely this that makes the Court effective: its ability to do both, albeit imperfectly. For others, a decision between the two is urgently required. Ultimately, this goes once more to the question of what the ECtHR is for, and how its purpose can be achieved.

CONCLUSION

Every formation of the Court can declare a judgment inadmissible, including the Grand Chamber.[54] As we have seen in this chapter, many decisions that are formally made by a formation of the Court are effectively pre-determined by Registry lawyers, a part of the Court we have already argued is opaque, under-studied, and vitally important to the work of the Court. This is of concern not just because of the lack of transparency, but because, as we have shown, every criterion of admissibility allows some exceptions and the Court can adjust these criteria if circumstances require it. Admissibility criteria range between those which allow very broad discretion and are akin to decisions on merits (such as manifestly ill-founded complaints or abuse of the right to individual petition) and those which are less open to interpretation but still allow some creative decision making from the Court (such as the six-month rule or the rule against anonymous applications). Not only that, but admissibility is a key stage in the management of the work – and the function – of the Court, which must sometimes decide between constitutionalism and adjudication.

FURTHER READING

de Londras, 'Dual Functionality and the Persistent Frailty of the European Court of Human Rights' (2013) *European Human Rights Law Review* 38.

Dzehtsiarou and Greene, 'Restructuring the European Court of Human Rights: Preserving the Right of Individual Petition and Promoting Constitutionalism' (2013) *Public Law* 710.

Greer and Wildhaber, 'Revisiting the Debate about 'Constitutionalising' the European Court of Human Rights' (2012) 12 *Human Rights Law Review* 655.

Phuong, 'The Relationship between the European Court of Human Rights and the Human Rights Committee: Has the Same Matter Already Been Examined?' (2007) 7 *Human Rights Law Review* 385.

Shelton, 'Significantly Disadvantaged? Shrinking Access to the European Court of Human Rights' (2016) 16 *Human Rights Law Review* 303.

Tickell, 'Dismantling the Iron-Cage: The Discursive Persistence and Legal Failure of a "Bureaucratic Rational" Construction of the Admissibility Decision-Making of the European Court of Human Rights' (2011) 12 *German Law Journal* 1786.

---

[54] *Banković and Others v Belgium and Others* (dec.) [GC], no. 52207/99, ECHR 2001-XII, *Behrami v France* and *Saramati v France, Germany and Norway* (dec.), no. 71412/01 and 78166/01, 2 May 2007.

CHAPTER 4

Evolution or Revolution?

Interpretation of the Convention by the European Court of Human Rights

The European Court of Human Rights (ECtHR or the Court) has long held that the European Convention on Human Rights (ECHR or Convention) is a living instrument to be interpreted in the light of present-day conditions. What this means, in essence, is that the Convention is subject to evolutive interpretation, i.e. its meaning can 'evolve' over time. As one might imagine, this is hardly without controversy. Not only does it raise questions about the appropriate role of judges in 'making' law (as it is sometimes put) but also about whether what the Convention is now said to mean (having been subject to evolutive interpretation) is what the states actually signed up to. In other words, to return to Chapter 1, is it *legitimate* when we consider what states consented to when they ratified the Convention? Does evolutive interpretation mean that states are being held to international standards to which they have never truly consented? Or should states be presumed to consent to a human rights instrument and its associated system of application and enforcement (such as the ECHR and its infrastructure) *as interpreted and applied* by its assigned adjudicator (in this case, the Court and, before that, the Commission and the Court)? If so, how can this presumption can be justified?

Even if it is the case that states should be seen as consenting broadly to the *system* as it develops and is applied (just as, for example, is the case with the world trade system as understood, interpreted, and applied within the WTO's infrastructure of adjudication), it is clear that evolutive interpretation has the potential to create tensions between the Court and the Contracting Parties. At the very least, states may raise a metaphorical eyebrow when the Court finds them to have obligations under the Convention that were not and could not have been foreseen when they signed up to it; at its peak, this can underpin damaging claims that the Court is illegitimate. Given this context, we might wonder why the Court engages in evolutive interpretation at all. Why does it open itself up to claims of illegitimacy? What is the value that evolutive interpretation brings to the Strasbourg system of human rights protection? This is the first debate that we will consider here. Even if evolution might be said to be valuable in a system designed to protect rights, determination of a 'tipping point' for such evolution can be hotly contested; the 'tipping moment' is the moment at which the law is ripe for evolution and the Court acts accordingly. So, the second debate we will consider relates to precisely this question: when does the Court decide it is time for evolution, and how does it come to that decision? It is often assumed that evolutive interpretation broadens the scope of human rights protection and improves human rights standards, but is evolutive interpretation necessarily progressive, or can rights protection be lowered by the application of the 'living instrument' doctrine? This is the third debate that we will look at in this chapter.

Debate 1

Is evolutive interpretation of the Convention necessary?

The argument against evolutive interpretation is, in essence, an originalist one: it is the claim that the document means what it meant when it was signed.[1] Any development beyond that is illegitimate because it involves a Court (perceived as undemocratic) 'making law'. This is a common argument in relation to written domestic constitutions, for example, but it is one to which there is a compelling response in that context. Let us, for these purposes, analogise the Convention to a constitution for a moment. Constitutions should have a certain chrononomy: they should be able to account for the past, govern the present, and accommodate the future.[2]

As society evolves, and as new governance challenges emerge, it is unlikely that a strictly originalist approach to any text would allow for it to meet that standard of chrononomy, and so one of three things must happen: the Constitution must be formally changed to account for social change and new governance challenges; the Constitution must evolve (through judicial interpretation and everyday constitutional practice) to govern contemporary society; or the Constitution must be left to be unfit for purpose, governing only the phenomena that can be squeezed into the text as it was at the time that it was written and therefore failing to deal properly with social and legal phenomena that subsequently develop. Each of these positions has its value and its drawbacks. The first allows for popular rejuvenation of the constitutional landscape, although it also brings a certain degree of instability. It can also be manifestly late and ineffective in dealing with complex current legal issues, as formal legal change is often time consuming and (for good reasons) difficult to achieve. The second allows for constitutions to evolve in order to ensure that all areas of government activity are effectively governed by the constitutional *acquis*. Having said

---

[1] The arguments of originalism are widely used in debates regarding the meaning of the US constitution. See, for example, McGinnis and Rappaport, *Originalism and the Good Constitution* (Harvard University Press, 2013).

[2] Kay, 'Constitutional Chrononomy' (2000) 13 *Ratio Juris* 31.

that, judicial interpretation resembles law-making and opens the courts to criticism. The third option brings the virtue of legal stability and certainty whilst also limiting the possibility of what some (derisorily) term 'judicial activism'.[3] The effectiveness of such documents is very limited as it is often impossible to apply concepts that are over 50 years old to the current events.

Of course, the ECHR is not a constitution per se but some of these same arguments might be said to arise in respect of it. The Convention emerged in a very particular set of circumstances; when the continent of Europe (and beyond) had just emerged from World War II and the Holocaust, when Europe (and the world) was dividing into 'the West' and 'the Rest' in political terms, and when political stability and peace were far from guaranteed. The Convention, then, had a certain context and was intended – as we said in Chapter 1 – to achieve a particular outcome: to protect us from the re-emergence of totalitarianism and to firmly identify human rights as having the capacity to *limit* states' desired actions. An originalist view of the Convention would say that this is what the Convention was designed to do, and that this is *all* the Convention is designed to do, so that using it to prevent the state from deporting a suspected terrorist, or to require the state to recognise someone's true gender, is taking it too far. It is not what the states consented to.

Of course, whether this is right or not depends on one's perspective on what the Convention was for. Was the Convention designed in order to simply protect the rights specified therein in the manner understood at the time? Or was the Convention drafted to ensure that human rights would be an effective limitation on state power? If the latter, then evolution of our understanding of the rights therein is not only legitimate but also, arguably, *necessary*. Without it, we might wonder whether, for example, rights implications arising from developments in technology (e.g. internet surveillance, advances in genetics, and assisted human reproduction) could be effectively addressed by application of the Convention. A literal originalist approach to the meaning of the Convention would suggest that the Court should not deal with any of those issues, at least inasmuch as they give rise to novel questions of rights that did not arise and would not have been contemplated in 1950; that the text of the Convention has a clear and 'true' meaning, to which judges should limit themselves.[4] Even some enthusiasts of a restrained judiciary accept that the shortcomings that would flow from such propositions show evolution in some senses is necessary.[5]

---

[3] For a full account of the role and value of judicial innovation in constitutional evolution see de Londras, 'In Defence of Judicial Innovation and Constitutional Evolution' in Cahillane, Gallen and Hickey (eds), *Judges, Politics and the Irish Constitution* (Manchester University Press, 2017).

[4] For a powerful critique in the ECHR context see Fredman, 'Living Trees or Deadwood: The Interpretive Challenge of the European Convention on Human Rights' in Barber, Ekins and Yowell (eds), *Lord Sumption and the Limits of the Law* (Hart Publishing, 2016).

[5] See, for example, Hoffmann, 'Judges, Interpretation, and Self-Government' in Barber, Ekins and Yowell (eds), *Lord Sumption and the Limits of the Law* (Hart Publishing, 2016).

It is worth noting, also, that the Convention's status as an international treaty also makes it ripe for evolutive interpretation. Given the role of consent in creating intentional obligations, this may at first seem counter-intuitive, but international law does not require a strict adherence to the idea of *original* consent as the *sole* basis for obligation. Article 31(1) of the Vienna Convention on the Law of Treaties provides that '[a] treaty shall be interpreted in good faith in accordance with the ordinary meaning to be given to the terms of the treaty in their context and in the light of its object and purpose'. The context is expressly said to include '[a]ny subsequent practice in the application of the treaty which establishes the agreement of the parties regarding its interpretation'.[6] Based on this, the established practice of Contracting Parties in executing judgments of the Court *including those featuring evolutive interpretation* and in not enacting Protocols to reverse or undo evolutive understandings of the Convention at least suggests that states were consenting not only to what the Convention might be said to have meant in 1950 but also to it being developed, understood and interpreted in a manner that allowed for evolution. This is not entirely unusual in international law; indeed, it might be said to be a common approach to human rights treaties, which are generally considered to be dynamic in nature.[7] Wessel argued that one could arrange all treaties across a spectrum ranging from, on the one extreme, 'dynamic' treaties and, on the other extreme, 'end of game' treaties.[8] The former treaties are concluded between cooperating parties in order to promote common values; the latter are concluded to freeze a given set of relations in existence at a certain moment in time. For Wessel: '[d]ynamic treaties [...] should be interpreted using relational contract principles, such as the parties' current practice'.[9] The ECHR is clearly a dynamic treaty, which was created to spread common values among the Contracting Parties.[10] The Preamble points out that it was concluded to further realise cooperation of the Contracting Parties in the area of human rights protection. Therefore, their subsequent practice in this area should be reflected in the judgments of the ECtHR and the argument of 'consent' cannot, alone, sustain a claim of illegitimacy.

That said, not all evolution is the same, and the extent to which one might question the legitimacy of evolutive interpretation can differ depending on the

---

[6] Article 31(3)(b).

[7] In connection to the practice of interpretation under the American Convention on Human Rights see Lixinski, 'Treaty Interpretation by the Inter-American Court of Human Rights: Expansionism at the Service of the Unity of International Law' (2010) 21 *European Journal of International Law* 585.

[8] Wessel, 'Relational Contract Theory and Treaty Interpretation: End-Game Treaties v. Dynamic Interpretation' (2004) 60 *Annual Survey of American Law* 149, 149.

[9] Ibid., 150.

[10] Fitzmaurice, 'Dynamic (Evolutive) Interpretation of Treaties (Part II)' in Lammers (ed.), *Hague Yearbook of International Law* (Martinus Nijhoff Publishers, 2009), para. 26.

kind of originalism being adopted.[11] Put relatively simply, one form of originalism demands that the text in question (here, the Convention) remain cryogenically frozen as at the time it was written so that it means *only* what it meant then. It necessarily flows that such a claim is underpinned by an understanding of terms that are used in human rights treaties, such as 'torture' or 'arbitrary detention', having a clear and objectively determinable meaning; a claim that is strongly disputed.[12] In truth, a literal approach to originalism is somewhat uncommon. Taken to its logical end point, it would require the Convention to either be unfit for purpose, or constantly subjected to formal amendment which, as we saw in Chapter 1, takes place by means of protocols and is a long and difficult process which states can try to hold up for reasons that are not always entirely bona fide.

A looser, and more common, approach to originalism holds that the meaning of a text can be developed but only inasmuch as that reflects the original intent of the founders/original drafters. This kind of originalism will be familiar to those who have studied US constitutional law, in particular, although it is not limited to that jurisdiction. It accepts that texts of a constitutional or quasi-constitutional nature do need to have some capacity for evolution and interpretation, but limits that to what was originally intended by the text and thus, in an international law setting in particular, to what might be said to have been reasonably within the contemplation of the state at the point at which consent was given. This type of originalism is also problematic, as it is often unclear what the intention of the drafters of the Convention (or similar text) might have been.

In the earlier days of the Court, it used evolutive interpretation to extend protection under Article 8 to 'illegitimate' children in a case that illustrates how thin the line between 'interpreting in line with original intent' and 'evolving the Convention' can be: *Marckx v Belgium*.[13] At that time, Belgium treated children whose biological parents were unmarried less favourably than children whose biological parents were married. The Court had to consider whether this violated the Convention, but of course the Convention said nothing about it directly (although it does protect the rights to private and family life in Article 8), and the Belgian government argued that when the Convention was ratified such differences were considered appropriate and, thus, acceptable by the Convention standards. The Court disagreed:

> It is true that, at the time when the Convention of 4 November 1950 was
> drafted, it was regarded as permissible and normal in many European countries
> to draw a distinction in this area between the 'illegitimate' and the 'legitimate'

---

[11] There is a voluminous literature on originalism, but the key competing accounts are well presented in Solum, 'What is Originalism? The Evolution of Contemporary Originalist Theory' in Huscroft and Miller (eds), *The Challenge of Originalism: Theories of Constitutional Interpretation* (Cambridge University Press, 2011), 12.

[12] Fredman, 'Living Trees or Deadwood' (above, n. 4).

[13] *Marckx v Belgium*, 13 June 1979, Series A no. 31.

family. However, the Court recalls that this Convention must be interpreted in the light of present-day conditions. In the instant case, the Court cannot but be struck by the fact that the domestic law of the great majority of the member States of the Council of Europe has evolved and is continuing to evolve, in company with the relevant international instruments.[14]

There was, thus, a violation of the Convention. One might argue that this is in line with the original intent of the Convention (to protect family and private life, including the family life of people whose families were not based on marriage), whilst another might say that it represented evolution because the states accepted that 'illegitimate' children could be treated less favourably at the time that the Convention was drafted. This kind of case – one that can arguably be defended by reference to relatively plausible claims of original intent – is not the kind of case most commonly singled out for criticism. Rather, cases where the Court applies an evolutive approach in order either to depart from its earlier decisions or to find Convention protection in respect of 'emerging' areas or claims not clearly contemplated by the Convention text are most heavily criticised.

It is not entirely unusual for the Court to hold that its interpretation of the Convention in an earlier case should be set aside in favour of a new interpretation that has 'evolved' by reference to, for example, changing practice across states or changing social and scientific understandings. Later in this chapter, we will expressly consider the role of 'European consensus' in such cases, but for now we can focus on the principled issue of evolution per se without necessarily considering *how* the evolution is justified. The Court's understanding of what the Convention requires may develop over time. The best example is, perhaps, the Court's jurisprudence on whether one has a right to have one's true gender recognised by the state when one has a transgender identity.

In a line of cases, largely against the UK, that started in the 1980s[15] the Court was asked to consider whether the UK's failure to fully recognise a preferred gender identity for post-operative applicants violated the Convention. Under national law, some legal documents such as birth certificates could not be changed even after gender reassignment surgery, and even though such surgery could be provided on the National Health Service (i.e. by the state). For more than a decade, the Court repeatedly found that the Convention did not *require* full documentary recognition of reassigned gender; instead, whether to recognise the reassigned gender was within the UK's margin of appreciation and was not required by Article 8. However, in these cases the Court hinted that this would not always be the case; as law, science and society developed this would not always remain within states' discretion. This point was reached in *Christine Goodwin v the United Kingdom* when the Court held:

---

[14] Ibid., para. 41.

[15] *Rees v the United Kingdom*, 17 October 1986, Series A no. 106; *Cossey v the United Kingdom*, 27 September 1990, Series A no. 184.

[T]he very essence of the Convention is respect for human dignity and human freedom. Under Article 8 of the Convention in particular, where the notion of personal autonomy is an important principle underlying the interpretation of its guarantees, protection is given to the personal sphere of each individual, including the right to establish details of their identity as individual human beings [...]
In the twenty first century the right of transsexuals to personal development and to physical and moral security in the full sense enjoyed by others in society cannot be regarded as a matter of controversy requiring the lapse of time to cast clearer light on the issues involved. In short, the unsatisfactory situation in which post-operative transsexuals live in an intermediate zone as not quite one gender or the other is no longer sustainable.[16]

Thus, the Convention's Article 8 protection of private life was finally evolved to positively protect the right to be recognised, officially, in one's preferred gender.

All approaches to evolution attract criticisms. One key objection is that evolution creates instability in the law: a legal standard may change, even though Contracting Parties have taken steps to ensure that its previous understanding has been effectively incorporated into domestic legal standards. In this telling, states cannot be sure what legal standard to apply for fear that it may change as a result of judicial interpretation. There are at least three responses to this pragmatic claim against evolutive interpretation.

First, it is not certain that such pragmatic considerations should be determinative for the Court. Letsas has argued that the judges of the Court should not enter into a cost-benefit calculation in deciding their approach to interpretation; for him, problems associated with the lack of predictability must be trumped by the moral value of human rights.[17] However, one does not need to endorse such a strong position in order to accept that pragmatic considerations need not be determinative; this is not to say that they should never be accounted for at all (after all, legal certainty *is* a value, and maintaining legitimacy through consistency has positive implications for the Court's overall capacity to protect rights), but simply that they should not be given such weight as to always prevent evolution where it seems normatively acceptable to undertake it. So, a concern with legal certainty might ground the claim that the Court should engage in evolution *carefully* and in a *reasoned* manner, but it should not stop the Court from applying evolutive interpretation when that is necessary to ensure effective rights protection.

Second, the fact that evolutive interpretation is used does not mean the Convention is volatile. Often the possibility of evolution is signposted to Contracting Parties in earlier cases. For example in the case of *S.H. and Others v Austria* the Court considered whether the Austrian ban on using sperm and

---

[16] *Christine Goodwin v the United Kingdom* [GC], no. 28957/95, ECHR 2002-VI, para. 90.
[17] Letsas, *A Theory of Interpretation of the European Convention on Human Rights* (Oxford University Press, 2007), 74.

ova donation for in vitro fertilisation violates the Convention.[18] The Grand Chamber of the Court decided that it does not but informed the respondent party that it needs to keep under review the developments in science and law in this area,[19] clearly signalling a potential evolution on this question in the future. Thus, although the Court did not evolve the Convention in this case, it made it clear that states must be prepared for this in the future, thus giving 'fair warning' of future potential change and dampening claims of volatility at the time when that change comes.

However, in giving those signals, it is important that the Court maintains consistency across its case law in an area, so that states know what the Court might be looking out for in deciding whether the tipping point has been reached. It does not always succeed in doing so. Let us return to the transgender cases to illustrate this. In *Sheffield and Horsham v the United Kingdom* the Court found that the failure to recognise preferred gender on state documents did not violate the Convention, pointing to the lack of European consensus on the matter.[20] However, it signalled to the UK that it would monitor the situation, indicating that should a European consensus develop this would feed into a change in the Court's consideration of whether the Convention had been violated. Only four years later, in *Christine Goodwin v the United Kingdom*, the Court did find a violation,[21] but on the basis of an international trend and *not* a European consensus, thus opening itself up to criticism for seeming to vary the benchmarks between cases on the same issue.[22] Perhaps in recognition of this, a similar 'switch' has not since occurred in any other area of evolutive interpretation.

Third, even where the legal standard evolves with little advance warning, the Contracting Party will in reality have some time to adjust its practices in order to accommodate it: execution of a judgment is not expected overnight. Indeed, quite unlike many national constitutional systems where a finding of rights violation can result in the immediate strike down of a statute and a resultant legal 'gap' that often needs to be filled quickly, a finding of violation does not automatically disturb the national legal system which must, instead, be expressly adjusted to execute the judgment. The claims as to certainty, then, seem insufficient to ground a strong case against evolution.

On all bases, then, it seems difficult to sustain an argument of simple illegitimacy for evolution per se, but this does not mean that there are no real concerns here, particularly on the question of *when* the tipping point has been reached and how the Court determines that. It is to this that we now turn.

---

[18] *S.H. and Others v Austria* [GC], no. 57813/00, ECHR 2011.

[19] Ibid., para. 118.

[20] *Sheffield and Horsham v the United Kingdom*, 30 July 1998, Reports of Judgments and Decisions 1998-V.

[21] *Christine Goodwin v United Kingdom* (above, n. 16).

[22] For a more in-depth discussion see Dzehtsiarou, *European Consensus and the Legitimacy of the European Court of Human Rights* (Cambridge University Press, 2015), 65–71.

Debate 2

How does the Court determine the moment of evolution?

As indicated above, the Court generally claims to be reflecting societal and technological developments when it applies an evolutive approach to interpretation, but of course this does not mean that the exercise is simply technocratic. Instead, the Court must apply its *judgement* in identifying the moment when there is sufficient development to justify evolutive interpretation and, as a result, the Court clearly has significant discretion here. Depending on how it interprets the prevailing conditions, the Court can speed up, slow down or even veto certain developments in rights protection that could only be achieved through evolutive interpretation.

Finding the right moment for evolution is crucially important for the effectiveness and legitimacy of the Court: push for evolution too early and the judgment might be never executed, do it too late and the Court might be perceived as irrelevant and unwilling to address real-life rights violations. Whilst, as outlined below, the Court applies different approaches to 'consensus' in order to try to identify whether the moment for evolution is ripe, the truth is that this is ultimately a matter of *judgement*: it cannot be 'scientifically' determined.

In exercising its judgement on this matter, then, the Court is open to allegations of illegitimacy both from Contracting Parties (along the lines outlined in Debate 1) and from applicants and other interested parties who may complain that the Court is going too fast, too slow, or in the wrong direction. The clearest way to address these kinds of criticisms is to apply rigour, method and clarity of reasoning in the decision to take an evolutive approach (or not). The key technique that the Court uses in this respect is 'consensus'.[23] Although this does not mean that the Court is applying discretion, it does provide it with some indicia through which its assessment might be said to be grounded in reality and, thus, its reasoning more persuasive. In other words, using consensus reasoning can help to ensure that the Court is *reflecting* reality, rather than *creating* law; i.e. to show judicial self-restraint in evolution.[24]

The Court uses four different kinds of consensus in doing this: European consensus, international consensus, internal (i.e. domestic) consensus and consensus among experts. Let us consider each in turn.

European Consensus

European consensus is a method of interpreting the ECHR that relies on comparative analysis of the law and practice of the Contracting Parties to the Convention, which analysis may then justify evolutive interpretation. If the Court

---

[23] Dzehtsiarou, 'European Consensus and the Evolutive Interpretation of the European Convention on Human Rights' (2011) 12 *German Law Journal* 1730.

[24] de Londras and Dzehtsiarou, 'Managing Judicial Innovation in the European Court of Human Rights' (2015) 15 *Human Rights Law Review* 523.

concludes that there is no European consensus on the rights-protection claim that is before it, it usually decides that this is an issue on which Contracting Parties enjoy a broad margin of appreciation. We will consider the margin of appreciation in Chapter 5, but for now it is sufficient to say that where something falls within the state's margin of appreciation it will have considerable discretion to decide on its domestic legal and policy position in respect of it: a range of different approaches will be permissible under the Convention, provided they comply to the basic requirements of the Article in question (e.g. are limited by reference to what is 'necessary in a democratic society' etc.).

The case of *Bayatyan v Armenia* is a good illustration of how European consensus can work.[25] Here, the Court considered whether Article 9 was violated where someone was punished for refusal to perform military service in contravention of his beliefs as a Jehovah's Witness. Accommodation of conscientious objection had not previously been considered by the Court as a requirement of the freedom of religious belief under Article 9.[26] In *Bayatyan* the Court found that a large number of Contracting Parties allowed for an alternative to military service in order to respect conscientious objections. Thus, failure to do so violated the Convention:

> [T]he Convention is a living instrument which must be interpreted in the light of present-day conditions and of the ideas prevailing in democratic States today. Since it is first and foremost a system for the protection of human rights, the Court must have regard to the changing conditions in Contracting States and respond, for example, to any emerging consensus as to the standards to be achieved.[27]

The Court noted that in the late 1980s and the 1990s there was an obvious trend among European countries, both existing Council of Europe member states and those which joined the organisation later, to recognise the right to conscientious objection. All in all, 19 of those States which had not yet recognised the right to conscientious objection introduced such a right into their domestic legal systems around the time when the Commission took its last decisions on the matter. Hence, at the time when the alleged interference with the applicant's rights under Article 9 occurred, namely in 2002–2003, only four other member states, in addition to Armenia, did not provide for the possibility of claiming conscientious objector status. Furthermore, three of those had already incorporated that right into their Constitutions but had not yet implemented that by law. Thus, already at the material time there was nearly a unanimous consensus among all Council of Europe member states, the

---

[25] *Bayatyan v Armenia* [GC], no. 23459/03, ECHR 2011.
[26] *Grandrath v Germany*, no. 5591/72, Commission decision of 2 April 1973, Collection 43, p. 161 and *G.Z. v Austria* (dec.), no. 5591/72, Commission decision of 2 April 1973, Collection 43, p. 161.
[27] *Bayatyan v Armenia* (above, n. 25), para. 102.

overwhelming majority of which had already recognised in their law and practice the right to conscientious objection.

The growth in the legal recognition of conscientious objections within the Contracting Parties allowed the Court to justify departing from its previous case law and establishing this standard of rights protection. This illustrates the fact that European consensus can help to rebut the argument that evolution means uncertainty as developing trends across the Contracting Parties can alert states to the possibility that the Court will evolve in jurisprudence in this fashion. In this case, the developing tendency to recognise conscientious objection was manifest: Armenia was one of only a handful of Contracting Parties that failed to accommodate such objections. Attention to the developing European consensus here would have mitigated any putative 'surprise' element.

This is not to suggest that European consensus is without criticism. It is, for example, quite a conservative way to approach evolution: rather than lead the way in developing human rights protection, the Court 'follows' trends in the Contracting Parties. Whilst this may be considered appropriate given the fact the Court is subsidiary, and the perceived limitations of appropriate judicial activity, for some this approach is problematic. For these commentators, human rights are standards that should be developed by reference to something more normatively rich than the sum of approaches that are taken by the Contracting Parties. European consensus, or the 'counting of states', does not seem to allow the Court to develop rights per se, but rather lets national trends determine supra-national standards.[28]

This relates to a further critique of European consensus: that it is effectively a majoritarian approach to human rights which should not, by their nature, be determined by such an approach.[29] This argument rests on the fact that one of the roles of human rights law is to protect those persons and groups who are underrepresented in democracy. Marginalities such as convicted criminals, children or national, religious or sexual minorities do not always have the 'clout' to establish protection through national political or, indeed, judicial processes and part of the role of institutions such as the ECtHR is to address that deficit and protect their rights, even if that is unpopular within the relevant polity. European consensus cuts across this by seeming to acquire its legitimacy from reflecting domestic trends. There are three possible counter-arguments to this undoubtedly strong point. First, the Court has in fact used European consensus to protect the rights of these very marginalities: religious minorities,[30] lifelong prisoners,[31] 'illegitimate' children[32] and homosexual men,[33] for example,

---

[28] For analysis of criticism of European consensus see Dzehtsiarou, *European Consensus* (above, n. 22), 115–142.

[29] See Benvenisti, 'Margin of Appreciation, Consensus, and Universal Standards' (1999) 31 *Journal of International Law and Politics* 843.

[30] *Bayatyan v Armenia* (above, n. 25).

[31] *Vinter and Others v the United Kingdom* [GC], nos 66069/09 and two others, ECHR 2013.

[32] *Fretté v France*, no. 36515/97, ECHR 2002-I.

[33] *Dudgeon v the United Kingdom*, 22 October 1981, Series A no. 45.

have succeeded before the Court through leveraging a European consensus approach. Second, consensus ensures the minimal standard of human rights protection and the Contracting Parties are free to set a higher standard. Finally, European consensus is not an automatic or strictly binding concept; the Court can set it aside if there are convincing reasons to do that. Perhaps, in cases of protection of some vulnerable minorities the Court might decide that in spite of consensus the state may go beyond to go beyond or stay below the standard of consensus because, for example, the state is in a situation of transition,[34] or the Court is satisfied that the people of the state in question hold a particular moral position on an issue of profound moral disagreement.[35] Furthermore, the inquiry into whether or not a consensus exists is not necessarily the end of the Court's assessment; it has been known to question *why* an apparent European consensus either does or does not exist *as a matter of fact*, and whether Contracting Parties are considering introducing similar laws, to determine whether a European consensus exists *as a matter of judicial reasoning*. This is well illustrated by the Court's judgment in the controversial case of *S.A.S. v France*.[36]

In this case, the Court had to decide whether the French ban on wearing full-face veils in public places violated Article 8 of the ECHR. The Court's consideration of comparative law in this case is particularly curious. It established that '[t]o date, only Belgium has passed a law that is comparable to the French Law of 11 October 2010, and the Belgian Constitutional Court has found it compatible with the right to freedom of thought, conscience and religion'.[37] In other words, there was manifestly *no* consensus across the Council of Europe in support of such a ban. In the past, the Court had stated that when only two states deviate from the commonly accepted standard this indicates a very strong consensus *against* the respondent state's position.[38] In *S.A.S.*, however, the Court observed that the issue of religious dress (especially full-face coverings) is more pressing in some states than in others and that this has to be taken into account when analysing the results of comparative legal research,[39] so that the lack of consensus in favour of allowing such a law did not stand against a finding that such a law was compatible with the Convention. This was notwithstanding the fact that there are clearly more than only two countries in Europe with a substantial Muslim population,[40] and these other states have not determined that such a ban is required. The percentage of the population that identifies

---

[34] *Tănase v Moldova* [GC], no. 7/08, ECHR 2010.

[35] See, for example, the decision relating to abortion in *A, B and C v Ireland* [GC], no. 25579/05, ECHR 2010.

[36] *S.A.S. v France* [GC], no. 43835/11, ECHR 2014.

[37] Ibid., para. 40.

[38] *A, B and C v Ireland* (above, n. 35), para. 235.

[39] *S.A.S. v France* (above, n. 36), para. 156.

[40] Data is taken from Pew Forum on Religion and Public Life. See 'Muslim Populations by Country: How Big Will Each Muslim Population Be by 2030?', *The Guardian*, available at https://www.theguardian.com/news/datablog/2011/jan/28/muslim-population-country-projection-2030#data.

as Muslim in the following Contracting Parties illustrates this well: Azerbaijan 98.4 per cent, Cyprus 22.7 per cent, Albania 82.1 per cent, Austria 5.1 per cent, Bosnia and Herzegovina 41.6 per cent, Bulgaria 13.4 per cent, Georgia 10.5 per cent, Germany 5 per cent, Montenegro 18.5 per cent, the Netherlands 5.5 per cent, Macedonia 34.9 per cent, Russia 11.4 per cent, Sweden 4.9 per cent and Switzerland 5.7 per cent. None of these countries introduced such a ban. By means of comparison, 7.5 per cent of the French population and 6 per cent of the Belgian population identify as Muslim. However, the Court determined that the lack of such a law in other states did *not* indicate a European consensus *against* the ban of public display of religious headscarves:

> [C]ontrary to the submission of one of the third-party interveners, there is no European consensus against a ban. Admittedly, from a strictly normative standpoint, France is very much in a minority position in Europe: except for Belgium, no other member State of the Council of Europe has, to date, opted for such a measure. It must be observed, however, that the question of the wearing of the full-face veil in public is or has been a subject of debate in a number of European States. In some it has been decided not to opt for a blanket ban. In others, such a ban is still being considered.[41]

Although the Court's reasoning in *S.A.S. v France* is open to criticism it shows that the Court does not apply consensus automatically. European consensus acts as a rebuttable presumption in favour of evolutive interpretation; namely, if there is consensus or an identifiable trend then the Court will allow evolutive interpretation of the Convention. This presumption can be rebutted if there are reasons for which the respondent state can justifiably deviate from the established trend.

International Consensus

The second type of consensus is consensus based on international law (international consensus), determined by analysis of international treaties mostly signed and ratified by the Contracting Parties to the ECHR and the law and practice of other international tribunals. Clearly, this is quite different to the European consensus approach: rather than consider legal and policy positions across individual states, the Court looks to international law per se.

The Court has used developments in international law to justify evolutive interpretation on a number of occasions, including in its earlier cases. In *Marckx v Belgium*, for example, the Court referred to two international conventions (the Brussels Convention of 12 September 1962 on the Establishment of Maternal Affiliation of Natural Children, and the European Convention of 15 October 1975 on the Legal Status of Children born out of Wedlock) in determining that differential treatment of 'illegitimate' children was prohibited

---

[41] *S.A.S. v France* (above, n. 36), para. 156.

by the Convention.[42] Interestingly, neither of these was yet in force at the time; rather they showed an emerging understanding and consensus across international law that children whose parents were not married should not be treated differently in law.

In a more recent case of *Mamatkulov and Askarov v Turkey* the Court has also relied on developments in international law to justify evolutive interpretation of the Convention.[43] The key issue in this case was the legal force of interim measures issued by the Court, i.e.:

> urgent measures which, according to the Court's well-established practice, apply only where there is an imminent risk of irreparable harm. Such measures are decided in connection with proceedings before the Court without prejudging any subsequent decisions on the admissibility or merits of the case in question.[44]

The vast majority of interim measures are of negative character; they oblige the respondent state not to worsen the situation of the applicant. The most common example is when the applicant is about to be removed to a country in which she may be the subject of ill-treatment contrary to Article 3 of the Convention; the Court can request the respondent state not to remove her before the Court's judgment in this case. More rarely, Contracting Parties are asked to fulfil certain duties under interim measures. For example, the Court can request the respondent party to transfer a sick inmate to a civil hospital.

In its earlier case law the Court held that interim measures were not legally binding;[45] however, it changed this position in *Mamatkulov and Askarov*.[46] Having regard 'to general principles of international law and the view expressed on this subject by other international bodies since *Cruz Varas and Others* [in which the Court stated that violation of interim measures does not violate the Convention]',[47] the Court decided its interim measures should have legally binding character. In reaching this decision, the Court expressly relied on the practice of international tribunals such as the Inter-American Court of Human Rights, UN Human Rights Committee, and International Court of Justice.

The use of international consensus to underpin evolutive interpretation has a number of benefits. The Court itself has emphasised the importance

---

[42] *Marckx v Belgium* (above, n. 13).

[43] *Mamatkulov and Askarov v Turkey* [GC], nos 46827/99 and 46951/99, ECHR 2005-I.

[44] Press Unit, *Factsheet: Interim Measures* (2016), Rule 39, Rules of Court. See also Keller and Marti, 'Interim Relief Compared: Use of Interim Measures by the UN Human Rights Committee and the European Court of Human Rights' (2013) 73 *Zeitschrift für ausländisches öffentliches Recht und Völkerrecht* 325; Haeck, Burbano Herrera and Zwaak, 'Strasbourg's Interim Measures under Fire: Does the Rising Number of State Incompliances with Interim Measures Pose a Threat to the European Court of Human Rights?' (2011) *European Yearbook of Human Rights* 375.

[45] *Cruz Varas and Others v Sweden*, 20 March 1991, Series A no. 201.

[46] *Mamatkulov and Askarov v Turkey* (above, n. 43).

[47] Ibid., para. 110.

of external sources by pointing out that '[t]he Convention and its Protocols cannot be interpreted in a vacuum but must be interpreted in harmony with the general principles of international law of which they form part'.[48] In *Demir and Baykara v Turkey* the Court stated that it has 'never considered the provisions of the Convention as the sole framework of reference for the interpretation of the rights and freedoms enshrined therein'.[49] The ECHR is a part of international law and some provisions of the Convention explicitly refer to it.[50] Thus, it is quite sensible for the Court to attempt to ensure that the Convention is developed in a manner that is consistent with international law.

This has the additional benefit of attempting to ensure 'systemic integration' between international instruments and principles of international law, rather than creating or exacerbating potential conflicts between them.[51] We already saw in Chapter 2 that states have multiple international obligations at any given time, and that these may appear to be in conflict with one another, so that bearing international law and practice in mind when developing the Convention helps to create harmony between these obligations per se. This is not only of benefit to the Contracting Parties, but also to international law itself of which, of course, the Convention is a party; it is a way in which the Court can contribute to the difficult but important task of trying to avoid the unnecessary and/or unproductive 'fragmentation' of international law – a major concern in that field.[52]

This is not to suggest that there are no potential criticisms of the Court relying on international consensus in its decision making. Why should, for example, an international treaty to which the respondent state is not a party be taken into account in determining the nature and scope of its Convention obligations? What about customary international law to which the state has consistently objected? And how does the Court decide which international treaties, or principles of international law, or (quasi-) judicial decisions it will take into account from the vast field that is 'international law'? All of this, combined with the fact that the role of the Court is to develop, apply and interpret the *Convention* and not to contribute to the development of international law per se, suggests that the Court ought to tread softly in the field of international consensus, applying it in conjunction with a European consensus analysis.

---

[48] *Marguš v Croatia* [GC], no. 4455/10, ECHR 2014, para. 129.

[49] *Demir and Baykara v Turkey* [GC], no. 34503/97, ECHR 2008, para. 67.

[50] Articles 7, 15 and 35 of the Convention. The CDDH has discussed a proposal to include 'the general principle that the Convention as a whole should be interpreted in harmony with other principles of international law' into the Preamble to the Convention. It has, however, rejected this proposal because it would be time consuming whilst added value would be limited. Report of the Steering Committee for Human Rights (CDDH), 101.

[51] On the general importance of this see Koskenniemi, ILC, 'Fragmentation of International Law: Difficulties Arising from the Diversification and Expansion of International Law' (2006) UN Doc A/CN.4/L.682.

[52] Ibid.

Internal Consensus

The third type of consensus is internal consensus. In this type of consensus, which is very rarely deployed, the Court attempts to establish a prevailing position within the respondent state, which may then justify the state's approach being found compatible with the Convention *even if* it is in contrast with European and/or international consensus. Establishing such an internal consensus is fundamentally challenging. In some cases, the national position may have been determined by referendum of the people, so that the referendum results are used to establish the internal consensus. However, even then the meaning of referendum results is not always straightforward. Where a populace is given a choice between, for example, Option A and Option B in a referendum all the result tells us is which of these options the majority of those who voted preferred, not whether the 'real world' consensus is really in line with a putative Option C for which they never had the opportunity to vote. This is well illustrated by the *A, B and C v Ireland*.[53]

In this case, the Court considered whether Ireland's extremely restrictive abortion regime (where abortion is available only where there is 'real and substantial risk' to the life of a pregnant woman) was compatible with the Convention. Only three countries in Europe have a more restrictive abortion law than Ireland: Andorra, Malta and San Marino. In contrast, 40 Contracting Parties allow abortion if there is a risk to the mother's health, suggesting that there is European consensus towards allowing abortion on broader grounds than available in Ireland. However, Ireland's restrictive approach to abortion is entrenched in the Irish Constitution and was placed there in 1983, by referendum of the People.[54] In subsequent referenda (in 1992 and 2002) the People had voted on whether to restrict access to abortion further by expressly prohibiting it in cases where the risk to the pregnant woman's life emanated from the risk of suicide, but this had twice been rejected. The People had never been given an opportunity to vote to liberalise Ireland's abortion law. Furthermore, when negotiating both the Maastricht and Lisbon treaties at EU level, Ireland had secured protocols to allow for the maintenance of the status quo regarding abortion, seemingly in response to popular demand.[55]

Based on this, the Irish government argued that the law in Ireland represented the profound moral position of the Irish people and that this internal consensus should mean that Ireland can maintain its particular stance on abortion, in spite of the fact that it was out of line with the apparent European consensus. Rather than focusing on the alignment in legal provision of abortion across the 40 Contracting Parties that allow for abortion in cases where

---

[53] See above, n. 35.

[54] Article 40.3.3, Constitution of Ireland.

[55] On the constitutional position on abortion in Ireland see, for example, de Londras, 'Constitutionalizing Fetal Rights: A Salutary Lesson from Ireland' (2015) 22 *Michigan Journal of Gender and Law* 243.

the pregnant woman's health is at risk, the Court noted that there is no consensus (of any kind) on the question of when life begins. As this is central to the question of whether and to what extent abortion might be made available in law, states enjoy a wide margin of appreciation and where, as the Irish government claimed was the case in Ireland, there was an internal consensus that could determine a restrictive abortion law regime that would be compatible with the Convention.

We have previously argued that this case illustrates the Court identifying a 'trumping internal consensus' for the first time in its jurisprudence, i.e. an internal consensus that could trump the established European *legal* consensus.[56] Here the Court avoided evolving the Convention to protect a right to access abortion, even though a European consensus appeared to exist. Clearly, the concept of 'trumping internal consensus' is a dangerous one. On the one hand, it allows the Court to avoid 'forcing the hand' of a state on a matter of particular sensitivity, such as abortion. On the other hand, the idea that a national sentiment could override an international standard found in the Convention seems to fly in the face of supra-national rights protection per se. Unquestionably, the fact that this case related to abortion was relevant: this *is* an area on which there is profound moral disagreement so that the Court might either have considered it inappropriate to 'interfere' or, indeed, might have used the concept of consensus in some way to elide the fact that the judges on the Court could not reach a consensus themselves on the difficult moral question at hand.

Given the clear difficulties with using 'trumping internal consensus' it is perhaps unsurprising that *A, B and C* is actually the only time it has been deployed by the Court, although it is certainly not the only time a Contracting Party has made such an argument. In the very first case in which the Court deployed evolutive interpretation – *Tyrer v the United Kingdom* – the UK attempted to rely on internal consensus. In this case, the Court considered whether corporal punishment ('birching') of an underage offender in the Isle of Man violated Article 3 of the ECHR.[57] The government argued that 'the judicial corporal punishment at issue in this case was not in breach of the Convention since it did not outrage public opinion in the Island'[58]; in other words, birching was an accepted form of punishment there and, if the populace was not outraged, should not be considered to violate Article 3. The Court disagreed:

> [E]ven assuming that local public opinion can have an incidence on the interpretation of the concept of 'degrading punishment' appearing in Article 3 (art. 3), the Court does not regard it as established that judicial corporal punishment

---

[56] de Londras and Dzehtsiarou, 'Grand Chamber of the European Court of Human Rights, A, B and C v Ireland' (2013) 62 *International and Comparative Law Quarterly* 250.

[57] *Tyrer v the United Kingdom,* 25 April 1978, Series A no. 26.

[58] Ibid., para. 31.

is not considered degrading by those members of the Manx population who favour its retention: it might well be that one of the reasons why they view the penalty as an effective deterrent is precisely the element of degradation which it involves. As regards their belief that judicial corporal punishment deters criminals, it must be pointed out that a punishment does not lose its degrading character just because it is believed to be, or actually is, an effective deterrent or aid to crime control. Above all, as the Court must emphasise, it is never permissible to have recourse to punishments which are contrary to Article 3 (art. 3), whatever their deterrent effect may be. The Court must also recall that the Convention is a living instrument which [...] must be interpreted in the light of present-day conditions. In the case now before it the Court cannot but be influenced by the developments and commonly accepted standards in the penal policy of the member States of the Council of Europe in this field.[59]

The approach in *Tyrer* is much more in line with how the Court has tended to respond to arguments that 'internal consensus' might justify a position that seems contrary to the Convention. This is not to say that internal consensus is totally irrelevant. It may well be that where the Court is asked to apply evolutive interpretation the internal consensus might be one factor in considering whether the moment for possible evolution is ripe.

Expert Consensus

Finally, the most rarely used type of consensus is expert consensus. The Court typically uses this type of consensus when it has to assess scientific developments in Europe and worldwide. For instance, in *L. and V. v Austria*, the applicants challenged Article 209 of the Austrian Criminal Code, which provided for a higher minimum age for consensual homosexual intercourse than for heterosexual intercourse.[60] The Court affirmed the decision of the Commission in *Sutherland v the United Kingdom*.[61] This referred to 'recent research according to which sexual orientation is usually established before puberty in both boys and girls and to the fact that the majority of Member States of the Council of Europe have recognised equal ages of consent'. It explicitly stated that it was 'opportune to reconsider its earlier case-law in the light of these modern developments'.[62] Although expert consensus can support the Court's decision to resort to evolutive interpretation it is unlikely that it will be the only or even the most conclusive argument used by the Court; rather, expert consensus seems mostly to be used to provide broader context for the Court's decision.

---

[59] Ibid., para. 31.
[60] *L. and V. v Austria*, nos 39392/98 and 39829/98, ECHR 2003-I.
[61] *Sutherland v the United Kingdom*, no. 25186/94, Commission's report of 1 July 1997, unpublished.
[62] *L. and V. v Austria* (above, n. 60), para. 47.

Debate 3

Is evolution necessarily progressive?

We often think about evolution as a linear process that improves human rights standards and never allows for regression in rights protection; in other words, as a progressive technique. However, this is not necessarily the case. In fact, evolution can indeed be regressive, either because the Court has experienced serious backlash in respect of an attempted progressive evolution, or because there is a trend towards regression in a certain area that the Court is not willing to try to halt. Prisoner voting neatly illustrates the first of these, whilst the Court's case law on Islamic dress illustrates the latter.

In *Hirst v the United Kingdom (no. 2)*[63] the Court ruled that the UK's blanket ban on prisoner voting violates the Convention, but it did not clearly outline what *would* be compatible with the Convention. It appeared clear that the Convention did not require *all* prisoners to be allowed to vote, but there is a considerable space between a blanket ban and blanket permission. The Court addressed this in the next case it decided about prisoners' right to vote: *Frodl v Austria*.[64] In this case it held that disenfranchisement of a prisoner would be Convention-compatible only if it had been decided by a judge in the individual case. This was, clearly, a burdensome standard requiring the question of disenfranchisement to be individually considered for every prisoner. As we have already discussed in Chapter 2, the Court's early approach to prisoner voting resulted in significant backlash, not least from the UK. It was in this context that the Court appeared to evolve its position *regressively* in *Scoppola v Italy (no. 3)*.[65] In Italy those who are in prison for less than three years can vote: this is clearly not a blanket ban, but it is also not the individual determination seemingly required by *Frodl*. In this case, the Court decided that it had gone too far in *Frodl* and found the Italian system compatible with the Convention. In doing so, it stated that its reasoning in *Frodl*

> takes a broad view of the principles set out in Hirst, which the Grand Chamber does not fully share. The Grand Chamber points out that the Hirst judgment makes no explicit mention of the intervention of a judge among the essential criteria for determining the proportionality of a disenfranchisement measure. The relevant criteria relate solely to whether the measure is applicable generally, automatically and indiscriminately within the meaning indicated by the Court. While the intervention of a judge is in principle likely to guarantee the proportionality of restrictions on prisoners' voting rights, such restrictions will not necessarily be automatic, general and indiscriminate simply because they were not ordered by a judge. Indeed, the circumstances in which the right to vote is forfeited may be detailed in the law, making its application conditional on such factors as the nature or the gravity of the offence committed.[66]

---

[63] *Hirst v the United Kingdom (no. 2)* [GC], no. 74025/01, ECHR 2005-IX.

[64] *Frodl v Austria*, no. 20201/04, 8 April 2010.

[65] *Scoppola v Italy (no. 3)* [GC], no. 126/05, 22 May 2012.

[66] Ibid., para. 99.

In other words, the Grand Chamber in *Scoppola no. 3* ruled that the Chamber in *Frodl* erred in its reading of what *Hirst no. 2* required. This illustrates the Court 'evolving' its own jurisprudence to seemingly reduce the level of rights protection.

The Court's jurisprudence on religious dress (and particularly Islamic dress) demonstrates the second form of regression through evolution. Article 9 of the Convention protects the right to freedom of religious belief, including the right 'to manifest [...] religion or belief'. In the ECHR (as in other international human rights systems) there is a distinction between the right to *hold* a religion or belief (which is unlimited) and the right to *manifest* that religion or belief (which can be limited, under Article 9(2) by 'such limitations as are prescribed by law and are necessary in a democratic society in the interests of public safety, for the protection of public order, health or morals, or for the protection of the rights and freedoms of others').[67] On the face of it, manifesting religious belief through one's dress seems relatively uncontroversial: it is difficult to see how wearing a kippah, crucifix or niqab might endanger public safety, public order or the rights and freedoms of others, so that one might reasonably expect that to have a right to freedom of conscience or belief includes having a right to dress in a manner that one considers to be compliant with one's religious belief. However, it now appears increasingly clear that this is not the case under the ECHR, especially if you happen to be a Muslim woman who wishes to be covered in public.

In *Leyla Şahin v Turkey*[68] and the previously discussed case of *S.A.S. v France*[69] the Court upheld prohibitions on the wearing of hijab in public universities (in Turkey) and face coverings in public (in France), finding them to be permissible limitations on the right of freedom of religion. As already discussed, in *S.A.S. v France* this was the case seemingly in contrast with the apparent European consensus, whilst in *Şahin* the decision was related to Turkey's secular constitutional identity. In *Şahin*, European consensus was also a point of disagreement between the majority of the Court and the dissenting judges. The Court claimed that there is no consensus in Europe in respect to wearing headscarves in educational establishments. However, if the enquiry were limited to religious dress in universities only (excluding schools, nurseries etc.), then there were only three states in which such prohibition exists.[70] In the same time period, the mandatory display of the crucifix in Italian schools was said not to violate Article 9 because, the Grand Chamber found, the crucifix is not necessarily a religious symbol.[71] These decisions illustrate that as the Convention develops, or evolves, it does not necessarily do so in a progressive

---

[67] See generally Sandberg, *Law and Religion* (Cambridge University Press, 2011), Chapter 5.
[68] *Leyla Şahin v Turkey* [GC], no. 44774/98, ECHR 2005-XI.
[69] *S.A.S. v France* (above, n. 36).
[70] Turkey, Azerbaijan and Albania. See *Leyla Şahin v Turkey* (above, n. 68), para. 116.
[71] *Lautsi and Others v Italy* [GC], no. 30814/06, ECHR 2011.

way; rather it may happen in a way that fundamentally undermines the capacities of people – especially women – to fully exercise their citizenship, broadly construed, by expressing (sometimes complex) personal identities and engaging in the public square.

Cases about Islamic dress are not *solely* about whether a state can tell a woman what she may wear, but also about the overall potential costs in rights terms of prohibiting a woman from wearing clothing that she considers to be required by her religious beliefs. Where a woman is told, for example, that she may not cover her face in public but considers herself bound by how she interprets her religious belief to do so, she must make a stark choice: to break the law, to act in conflict with her conscience and religious belief, or to shirk the public square and all of the richness of life – and exercise of rights such as association and expression – that comes with it. Thus, cases of this kind have implications that are unquestionably regressive in both doctrinal and 'real' terms, with disproportionate impacts on people who are already often marginalised, in this case Muslim women who wish to dress in a manner that they consider consistent with their religious beliefs.

CONCLUSION

In this chapter, we discussed the need for evolutive interpretation. Although when deploying evolutive interpretation the ECtHR is open to the criticism of judicial activism, the alternative to evolution is that the ECHR will not be able to respond to contemporary developments, thus risking ineffectiveness and related illegitimacy. In order to counter claims of illegitimate activism, the Court adopts techniques such as European consensus to assess whether evolution on any particular issue or at a particular point of time might be apposite. The consensus argument is not homogenous and the Court uses different evidence to justify the existence of consensus including comparative legal analysis of the laws and practice of the Contracting Parties, international treaties, expert opinions and popular opinions. Finally, evolution is not necessarily progressive; there are incidents of evolution in fact acting regressively and narrowing the scope of protection allowed by the ECHR.

FURTHER READING

Dzehtsiarou, *European Consensus and the Legitimacy of the European Court of Human Rights* (Cambridge University Press, 2015), Chapters 2 and 3.

Fitzmaurice, 'Dynamic (Evolutive) Interpretation of Treaties (Part I)' in Lammers (ed.), *Hague Yearbook of International Law* (Martinus Nijhoff Publishers, 2008).

Fredman, 'Living Trees or Deadwood: The Interpretive Challenge of the European Convention on Human Rights' in Barber, Ekins and Yowell (eds), *Lord Sumption and the Limits of the Law* (Hart Publishing, 2016).

Hoffmann, 'Judges, Interpretation, and Self-Government' in Barber, Ekins and Yowell (eds), *Lord Sumption and the Limits of the Law* (Hart Publishing, 2016).

Letsas, *A Theory of Interpretation of the European Convention on Human Rights* (Oxford University Press, 2009), Chapter 3.

Mowbray, 'An Examination of the European Court of Human Rights' Approach to Overruling its Previous Case Law' (2009) 9 *Human Rights Law Review* 179.

CHAPTER 5

Accounting for Difference: Proportionality and the Margin of Appreciation

We have already seen that the European Convention on Human Rights (ECHR or Convention) sprang from, and purports to reflect, the common heritages and values of European states (Chapter 1). However, this does not mean, of course, that the 47 states of the Council of Europe are the same; some states will have a particular constitutional commitment to secularism, and some not; some will have endemic problems with political violence, others will not; and so on. The Contracting Parties will also have different views on what the right way of managing contentious issues is; where does the balance lie between the state interest in, for example, secularism and the individual interest in wearing a crucifix in public? There is more than one answer to this, just as there is to a whole host of different questions relating to human rights, even within the common politico-geographical space of the Council of Europe.

The European Court of Human Rights (the ECtHR or Court), then, has had to develop ways of accounting for difference; of acknowledging that in some cases there might be multiple potential approaches to managing a human rights question, and that an approach may be rights compliant even if it is not considered to be optimal. This chapter focuses on such techniques the Court has developed: proportionality and the margin of appreciation.

The margin of appreciation might be broadly understood as the discretion that states retain to determine their own legal and policy approaches to questions (usually of particular contention), even where those approaches have implications as to rights. It is the 'space for manoeuvre' that the Court is willing to afford the Contracting Parties in fulfilling their obligations under the Convention.[1] The margin of appreciation is closely linked to the test of proportionality. This is essentially a 'test' or a 'principle' that requires that, in acting in a manner that interferes with rights, the state must (a) have a

---

[1] Yourow, *The Margin of Appreciation Doctrine in the Dynamics of European Human Rights Jurisprudence* (Springer, 1995), 13; Greer, *The Margin of Appreciation: Interpretation and Discretion under the European Convention on Human Rights* (Council of Europe, 2000), 5.

legitimate objective in mind, (b) be acting in a manner that is related to this objective, (c) interfere no more than is necessary to achieve that objective, and (d) strike a reasonable balance between the need to achieve the objective and the interference with rights. The Court will apply this test with varying degrees of strictness depending on the circumstances: for example, interference with political speech will be subjected to a heightened standard of scrutiny than interference with commercial speech.[2] Even where the Court has acknowledged that a state has a margin of appreciation in respect of the particular issue under consideration, it will usually deploy the proportionality test to assess whether the action complained of remains within, or exceeds, that margin of appreciation. Thus, the margin of appreciation impacts on the strictness of scrutiny under the proportionality principle.

The margin of appreciation and proportionality are arguably the most academically contentious of the Court's methods of the Convention interpretation, having generated a great many books, articles and collections.[3] This is partly because they may lead to different answers to similar questions asked in different situations, and thus appear to endanger consistency of approach and rights protection across the Contracting Parties. Furthermore, ascertaining (dis)proportionality and identifying the margin of appreciation are hardly exact sciences: in taking into account variable conditions such as national traditions, legal cultures, religious and developmental particularities and so on, the Court seems to be treating different people's claims to rights differently and in a way that is not always foreseeable.

Ultimately, a proportionality analysis seeks to determine whether an appropriate 'balance' has been struck between competing interests. This is not something that is amenable to scientific determination. It is, rather, a matter of *judgement*, in the fullest sense of the word. The resulting lack of precision is one of the primary concerns that might be expressed in relation to proportionality, but it is also one the structure of the test itself attempts to address. The proportionality analysis does not ask whether the optimal or perfect balance has been struck; only whether a *proportionate* balance has been found. Thus, through this analysis the Court is trying to account for difference (of context, experience, expertise etc.), but to do so in a transparent manner so that at the very least the weighting given to the various factors (e.g. the alleged legitimate objective being pursued) is made clear.

This is not to say, however, that the Court will always be able to determine the question of balance; sometimes it will recognise that a topic is of such

[2] Compare, for example, *Bowman v the United Kingdom*, 19 February 1998, Reports of Judgments and Decisions 1998-I and *Colman v the United Kingdom*, 28 June 1993, Series A no. 258-D.

[3] Just to mention a few examples: Arai-Takahashi, *The Margin of Appreciation Doctrine and the Principle of Proportionality in the Jurisprudence of the ECHR* (Intersentia, 2002); Benvenisti, 'Margin of Appreciation, Consensus, and Universal Standards' (1999) 31 *Journal of International Law and Politics* 843; Kratochvil, 'The Inflation of the Margin of Appreciation by the European Court of Human Rights' (2011) 29 *Netherlands Quarterly of Human Rights*, 324.

sensitivity, such profound disagreement, and such centrality to 'national' or 'constitutional' identity that the state ought to be allowed a wide margin of appreciation in relation to it. Once the state, then, stays within that margin of appreciation, its actions will pass Convention muster. This is certainly considered important by the Contracting Parties, which seem to want to nudge the Court towards displaying ever more deference towards the decisions of the national authorities. This is reflected in the symbolically important decision to mention subsidiarity and the margin of appreciation in the Preamble once Protocol 15 comes into force.

The margin of appreciation is not limited to the qualified rights in Articles 8–11 of the Convention which are naturally fit for proportionality analysis; the margin of appreciation can also exercise an independent function within the Convention jurisprudence. Let us take Article 3, the right to be free from torture, inhuman and degrading treatment or punishment, as an example. This is an absolute right that contains at least three levels of protection: first, the state's negative obligation to refrain from torture, inhuman or degrading treatment or punishment; second, its positive substantive obligation to protect people from ill-treatment from other individuals; and, third, its positive procedural obligation to investigate situations of torture, inhuman or degrading treatment or punishment. There is no margin of appreciation as regards the negative obligation, but the Court has suggested that states do have some margin of appreciation when it comes to the positive obligations.[4]

The key issues that will be discussed in this chapter are the issues of shape and limits. We will first look into the test of proportionality. We will consider if this test is needed and desirable in human rights adjudication: commentators tend to treat it variously as a useful tool, a necessary evil, or an 'assault on human rights'.[5] In Debate 1 we return to the baseline question of whether we need a proportionality approach to assessing rights claims. The margin of appreciation is no less controversial than the test of proportionality; commentators writing on it can be divided on those who think that there is no place for any margin of appreciation in human rights adjudication,[6] and those who think that this is an appropriate concept that might be spread beyond the ECtHR.[7] Debate 2 therefore will shed some light on the reasons behind these conflicting

---

[4] See, for example, *Vinter and Others v the United Kingdom* [GC], nos 66069/09 and two others, ECHR 2013, para. 120.

[5] Tsakyrakis, 'Proportionality: An Assault on Human Rights?' (2009) 7 *International Journal of Constitutional Law* 468.

[6] Examples are multiple including Benvenisti, 'Margin of Appreciation' (above, n. 3), Letsas, *A Theory of Interpretation of the European Convention on Human Rights* (Oxford University Press, 2009).

[7] See Shany, 'Toward a General Margin of Appreciation Doctrine in International Law?' (2005) 16 *European Journal of International Law* 907; see also Gerards, 'Pluralism, Deference and the Margin of Appreciation Doctrine' (2011) 17 *European Law Journal* 80, McGoldrick, 'A Defence of the Margin of Appreciation and an Argument for its Application by the Human Rights Committee' (2016) 65 *International and Comparative Law Quarterly* 21.

views. One of the key reasons for criticism of the margin of appreciation is that its scope is difficult to define as its boundaries are set on a case-by-case basis. Debate 3 addresses these concerns.

Debate 1
Do we need a proportionality analysis for rights adjudication?

Assessing whether or not a particular law, policy or state action is a proportionate interference with rights involves a number of stages of analysis, and a violation of the Convention can be established at any one of these stages. Usually, we think about the stages of proportionality as being broken down into questions, considered by the Court in turn. The questions are:

1. Was there an interference with an ECHR right?
2. Was the interference legal?
3. Did the interference pursue a legitimate aim?
4. Is the interference necessary in a democratic society?
5. Did the authorities balance the relevant public and private interests properly when they considered the interference?

The Court does not always address each of these steps expressly when considering a claim of disproportionate interference with rights (because, for example, the interference is apparent and not disputed, or the legitimacy of the aim pursued is accepted by all parties), but it is useful, when analysing the facts of a particular case, to use them as the framework for assessing proportionality. Let us therefore address them in turn.

Was there an Interference with an ECHR Right?

This stage can be called the 'preliminary' stage of proportionality, where the Court assesses whether any Convention right is engaged by the impugned action. If there was no interference by the respondent state then the Court can either find no violation or declare an application inadmissible. In truth, it is rare for the parties to dispute whether there was an interference. Usually, the respondent state accepts the claim of interference, but argues that it was justified. This is not to say that this preliminary question is never disputed. In *S. and Marper v the United Kingdom*, concerning the retention of DNA data about suspected criminals, the UK government argued that there was no interference because the fingerprints and DNA samples collected during the criminal investigation against the applicant were not used but only retained.[8] The criminal investigation in question did not lead to a conviction. The Court

---

[8] *S. and Marper v the United Kingdom* [GC], nos 30562/04 and 30566/04, ECHR 2008, para. 63.

disagreed and found that Convention rights had been interfered with because the samples might be used in future, and could provide sensitive personal information about the applicants. In *S. and Marper* the Court then moved on to the following stages of the test of proportionality and ultimately found a violation of the Convention. In general, if the Court is satisfied that there was an interference then it moves on to the second stage of the test of proportionality.

Was the Interference Legal?

This stage can be called a 'legality' stage of proportionality, and reflects the requirement in Articles 8–11 that interferences would be 'in accordance with the law' (Article 8(2)) or 'prescribed by law' (Article 9(2), Article 10(2), Article 11(2)). At this stage, the Court only assesses whether the respondent state complied with its national law; a lack of legal basis in domestic law will lead to a finding that the Convention has been violated. In *Giacomelli v Italy*, for example, the Court found a violation because the authorities continued to operate a hazardous waste plant although they were obliged to close it under the national law.[9] Thus, if there is no legal basis for the action the test of legality is failed and a violation is established; unlawful action cannot be proportionate. Conversely, if the interference is legal under the national law then the Court moves to the next stage of the test of proportionality.

Did the Interference Pursue a Legitimate Aim?

This stage can be called a 'legitimacy' stage of proportionality, at which the state identifies an objective that was being pursued by the impugned action. If no legitimate aim is identified the Court will find a violation of the Convention. The legitimate aims are usually listed in the qualifying clauses of the relevant right in the Convention, e.g. Article 8(2), Article 9(2), Article 10(2) and Article 11(2). By means of example, Article 9(2) provides:

> 2. Freedom to manifest one's religion or beliefs shall be subject only to such limitations as are prescribed by law and are necessary in a democratic society *in the interests of public safety, for the protection of public order, health or morals, or for the protection of the rights and freedoms of others* (emphasis added).

The ECtHR applies a very light touch approach to governments' claims that they pursued a legitimate aim. A violation will only be established at this stage where no aim is identified, or where the interference cannot be even remotely linked to any of the legitimate aims. This is rare, although not unheard of. For example, in *Catan and Others v the Republic of Moldova and Russia* the applicants lived on a territory of the self-proclaimed Republic of Transnistria, which is *de jure* a part of Moldova. The authorities of Transnistria decided to close

---

[9] *Giacomelli v Italy*, no. 59909/00, ECHR 2006-XII.

some schools on its territory in which instruction was through Romanian, the official language of Moldova. The Court held that these schools were closed as part of 'entrenching the separatist ideology' of Transnistria and not in pursuit of a legitimate aim. As a result, the Convention had been violated.[10] Conversely, if a legitimate aim can be identified (even presumptively) the Court moves on to the next stage of the proportionality analysis.

Is the Interference Necessary in a Democratic Society?

This stage can be called the 'necessity' stage of proportionality. Articles 8–11 of the ECHR provide that every interference with the rights enshrined in these Articles should be 'necessary in a democratic society'. In considering necessity, the Court, having assessed whether there was a legitimate aim, assesses whether there is a 'reasonable relationship of proportionality between the means employed and the aim sought to be realised'[11] and whether there were less intrusive ways of achieving the same result. For instance, in the case of *Alekseyev v Russia* the Court held that the authorities had resorted to measures that were not necessary in a democratic society when they banned a Gay Pride march.[12] Here, the government argued that this parade would provoke counter-demonstrations and cause public disorder. The Court noted that 'the authorities could have made arrangements to ensure that both events [pro-LGBTQI and anti-LGBTQI] proceeded peacefully and lawfully, allowing both sides to achieve the goal of expressing their views without clashing with each other'.[13] Doing that did not necessitate banning the Pride parade, which was therefore not necessary in a democratic society. This stage of analysis does not concern itself with whether the option taken is fair, or whether the interference is disproportionate to the public interest to be achieved; rather it is limited to questions of necessity, sometimes implicating effectiveness of the approach taken.[14] If the Court establishes that the measure is not necessary in a democratic society it finds a violation; otherwise it moves to the next stage of the proportionality test.

Did the Authorities Balance the Relevant Public and Private Interests Properly When they Considered the Interference?

This stage can be called a 'balancing' stage of proportionality. Somewhat controversially,[15] it is not uncommon for the ECtHR to merge the necessity and balancing stages, considering them both as part of its analysis of whether the

---

[10] *Catan and Others v the Republic of Moldova and Russia* [GC], nos 43370/04, 8252/05 and 18454/06, ECHR 2012.

[11] *Lithgow and Others v the United Kingdom*, 8 July 1986, Series A no. 102, para. 120.

[12] *Alekseyev v Russia*, nos 4916/07, 25924/08 and 14599/09, 21 October 2010.

[13] Ibid., para. 75.

[14] Gerards, 'How to Improve the Necessity Test of the European Court of Human Rights' (2013) 11 *International Journal of Constitutional Law* 466, 471.

[15] Gerards, 'How to Improve the Necessity Test' (above, n. 14), 472–473.

measures taken were 'necessary in a democratic society'.[16] The key difference is that during the balancing stage the Court is asking not whether the interference was necessary or effective, but rather whether it fairly weighed the competing interests against one another and reached a balanced conclusion. This complex analysis is not amenable to a scientifically 'correct' answer: rights are often in contest with one another, and finding the right 'balance' between them is always challenging.[17]

Von Hannover v Germany illustrates this well. In this case, the Court considered whether the applicant's right to privacy was breached. The applicant, a member of royal family of Monaco, was photographed without her consent and these photographs were published in a German tabloid. The German courts favoured freedom of expression in this case and did not interfere, finding that whilst there was an infringement of her privacy this was proportionate to the public interest in her life as a public figure. Of course, here such actions of the German authorities cannot be deemed as 'unnecessary in a democratic society'. Having balanced the competing interests of privacy for the applicant and freedom of speech for the tabloid, the Court decided that there was a violation of Article 8 of the Convention; that the interference with her privacy was disproportionate to the public interest in knowing about her private life.[18] Here, as ever, the question of whether an appropriate balance was struck finally determined the question of proportionality.

Critics of proportionality mount three major arguments relating to the test's utility, impact on human rights, and interference with substantive decision making on the national level.

The utility critique claims that proportionality is not a means of reasoning that helps effectively to resolve cases, but rather conceals discretionary and ad hoc reasoning. This relates to the fact that the structure of the proportionality analysis outlined above, and indeed the whole idea that a 'balance' can be identified with any certitude between different interests, suggests a kind of scientific precision for proportionality, when in truth only some elements of the test can be objectively verified (e.g. necessity, or legality) and the rest of the analysis is a structured, but subjective, assessment. As Fontanelli argues, proportionality 'is a myth in which the form draws its nourishment from an impoverished meaning'.[19] Thus, the heart of this criticism is that the ECtHR represents this as an objective test, and does not acknowledge that no precise scale for measuring incompatible interests can be identified. The criticism is not, then, that the assessment of proportionality is subjective per se; indeed, it is inevitably

---

[16] See, for example, *S.A.S. v France* [GC], no. 43835/11, ECHR 2014.

[17] Indeed, sometimes they might be said to 'clash'; see Smet and Brems (eds), *When Human Rights Clash at the European Court of Human Rights – Conflict or Harmony?* (Oxford University Press, 2017).

[18] *Von Hannover v Germany*, no. 59320/00, ECHR 2004-VI.

[19] Fontanelli, 'The Mythology of Proportionality in Judgments of the Court of Justice of the European Union on Internet and Fundamental Rights' (2016) 36 *Oxford Journal of Legal Studies* 630, 632.

so. It is, rather, that the Court denies this subjectivity when it pursues the appearance of objectivity through a proportionality test. The subjectivity of proportionality analysis is perhaps most clearly evident in the assignment by the Court of varying weights to different interests in any particular scenario. The recent Chamber judgment in *Osmanoğlu and Kocabaş v Switzerland* is an apposite illustration.[20]

The applicants in this case were Turkish immigrants in Switzerland who wanted their daughters to be exempted from mixed-sex swimming lessons. Their request was refused, which they claimed violated their rights under Article 9. They understood their Muslim faith as requiring a certain approach to raising children, which included not allowing their daughters to undertake swimming lessons together with boys. Switzerland argued that this was not compatible with the Swiss way of life, and that the interference with Article 9 was proportionate in pursuit of public order and morality. To determine the case, the Court ended up comparing the state's interest in integrating immigrants into their society against the applicants' religious beliefs. In this case, the Court considered the state interest to be a legitimate one, the action to be necessary, and the interference thus to be a proportionate interference with rights. In other words, the Court prioritised integration over religious belief. One can imagine, however, the Court coming to precisely the other conclusion; it is not clear why the Court here prioritises the integration rationale over religious belief. Either outcome is possible, and the inability to predict which will be arrived at in a particular case makes the outcome of a complaint difficult to foresee, and thus calls into question the effectiveness of the Convention in ensuring practical protection of rights, including at the stage of making the kinds of policy that mandate mixed-sex swimming lessons regardless of the likely objections of people who follow a more conservative approach to religious beliefs and for whom this would likely cause real difficulties, such as Orthodox Jews or devout Muslims. A similar observation could be made about cases in which the Court compares interests such as the right not to be indoctrinated against the need to maintain cultural traditions,[21] or when the right to acquire information clashes with personal privacy.[22] The criticism of proportionality here is not, then, that it arrives at the 'wrong' outcome – one might argue that balancing such interests is so difficult that a range of possible outcomes might be defended – but rather that its pretension to objectivity and exactitude elides the reality of subjective reasoning in any given case.

The second criticism – that of the impact of proportionality on the value of human rights – is somewhat more philosophical. Some commentators argue

---

[20] *Osmanoğlu and Kocabaş v Switzerland*, no. 29086/12, ECHR 2017.

[21] *Lautsi and Others v Italy* [GC], no. 30814/06, ECHR 2011.

[22] See *Von Hannover v Germany (no. 2)* [GC], nos 40660/08 and 60641/08, ECHR 2012.

that proportionality reduces the value of human rights to the level of comparing various interests.[23] In fact, they say, human rights should be more than just personal interests that can be equal or even sometimes subordinate to communal preferences; that they should trump any other competing considerations and the result of the case should follow from moral assessment of the situation involving human rights.[24] The ECtHR does not explicitly take this approach. As the *Osmanoğlu and Kocabaş* judgment shows, communal interests can trump human rights in some circumstances. Moreover, proportionality provides shortcuts for moral reasoning and does not explain the moral background of the decision taken. Tsakyrakis argues that

> The adoption of a balancing test, according to the principle of proportionality, risks neglecting the complexity of moral evaluation and, especially, the complexity of rights. More specifically, it tends to overlook, or at least not appreciate adequately, the fact that our moral universe includes ideas not amenable to quantification, with the result that these ideas are not given due consideration in our reasoning.[25]

This criticism is not accepted by all commentators. Moral reasoning as suggested by Tsakyrakis might lead to even more subjective, speculative and unpredictable results. People disagree about human rights and there is no universally acceptable morality. Therefore, sometimes moral reasoning presents itself in a form of imposing of personal biases of the judges sitting in the case. Such an approach undermines the legitimacy of human rights adjudication. The uncertainty and unpredictability of the results and seemingly ad hoc nature of the reasoning in this case will not even be furnished by a structure that proportionality provides.[26]

The final criticism of proportionality is that it involves the Court in a substantive review of decisions taken on the national level. Where the ECtHR considers proportionality, its analysis might be perceived as constituting substantive, rather than procedural, judicial review. This might exacerbate the kinds of tensions about the appropriate judicial role that we already canvassed in Chapter 2. By means of illustration, in the case of *Konstantin Markin v Russia* the Court considered whether the Russian law prohibiting male military personnel from taking paternity leave was compatible with the Convention. The Court had to balance the state's reasons for prohibiting paternity leave (which related to 'national traditions', military discipline and national security) against considerations of gender equality. The Russian Constitutional Court had already

---

[23] See, for example, Letsas, 'Rescuing Proportionality' in Cruft, Liao and Renzo (eds), *Philosophical Foundations of Human Rights* (Oxford University Press, 2015).
[24] Dworkin, *Taking Rights Seriously* (Harvard University Press, 1977), xi.
[25] Tsakyrakis, 'Proportionality' (above, n. 5), 475.
[26] For more see Dzehtsiarou, *European Consensus and the Legitimacy of the European Court of Human Rights* (Cambridge University Press, 2015), 116–119.

had a chance to balance the same considerations and decided against allowing male military servicemen to have access to parental leave; it considered that the state had struck a permissible balance.[27] The Chamber of the Court, however, forcefully disagreed, holding:

> [T]he core argument of the Constitutional Court in support of the limitation of the rights of servicemen was that military service imposed specific demands in so far as it required uninterrupted performance of duties by them and that, consequently, the taking of parental leave by servicemen on a large scale would have a negative effect on the fighting power and operational effectiveness of the armed forces. The Court finds that argument unconvincing. It notes the lack of concrete evidence to substantiate the alleged damage to national security. There is no indication that any expert study or statistical research was made to assess the number of servicemen who would be in a position to take three years' parental leave at any given time and would be willing to do so. There is accordingly no evidentiary basis for the assertion that the number of servicemen simultaneously taking parental leave would be so significant as to undermine the fighting capacity of the army. It follows that the Constitutional Court based its decision on a pure assumption, without attempting to probe its validity by checking it against statistical data or by weighing the conflicting interests of maintaining the operational effectiveness of the army, on the one hand, and of protecting servicemen against discrimination in the sphere of family life and promoting the best interests of their children, on the other.[28]

Contrary to the decision of the Russian Constitutional Court, then, the ECtHR decided that there was a violation of Article 8. For some, such an outcome raises serious questions about whether the ECtHR is adhering to its subsidiary character. In response, one might argue that the ECtHR can only identify violations of the Convention; it does not have any power to invalidate domestic laws and thus exercises an especially 'weak' form of judicial review that makes substantive review relatively unproblematic. However, that argument ignores the fact that the Court's decision is binding on the respondent state under Article 46(1) (which we consider further in Chapter 8), even if the state considers that the ECtHR has got the question of balance 'wrong' or the issue is one on which reasonable people might reasonably disagree so that a 'right answer' might not easily be discernible. Even if the ECtHR's review is 'weak', then, it is still legally binding, a situation that one might argue is particularly troublesome where the test being applied to assess whether there was a violation is an imprecise one, as proportionality is.

There are, then, seemingly compelling arguments against the Court's use of a proportionality analysis. Why, then, does it persevere with it? The truth is that proportionality analysis is a commonly deployed approach to the difficult question of 'balancing' competing rights and interests in tribunals all over the

---

[27] *Konstantin Markin v Russia* [GC], no. 30078/06, ECHR 2012.

[28] *Konstantin Markin v Russia*, no. 30078/06, 7 October 2010, para 57.

world.[29] This is not because any system considers that it is perfect or is unaware of the criticisms already outlined but rather because, to paraphrase a famous line of Churchill's, proportionality is the worst form of reasoning, except for all the others.

First, the structured nature of the proportionality analysis creates an analytical framework for the delicate assessments that competing interests and rights necessitate, which in turn facilitates *some* transparency. Even if the reader might not be convinced of why the Court came to a certain conclusion on the question of balancing, the structure of the analysis at least outlines how it came to that conclusion – or at least how it purports to have done so. If the balancing analysis as outlined is inadequate this is quickly apparent from the text of the judgment, and can form the basis of concerted scholarly engagement with the reasoning and future attempts to convince the Court to revisit its position.

Second, although the outcome of a proportionality analysis is sometimes unpredictable, the highly structured nature of the assessment does bring an element of foreseeability to how the analysis will proceed and to the arguments that a state will need to make to ground a claim of proportionality. This is significant not only in cases before the Court, but also potentially in the policy-making process where the likely assessment of a contentious law in the ECtHR (or a domestic court mirroring the Strasbourg framework of analysis) will require legality, legitimacy, necessity etc. to be established. Thus, the structure of the proportionality analysis in the Strasbourg jurisprudence may structure the policy-making process, potentially reducing the likelihood of a disproportionate law or policy being introduced in the first place.[30] This reflects also the fact that the judges and lawyers of the Court, the lawyers before it, and the lawyers and policy makers at domestic level are now generally familiar with proportionality as a method of reasoning: not only was the principle developed in Strasbourg after the example of, especially, the German Constitutional Court, but so too has its development in the ECtHR influenced the use of proportionality

---

[29] For a comparative overview see Pirker, *Proportionality Analysis and Models of Judicial Review* (Europa Law Publishing, 2013) and Stone Sweet and Mathews, 'Proportionality Balancing and Global Constitutionalism' (2008) 47 *Columbia Journal of Transnational Law* 73. Some key judgments on proportionality include the following from the European Court of Justice: *Internationale Handelsgesellschaft mbH v Einfuhr- und Vorratsstelle für Getreide und Futtermittel*, 1970 ECR 1125, 1136; UK: *R (Daly) v Secretary of State for the Home Department* [2001]; Germany: the German Constitutional Court began using this principle almost from the very beginning, see BVerfGE 3, 383 at 399 (1954); it is used in Israel: HCJ 2056/04 *Beit Sourik Village Council v The Government of Israel* PD 24 [2004]; and in Canada: *R v Oakes* [1986] 1 SCR 103 [Oakes].

[30] In both Ireland and the UK, for example, 'organs of the state' (Ireland) and 'public authorities' (UK) are required to undertake their work in accordance with the ECHR and can thus be expected to consider proportionality when making policies and proposing laws that have Convention implications. See s. 6, Human Rights Act 1998 (in the UK) and section 3, European Convention on Human Rights Act 2003 (in Ireland).

analysis in other Contracting Parties' domestic law. Very simply put, proportionality is now a familiar and in some jurisdictions fundamental approach to reasoning about rights that it would be difficult, if not impossible, to abandon.

Indeed, for all its difficulties as outlined above, proportionality has much to commend it as an approach to undertaking judicial review of the Convention-compatibility of state action whilst maintaining respect for the principle of subsidiarity. Although there are legitimacy concerns associated with the test of proportionality, it leaves ample space for subsidiarity and deference through the mode of margin of appreciation. As already mentioned, and further considered below, where the issue in question is one in relation to which states enjoy a broad margin of appreciation, the strictness with which the Court scrutinises proportionality will be lightened, whereas where there is a narrower margin of appreciation the analysis will be strict. Proportionality, thus, allows the Court to attempt to walk the very delicate line between supervising the Convention and not trespassing too far on the sovereignty of states.

Debate 2
Should national authorities have a margin of appreciation in respect of human rights protection?

The ECHR does not contain a definition of the margin of appreciation; indeed, as it stands the margin of appreciation is never mentioned within the text of the Convention (although it will appear in the Preamble once Protocol 15 comes into force). Moreover, the Court has never clearly given a definition of it. There are, however, many scholarly definitions. For O'Donnell, 'margin of appreciation refers to the latitude allowed to the member states in their observance of the Convention'.[31] Yourow defines the margin of appreciation in the following terms:

> The national margin of appreciation or discretion can be defined in the European Human Rights Convention context as the freedom to act; manoeuvring, breathing or elbow room; or the latitude of deference or error which the Strasbourg organs will allow national legislation, executive, administrative and judicial bodies before it is prepared to declare a national derogation from the Convention, or restriction, or limitation upon a right guaranteed by the Convention, to constitute a violation of one of the Convention's substantive guarantees.[32]

Letsas argues that the margin of appreciation as applied by the Court has at least two meanings: substantive and structural. A substantive margin is deployed when the Court considers whether the state rightly interfered with

---

[31] O'Donnell, 'The Margin of Appreciation Doctrine: Standards in the Jurisprudence of the European Court of Human Rights' (1982) 4 *Human Rights Quarterly* 474, 475.
[32] Yourow, *The Margin of Appreciation Doctrine* (above, n. 1), 13.

personal rights to protect collective goals such as public order or public health or morals. In contrast, the structural margin of appreciation reflects the need for institutional deference of the Court to the national authorities. For Letsas the latter may be justified, but the former is intensely problematic. He writes:

> The idea of the margin of appreciation in itself clearly lacks any normative force that can help us strike a balance between individual rights and public interest. Whether the complained acts fall within or outside the margin of appreciation, whether that is, the interference with the freedom is permissible all things considered, is what the Court in each case is asking.[33]

A structural approach to the margin of appreciation is, perhaps, more justifiable. The Court itself often points to this concept of the margin in its oft-repeated mantra that the national authorities are better placed than the Court to assess the situation and make relevant decisions.[34] The Court decides not to interfere here because the States know better how to secure human rights in a particular situation and therefore they enjoy a margin of appreciation. We will see this in particular in the context of (national) security in Chapter 6.

However, even the structural approach to the margin of appreciation raises questions as to how to justify the Court's deference to national authorities. Two primary arguments are advanced. The first is that it is the national authorities, rather than Strasbourg, which have democratic legitimacy to deal with complex human rights issues. Of course, this rests heavily on the assumption that all member states to the Council of Europe are well-functioning democracies, which is certainly not always the case. However, even if this were a sustainable assumption, one might note that a democratic mandate is not the only source of legitimacy that an institution can rely upon in making decisions as to rights.[35] Indeed, it might even be argued that rights are such that they, perhaps, ought not to be determined solely by majoritarian structures such as politics, and that instead process, participation and outcome might all be important sources of legitimacy. Thus, whilst the argument of democratic legitimacy provides a compelling grounding for the margin of appreciation it does not, alone, provide a complete justification.

The second argument for a margin of appreciation is that national authorities have more expertise to solve difficult human rights questions as they arise at the national level because they are better exposed to the national dynamics, debates and contexts which influence the 'real world' impact of political and legal decisions in sensitive right areas. The Court itself has tended to endorse this approach, holding that '[b]ecause of their direct knowledge of their

---

[33] Letsas, 'Two Concepts of the Margin of Appreciation' (2006) 26 *Oxford Journal of Legal Studies* 705, 711.
[34] Gerards, 'Pluralism, Deference and the Margin of Appreciation Doctrine' (above, n. 7), 104; see also Bakircioglu, 'The Application of the Margin of Appreciation Doctrine in Freedom of Expression and Public Morality Cases' (2007) 8 *German Law Journal* 711, 717.
[35] See, for example, Lever, 'Is Judicial Review Undemocratic?' (2007) *Public Law* 280.

society and its needs, the national authorities are in principle better placed than the international judge to appreciate what is "in the public interest"'.[36] This assumption, however, needs to be tested. Tsarapatsanis argues that whether the ECtHR is better or worse at deciding complex human rights dilemmas might depend on a myriad of factors, and without extensive empirical research it is difficult to make any conclusions. Moreover, such conclusions might differ in relation to different rights and different states, and even different institutions within the same state.[37] In other words, familiarity with the domestic context does not necessarily put the national authorities into a better position to determine questions of rights.

Why, then, does the Court continue to use the concept of the margin of appreciation? For some commentators, it is simply a technique for abdicating judicial responsibility and results in a denial of justice, leaving (often marginalised) people to the mercy of the decisions of the domestic authorities provided they are not manifestly and unanswerably disproportionate and absolute denials of Convention rights.[38]

In contrast, Legg argues that the margin of appreciation is best understood as a useful tool allowing the Court to take into account considerations that are contextual and not immediately relevant to the matter at hand, but at the same time worthy of being weighed in the balance. He defines the margin of appreciation as 'an adjudicatory technique enabling the [Court] to navigate a course through the competing considerations, and provides a vehicle through which lawyers for states and applicants can make their claims'.[39] Legg uses the theory of practical reasoning to argue that in arriving at a particular decision the ECtHR uses both first-order and second-order reasons. First-order reasons are immediately relevant to the case at hand; they relate directly to the questions raised. Second-order reasons are less manifestly relevant but determine the context in which the case is taking place, such as broader societal conditions or political structures. Legg uses an example of a person who 'because of tiredness decided not to assess whether or not to accept an investment proposal, thus losing the opportunity'.[40] In this example tiredness is the second-order reason since it is not directly relevant to the matter at issue but can have a substantive effect on the final decision. The first-order reasons would be the interest that would have been earned if the investment went ahead, the risk assessment, the availability of necessary funds and so on. Tiredness here is

[36] *James and Others v the United Kingdom*, 21 February 1986, Series A no. 98, para. 46.
[37] Tsarapatsanis, 'The Margin of Appreciation Doctrine: a Low-Level Institutional View' (2015) 35 *Legal Studies* 675.
[38] See Benvenisti, 'Margin of Appreciation' (above, n. 3), Macdonald, 'The Margin of Appreciation' in R. Macdonald et al. (eds), *The European System for the Protection of Human Rights* (Martinus Nijhoff 1993).
[39] Legg, *The Margin of Appreciation in International Human Rights Law* (Oxford University Press, 2012), 58.
[40] Ibid., 18.

an exclusionary second-order reason that prevents any considerations of the first-order reasons.[41] Within Legg's argument, second-order reasons can influence the significance (or weight) attached to first-order reasons: '[t]he [Court] considers the first-order reasons, and applies second-order reasons to them. The second-order reasons may cancel out, strengthen or reduce the ordinary weighting of first-order reasons'.[42] Under this approach, the margin of appreciation simply allows for decisions as to weighting to be made: where there is a broad margin of appreciation the first-order reasons for finding violation should be particularly weighty; where there is a narrow or no margin of appreciation much less convincing first-order reasons can justify a violation of the Convention.

Whilst Legg's argument is attractive in explaining *how* the margin of appreciation can assist in structuring the Court's reasoning, it does not fully address the major criticism that is levied against it: that its impact is such as to leave some people without relief before the Court simply because the rights, topic or context is such that the Court prefers to avoid making a decision as to rights. Macdonald opines that the Court uses the margin of appreciation when it does not want to provide reasons for its decision not to interfere;[43] Benvenisti argues that the margin of appreciation is a dangerous doctrine that undermines the universality of human rights because it introduces varying standards of human rights protection.[44] The criticism is not limited to scholarly reflection on the margin of appreciation. Judge De Meyer, for example, has famously argued that:

> The empty phrases concerning the State's margin of appreciation – repeated in the Court's judgments for too long already – are unnecessary circumlocutions, serving only to indicate abstrusely that the States may do anything the Court does not consider incompatible with human rights. Such terminology, as wrong in principle as it is pointless in practice, should be abandoned without delay.[45]

In spite of the criticism of the margin of appreciation, however, the Court continues to use it. Why? Simply put, the doctrine is deeply embedded in the reasoning of the Court and is considered important by the Contracting Parties; recall that they have insisted on its appearing in the Preamble once Protocol 15 comes into force. Any attempt to abandon the margin of appreciation now would seem incredibly difficult and would be likely to attract criticism from the member states. This is largely because the Court is a subsidiary body that needs to allow the Contracting Parties some space to deal

---

[41] For more examples, see Ibid., 18–23.

[42] Ibid., 195.

[43] Macdonald, 'The Margin of Appreciation' (above, n. 38), 85.

[44] Benvenisti, 'Margin of Appreciation' (above, n. 3).

[45] *Z. v Finland*, 25 February 1997, Reports of Judgments and Decisions 1997-I, dissenting opinion of Judge De Meyer.

with the local human rights challenges and carefully consider their decisions. Ideally, interaction between the Court and the national authorities would be non-hierarchical and dialogic, notwithstanding the fact that, as we discuss in Chapter 8, the Court's judgments are binding on the states to which they are addressed. This is because implementation of the Convention is based on a sense of collective responsibility between the ECtHR and national authorities. If there is a shared responsibility for protecting human rights, then – the argument goes – there should be a shared decision-making power between the Contracting Parties and the ECtHR. Should one accept this, one might argue that the margin of appreciation allows the Court to maintain effective implementation of the ECHR by not doing too much too soon, and thus avoids undermining trust and co-working between the national and European institutions.

Thus, whether one considers the margin of appreciation to be justifiable is, in essence, connected to how one conceives the role of the Court. If it is to grant individual justice in all cases that come before it there seems to be limited justification for the margin of appreciation. However, if the Court's role is more broadly to 'assum[e] a central coordinating role in implementing the ECHR, by closely cooperating with national institutional agents, which comprise legislatures, courts and administrative agencies'[46] the margin may seem a sensible, if not essential, principle for the Court to have developed and to continue to apply.

Debate 3

What are the boundaries of the margin of appreciation?

Even those who agree that the margin of appreciation is conceptually appropriate often criticise how it is applied in practice. Lord Lester famously called it 'slippery and elusive as an eel',[47] Yourow points out that 'the contours of margin analysis are too vague, that the substantive content of the doctrine is too elusive and that it can be invoked to reach both pro-rights and pro-state holdings without the benefit of developing substantive doctrinal consistency',[48] and Gerards opines that 'the court frequently just mentions the margin of appreciation test and some factors determining its width, without explaining what the precise scope of the margin in the concrete case should be'.[49] Thus, even if one accepts that the margin of appreciation might be sustainable, questions arise about how the breadth of the margin should be determined, and what factors should be taken into account.

---

[46] Tsarapatsanis, 'The Margin of Appreciation Doctrine' (above, n. 37), 684.
[47] Lester, 'Universality Versus Subsidiarity: A Reply' (1998) *European Human Rights Law Review* 73, 75–76.
[48] Yourow, 'The Margin of Appreciation Doctrine' (above, n. 1), 152.
[49] Gerards, 'Pluralism, Deference and the Margin of Appreciation Doctrine' (above, n. 7), 106.

The Nature of the Implicated Right

The first stage in deciding how wide the margin of appreciation should be in any case is to determine the quality of the implicated right as it relates to the margin. In this respect, one can suggest that the rights enshrined in the Convention can be divided into four groups.

First, the Court has never used margin of appreciation in relation to negative obligations under absolute rights. Having said that, the relativity that is often reflected in the Court's references to the margin of appreciation can even be found in relation to the most absolute of all rights: the prohibition of torture, inhuman and degrading treatment and punishment under Article 3,[50] for example when determining whether the treatment complained of has reached the minimal level of severity to engage Article 3.

The second group is positive obligations under any right of the Convention and its Protocols, in relation to which states do enjoy a margin of appreciation. This is true even in relation to the positive obligations that arise under Article 3: states can decide how to fulfil its obligation to protect people from torture, for example, with the Court intervening only if the actions are manifestly deficient. The case of *M.C. v Bulgaria* illustrates this well. The applicant was an underage victim of an alleged rape, which was not prosecuted by the Bulgarian authorities because the victim did not physically resist. It was alleged that this violated the positive obligation to protect people from torture, inhuman and degrading treatment or punishment. Although the Court held that actions of state authorities were so inadequate that they fell outside of Bulgaria's margin of appreciation, it stated that 'in respect of the means to ensure adequate protection against rape, States undoubtedly enjoy a wide margin of appreciation. In particular, perceptions of a cultural nature, local circumstances and traditional approaches are to be taken into account'.[51]

The third group is the qualified rights, in relation to which states enjoy a margin of appreciation. Shany identified three ways in which the Court applied the margin of appreciation to qualified rights: in the application of law to facts, in norm-balancing in law application, and in norm-balancing in law interpretation.[52] The margin of appreciation in the application of law to facts is evident in the so-called immigration cases under Article 8. According to the well-established case law, an immigrant cannot be expelled if his family life will

---

[50] In order to be prohibited by Article 3 certain treatment should reach a minimal level of severity. Compare the Chamber and Grand Chamber of the ECtHR in *Janowiec and Others v Russia* to see that judges disagree about what this level of severity actually means. *Janowiec and Others v Russia*, nos 55508/07 and 29520/09, 16 April 2012 and *Janowiec and Others v Russia* [GC], nos 55508/07 and 29520/09, ECHR 2013.

[51] *M.C. v Bulgaria*, no. 39272/98, ECHR 2003-XII, para. 154.

[52] Shany, 'All Roads Lead to Strasbourg?: Application of the Margin of Appreciation Doctrine by the European Court of Human Rights and the UN Human Rights Committee' (January 1, 2017). *Journal of International Dispute Settlement (Forthcoming); Hebrew University of Jerusalem Legal Research Paper No. 17–16*, available at SSRN: https://ssrn.com/abstract=2925652.

be disproportionately impacted as a result. In these circumstances, the states are given wide margin of appreciation in assessing whether the applicant has indeed established any family life in the host country, i.e. as to the determination of facts and subsequent application of law thereto.[53] The margin of appreciation in norm-balancing in law-application can be illustrated by reference to the accommodation of religious beliefs under Article 9. For instance, in *Lautsi and Others v Italy*[54] the Court decided that the Italian authorities could restrict the right of the applicant not to be exposed to religious symbols due to the breadth of the margin of appreciation the authorities enjoyed in accommodation of Article 9. Here, then, the authorities had a wide margin of appreciation in their application of the law (requiring the display of the crucifix in school) to the facts (of a non-Christian pupil's exposure to that crucifix). The margin of appreciation in norm-balancing in law interpretation arises where the state is determining the scope of a particular right. This is a particularly challenging aspect of the margin of appreciation, creating problematic differences in standards that in turn might undermine the universality of the human rights standards. The ongoing litigation on whether there is a right for same-sex couples to access marriage under Article 12 illustrates this well. In *Oliari and Others v Italy* the Court appeared to suggest that the Contracting Parties have a margin of appreciation in deciding whether to implement any legislative reforms as to recognition of homosexual relations, although here the Constitutional Court of Italy called for relationship recognition which was not provided, thus causing a violation.[55] A similar outcome was reached in *A, B and C v Ireland* where the Court held that the extent to which abortion should be legally available was within the margin of appreciation of the states, but that where the law did provide for access this must be facilitated and cannot be illusory.[56] The application of the margin of appreciation in terms of norm-balancing in law interpretation readily illustrates how it can help the Court to negotiate the narrow space between a rock and a hard place. Marriage equality, abortion and the right to choose the time and nature of one's dying are situations in which there are longstanding and unresolved tensions in ethics, politics and international law. It is clear that should the Court require Russia, for example, to legalise same-sex marriage, or Malta to make access to abortion available without restriction this would cause an enormous outbreak of criticism, and the judgments would likely not be executed. The key question, then, is whether the Court should be principled and ignore the reality of this likely reaction, or whether it should accommodate the differences in national context and tolerate varying levels of protection across the continent. Seeing those national contexts as second-order reasons, in Legg's argument, leads one

---

[53] Harris et al., *Harris, O'Boyle and Warbrick Law of the European Convention on Human Rights* (3rd edn, Oxford University Press, 2014), 577.

[54] *Lautsi and Others v Italy* (above, n. 21).

[55] *Oliari and Others v Italy*, nos 18766/11 and 36030/11, 21 July 2015.

[56] *A, B and C v Ireland* [GC], no. 25579/05, ECHR 2010.

certainly to favour the latter, although that unquestionably causes those likely to be least able to leverage national politics in their favour in homophobic, misogynistic and socially repressive domestic political environments wondering whether and how the ECtHR can truly be said to be a 'beacon of light' from their perspective.

The fourth group of rights is the so-called super-qualified rights in relation to which an even broader margin of appreciation is provided. Unlike qualified rights, legal provisions enshrining rights of this category do not list legitimate aims for which they can be restricted; rather they can be limited in pursuit of any aim provided that they do not cut into the core of the right. Because these rights are 'so' qualified, the states enjoy a remarkably broad margin of appreciation. Perhaps the best example is the right to free elections under Article 3 of Protocol 1. This provides:

> The High Contracting Parties undertake to hold free elections at reasonable intervals by secret ballot, under conditions which will ensure the free expression of the opinion of the people in the choice of the legislature.

The broad margin of appreciation enjoyed by states in organising their electoral systems under Article 3 of Protocol 1 is well illustrated by *Yumak and Sadak v Turkey*. At the time, Turkish law set a particularly high 10 per cent nationwide threshold for a party to enter parliament. The effect of this was that regional parties, which would practically never reach the threshold, could not enter the national Parliament and any seats they had won would be transferred to the bigger nationwide parties. Although the Court accepted that such a high threshold for entering the national parliament was unusual when compared to the other member states, it did not find a violation precisely on the basis of the wide margin of appreciation afforded to the respondent states.[57]

Beyond the Nature of the Implicated Right

Although the nature of the right is an important consideration in the Court's assessment of the scope of the margin of appreciation, it is not enough to determine its scope in each case. The Court listed the factors that determine the margin of appreciation in *S. and Marper v the United Kingdom*. These include (a) the nature of the Convention right, (b) the importance of the right for the individual, (c) the nature and the object of the interference, and (d) European consensus.[58] It seems that first three criteria are vaguely formulated and cannot determine the scope of the margin with much clarity,[59] and although (as discussed in Chapter 4) European consensus reasoning does not always

---

[57] *Yumak and Sadak v Turkey* [GC], no. 10226/03, ECHR 2008.

[58] *S. and Marper v United Kingdom* (above, n. 8).

[59] Gerards, 'Pluralism, Deference and the Margin of Appreciation Doctrine' (above, n. 7), 106.

introduce rigour and predictability, it can be used to help determine the first three factors. For example, in *Dickson v the United Kingdom* the Court pointed out that:

> Where [...] there is no consensus within the Member States of the Council of Europe, either as to the relative importance of the interest at stake or as to how best to protect it, the margin will be wider. This is particularly so where the case raises complex issues and choices of social strategy: the authorities' direct knowledge of their society and its needs means that they are in principle better placed than the international judge to appreciate what is in the public interest.[60]

The Democratic Process at the National Level

Factors like the democratic legitimacy of the legal provision in question or a higher level of expertise of national decision makers can also feature in determination of the scope of margin of appreciation. When a decision is taken by a legitimate national parliament through rigorous parliamentary procedures the margin of appreciation should be wider for the respondent state. Saul has observed that although there is considerable ambiguity as to how parliamentary procedures feature in determination of the scope of the margin of appreciation[61] it is possible to suggest that proper parliamentary decision-making process broadens the scope of the margin of appreciation. For example, in *Odièvre v France* the Court stated that broad margin of appreciation should be given to the national parliament which had to strike a balance between the interest of a child to know her parents and her mother to remain unknown.[62] Conversely, failure to discuss a particular issue in the parliament might significantly reduce the margin. The challenge here is whether mere discussion of a particular issue in the parliament would suffice to crucially broaden the margin or whether the quality of the discussion and debate would be taken into account and, if so, how that can be reconciled with the principle of subsidiarity. Moreover, it is unclear whether debating the issue in the parliament would be enough to execute the judgment after it was delivered.[63] This latter challenge became apparent in the case of *Hirst v the United Kingdom (no. 2)*. Here, the Court decided that total disenfranchisement of prisoners is a violation of

---

[60] *Dickson v the United Kingdom* [GC], no. 44362/04, ECHR 2007-V, para. 78.

[61] Saul, 'The European Court of Human Rights' Margin of Appreciation and the Processes of National Parliaments' (2015) 15 *Human Rights Law Review* 745.

[62] *Odièvre v France* [GC], no. 42326/98, ECHR 2003-III, para. 45. See also *Evans v the United Kingdom* [GC], no. 6339/05, ECHR 2007-I, para. 86; *Murphy v Ireland*, no. 44179/98, ECHR 2003-IX, para. 73; *Dudgeon v the United Kingdom*, 22 October 1981, Series A no. 45, para. 59.

[63] On rationality generally see Popelier and van de Heyning, 'Subsidiarity Post-Brighton: Procedural Rationality as Answer?' (2017) 30 *Leiden Journal of International Law* 5.

the Convention. Although this question had been considered by Westminster in the 1960s, the Court was not satisfied with the level of debate that took place then. It stated:

> there is no evidence that Parliament has ever sought to weigh the competing interests or to assess the proportionality of a blanket ban on the right of a convicted prisoner to vote. It is true that the question was considered by the multi-party Speaker's Conference on Electoral Law in 1968 which unanimously recommended that a convicted prisoner should not be entitled to vote. It is also true that the working party which recommended the amendment to the law to allow unconvicted prisoners to vote recorded that successive governments had taken the view that convicted prisoners had lost the moral authority to vote and did not therefore argue for a change in the legislation. It may be said that, by voting the way they did to exempt unconvicted prisoners from the restriction on voting, Parliament implicitly affirmed the need for continued restrictions on the voting rights of convicted prisoners. Nonetheless, it cannot be said that there was any substantive debate by members of the legislature on the continued justification in light of modern-day penal policy and of current human rights standards for maintaining such a general restriction on the right of prisoners to vote.[64]

In this case, it seems questionable that the Court should limit the scope of the margin of appreciation of Contracting Parties mainly on the basis of the absence of any recent consideration of the particular issue by the national parliament. Such a requirement seems very crude and formalistic. In 2011, the Westminster Parliament discussed the issue and concluded that prisoners should continue to be disenfranchised, but does the mere discussion of this expand the margin of appreciation and suggest execution of the *Hirst* decision? Surely not. Thus, a parliamentary debate is a necessary but not sufficient precondition for finding the disenfranchisement of prisoners legal under the Convention. Even the concurring Judges Tulkens and Zagrebelsky, who thought that there was no rational basis for blanket disenfranchisement, were critical of the Court's assessment of the nature of the parliamentary debates in the UK.[65] Of course, this is a variation on a more fundamental question for the Court about how far it can go in scrutinising the decisions of democratically legitimate national bodies. We return to this in earnest in Chapter 8.

The Complexity of the Issue

It might be argued that the limits of the Court's expertise should affect the scope of the margin of appreciation. According to this argument, the state should have a wider margin of appreciation in relation to complex technical

---

[64] *Hirst v the United Kingdom (no. 2)* [GC], no. 74025/01, ECHR 2005-IX, para. 79.
[65] Ibid., joint Concurring Opinion of Judges Tulkens and Zagrebelsky.

or scientific issues the full extent of which can only be understood by specially trained professionals. This is quite in line with the idea of deference on the basis of expertise often found in domestic law. Having said that, the Court could still narrow the margin of appreciation in relation to the procedural aspects of making law and policy relating to such complex technical issues. For example, in *Hatton and Others v the United Kingdom* the matter at issue was whether the decision of the UK authorities to allow night flights at Heathrow airport violated Article 8 rights of the applicants.[66] The Court accepted that the national authorities had a wide margin of appreciation in deciding on the means of economic development (which was implicated by decisions as to having open runways overnight), but it scrutinised the surrounding processes such as consultations during the decision-making process and decided that the authorities did not violate the Convention.

To sum up, although it is possible to identify some factors that determine the scope of the margin of appreciation such as the nature of the rights, European consensus and the character of the matter at issue and decision-making process it seems safe to conclude that the Court often operates in uncertain conditions. In some novel cases, it is almost impossible to predict what margin of appreciation will be afforded to the respondent state.

CONCLUSION

Proportionality and the margin of appreciation are key techniques of ECHR interpretation and, unsurprisingly, have generated a great amount of commentary. This is so because these techniques can accommodate differences in the application of human rights across contexts, even though in principle human rights are universal and, within the Convention system, would be expected to apply in the same way across the Council of Europe. Even if one agrees that the practice of human rights adjudication requires some scope for recognising and accommodating difference, the boundaries of that accommodation are contentious. Although both proportionality and margin of appreciation make a claim to objectively determine those boundaries, balancing is fundamentally subjective and the scope of the margin of appreciation sometimes seems to be determined on an ad hoc basis. The lack of clear and objective criterion to determine the scope of the margin of appreciation and outcome of a balancing exercise can call into question the foreseeability and effectiveness of the Convention and, thus, its legitimacy.

FURTHER READING

Arai-Takahashi, *The Margin of Appreciation Doctrine and the Principle of Proportionality in the Jurisprudence of the ECHR* (Intersentia, 2002), Part 1.
Çalı, 'Balancing Human Rights? Methodological Problems with Weights, Scales and Proportions' (2007) 29 *Human Rights Quarterly* 251.

---

[66] *Hatton and Others v the United Kingdom*, no. 36022/97, 2 October 2001.

Legg, *The Margin of Appreciation in International Human Rights Law* (Oxford University Press, 2012), Chapters 4–6.

Tsakyrakis, 'Proportionality: An Assault on Human Rights?' (2009) 7 *International Journal of Constitutional Law* 468.

CHAPTER 6

The Convention in Times of Insecurity

Insecurity poses challenges for human rights. Not only do situations of insecurity create conditions in which it can be more difficult for people to enjoy and exercise their rights, but so too can insecurity lead to the introduction by states of security measures with significant deleterious effects on rights. Thus, security and rights have a clear connection to one another, and one that is not often positive in its effects on rights protection.

Armed conflict (or war) is subject to a particular set of rules, known as international humanitarian law, and the extent to which international human rights law – including the European Convention on Human Rights (ECHR or Convention) – continues to operate in situations where these rules are being applied is a matter of some contention, which we consider in Debate 1. Even if (as we will find is the case) the Convention does continue to apply in times of armed conflict, a difficult question arises when that armed conflict takes place outside of the territory of the Contracting Party. Article 1 provides that the states parties to the Convention will secure the rights therein protected 'to everyone within their jurisdiction'. Thus, the question of whether the Convention has extraterritorial application is a highly controversial one. We address it here as Debate 2.

Insecurity does not only emanate from armed conflict. There can always be situations of 'public emergency' that, as Article 15 puts it, 'threaten[…] the life of the nation'. In such cases the Convention permits states to derogate from rights 'to the extent strictly required by the exigencies of the situation', but questions inevitably arise over whether (a) that should be the case at all, and (b) the European Court of Human Rights (ECtHR or Court) takes an effective approach to restraining state action under Article 15 or, instead, is deferential to claims of both the existence of an emergency and the appropriateness of the response thereto. In Debate 3 we consider these questions relating to Article 15.

Importantly, insecurity is not only something that takes place or is experienced at a grand/statist scale; insecurity is, instead, an alarmingly commonplace experience. Domestic violence and similar forms of interpersonal violence are a major public health concern in Europe and worldwide, and in Debate 4 we focus on the example of domestic violence to consider the extent to which the Convention protects people from everyday, interpersonal experiences of insecurity.

Debate 1

Does the ECHR apply in war?

We have already noted that the state of war has a particular applicable legal system: international humanitarian law. However, this does not mean that international human rights law ceases to operate during an armed conflict.[1] In the context of the Council of Europe, this means that the ECHR continues to apply to its Contracting Parties in war but that simple statement, generally accepted within international law and politics, should not be taken to mean that the application of both international humanitarian and international human rights law simultaneously is unproblematic. Indeed, it is anything but. This represents one of the key debates not only in the context of the ECHR but also in the context of international law. Questions arise as to whether, and if so when, one body of law stops applying in any given situation (international human rights law) and another begins exclusively to apply (international humanitarian law), or whether the two bodies of law should be read together in a more harmonious manner to apply concurrently throughout an armed conflict.[2] The potential for the two bodies of law to diverge, converge or be read together is well illustrated by the example of the right to be free from arbitrary detention.

Arbitrary detention is prohibited by human rights law (and Article 5 of the ECHR) and remains prohibited in war,[3] but in a situation of armed conflict how we determine whether a detention is arbitrary or not will be defined by the rules of international humanitarian law which permits, for example, the detention of prisoners of war without charge or trial until the cessation of hostilities, which may in real terms mean years of detention. These rules may permit detention in situations, and for durations, that international human rights law would not.[4] A key mechanism to manage these potential inconsistencies is to say that, in the context of armed conflict, compliance with the rules of international humanitarian law will often be sufficient to ensure compliance with international human rights law.

What, then, could possibly be controversial about saying that international human rights law is applicable in times of armed conflict? That a state could

---

[1] See, for example, *Legal Consequences of the Construction of a Wall in the Occupied Palestinian Territory* (Advisory Opinion) 2004, available at http://www.icj-cij.org/en/case/131 and *Armed Activities on the Territory of Congo (Democratic Republic of Congo v Uganda)* [2005] ICJ Rep 168.

[2] Orakhelashvili, 'The Interaction between Human Rights and Humanitarian Law: Fragmentation, Conflict, Parallelism, or Convergence' (2008) 19 *European Journal of International Law* 161.

[3] See, for example, Rule 99, ICRC Rules of Customary International Humanitarian Law; Article 42, Geneva Convention IV (1949); Rule 147, Geneva Convention IV (1940); Article 7(1)(e) Rome Statute of the International Criminal Court 1998.

[4] On the right to be free from arbitrary deprivation of liberty generally see, e.g., de Londras, *Detention in the War on Terror: Can Human Rights Fight Back?* (Cambridge University Press, 2011), Chapter 2.

be held accountable for its actions in violation of human rights obligations in a time of war? In essence, it is the possibility that civilians within an armed conflict situation might engage with human rights law enforcement mechanisms in order to try to secure a remedy for rights violations during war that causes this controversy; in the context of the ECHR, that is to make a complaint to the ECtHR in respect of alleged rights violations in armed conflict.

As we will see below, the Court's willingness to adjudicate alleged human rights violations in times of armed conflict that are said to come within the jurisdiction of Contracting Parties is controversial indeed. However, the material point at this stage is that the Court has not shied away from asserting the continuing application of the Convention in times of war. This is consistent with the approach of other international courts, including the International Court of Justice,[5] and just as those courts have done, the ECtHR has shown a willingness to reconcile states' obligations under human rights law with their obligations under international humanitarian law and the perceived realities and necessities of armed conflict. So, for example, in *Jaloud v the Netherlands* (which we explore in more detail below) the Court accepted that a situation of armed conflict might be such that a state's duty to investigate the use of lethal force can be discharged with a less rigorous investigation and somewhat less careful evidence gathering etc. than would ordinarily be expected of it:

> The Court is prepared to make reasonable allowances for the relatively difficult conditions under which the Netherlands military and investigators had to work. In particular, it must be recognised that they were engaged in a foreign country which had yet to be rebuilt in the aftermath of hostilities, whose language and culture were alien to them, and whose population [...] clearly included armed hostile elements.[6]

The clear thrust of this is that the Court applies a looser test of proportionality in scenarios like this, allowing a broader decision-making margin to the respondent state. Importantly, however, *Jaloud* is representative of an approach that suggests that the Convention obligations continue to apply with as much substantive force in a military context as they do otherwise. However, it is not at all clear that this should be the case especially in situations of international armed conflict and occupation where international humanitarian law arguably permits more rights-restrictive activity than does the ECHR.

The question that arises here is whether a state's obligations under international humanitarian law ought to lead to an adjustment of how the Court assesses compliance with Convention rights; should Convention rights, in a sense, be 'refracted' through international humanitarian law (IHL)? Certainly, for some scholars, the Court ought to take a firm line; as Silvia Borelli has written,

---

[5] See further the jurisprudence cited in Orakhelashvili, 'The Interaction' (above, n. 2).

[6] *Jaloud v the Netherlands* [GC], no. 47708/08, ECHR 2014, para. 226.

where a State has failed to enter a derogation from its relevant ECHR obligations in relation to military action abroad, the Court should adopt a principled stance and assess the legality of its actions on the basis of the Convention alone, without seeking to qualify or interpret the State's obligations by reference to IHL standards.[7]

However, *Hassan v the United Kingdom*[8] suggests that the Court itself might not be quite so strict on this matter.

Hassan related to detention. As outlined above this is an area in which, on the face of it at least, there is significant divergence between the ECHR and international humanitarian law. Hassan had been arrested (by UK troops), detained (at a US-run facility) and interrogated (by UK intelligence agents) in Iraq, and claimed a violation of Article 5 of the ECHR. Article 5(1) lists a clearly constrained set of circumstances in which detention is permitted; in contrast, international humanitarian law allows detention on much wider bases. The UK argued that, as this was an armed conflict, compliance with IHL ought to be said to mean compliance with Article 5, notwithstanding the fact that this is not a basis for detention under Article 5 and that they had not derogated from the Article 5 rights. This was based on the argument that international humanitarian law was the *lex specialis* that 'might operate to modify or even displace'[9] a Convention provision.

Somewhat unexpectedly, the Court largely acceded to the UK's claims. It found that there was a clear state practice not to require derogation from Article 5 in order to allow for detention compliant with international humanitarian law in armed conflict, that it was obliged to understand and apply the Convention in a manner congruent with general public international law (citing the Vienna Convention on the Law of Treaties), and it was not therefore precluded from taking international humanitarian law into account when interpreting and applying Article 5. The Court claimed that 'even in situations of international armed conflict, the safeguards under the Convention continue to apply, albeit interpreted against the background of the provisions of international humanitarian law', and effectively 'read in' a provision allowing detention compliant with international humanitarian law to Article 5(1). In so doing, it rejected the UK's argument that *lex specialis* displaced the Convention, although it came to a remarkably similar conclusion to the one sought by the UK through that claim.[10]

Hassan is a radical step by the Court; it seems not only to take account of context and the challenges of armed conflict, but to go further than this and effectively equate legality under international law per se with Convention-compatibility. Whilst some have praised the Court for asserting its jurisdiction to

---

[7] Borelli, '*Jaloud v. Netherlands* and *Hassan v. United Kingdom*: Time for a Principles Approach in the Application of the ECHR to Military Action Abroad' (2015) 16 *Questions of International Law: Zoom In* 25, 27.

[8] *Hassan v the United Kingdom* [GC], no. 29750/09, ECHR 2014.

[9] Ibid., para. 88.

[10] On the importance of rejecting the *lex specialis* claim, see Hill-Cawthorne, 'The Grand Chamber Judgment in Hassan v. UK', *EJIL: Talk,* available at https://www.ejiltalk.org/the-grand-chamber-judgment-in-hassan-v-uk/.

hear the case in the first place,[11] there are powerful critiques of the decision, not least in the dissenting opinions which argue that states such as the UK not only failed to derogate from Article 5 and yet tried to rely on a lower legal standard, but also consistently resist the extraterritorial application of the Convention. In other words, the implicit critique is that in *Hassan* the Court concedes too much to states; that, as Borelli argues, the way to avoid Article 5 obligations here is to derogate,[12] not to attempt to undermine the Convention protection per se through argumentation of this kind. Whilst for some the Court's 'symbiotic' approach in *Hassan*, reading international humanitarian law and international human rights law together, is commendable,[13] for others it is human rights law that loses out here, providing to states a way to release themselves from rights obligations in practice, if not in law, when acting militarily abroad.

However, even *Hassan* has not been enough to quell concerns in the United Kingdom, in particular, about the Court's approach to applying the Convention to military operations abroad. As considered further in respect of Debate 2 below, there is a view among some in the UK that the Convention ought not to be applicable to such conflicts, which should instead be governed exclusively by international humanitarian law. Partly emanating from this, former UK Defence Secretary Michael Fallon announced that he would apply a 'presumption to derogate' in all future military conflicts,[14] although, as we will discuss in Debate 3, derogation under Article 15 is subject to a number of rules that would have to be complied with in any particular conflict situation.

Although the Court has reserved some space for its involvement in situations of an armed conflict, and therefore rejected the argument of the respondent state in relation to its jurisdiction, it has strategically accepted the UK's argument as to the substance of the violation. This strategic approach to human rights allows the Court to expand its substantive understanding of human rights without changing its approach to its jurisdiction.

Debate 2

Does the ECHR have extraterritorial effect?

A particular challenge of human rights protection arises in respect of extraterritorial military operations, including those undertaken under a mandate from the UN Security Council. This raises an interesting and controversial question

---

[11] Ibid.

[12] See Borelli, '*Jaloud v. Netherlands* and *Hassan v. United Kingdom*' (above, n. 7).

[13] De Koker, 'Hassan v. United Kingdom: The Interaction of Human Rights Law and International Humanitarian Law with Regard to the Deprivation of Liberty in Armed Conflicts' (2015) 31 *Utrecht Journal of International and European Law* 90.

[14] Fallon, *Speech to the Conservative Party Conference*, Birmingham, 4 October 2016. For analysis see Dzehtsiarou, 'Different Human Rights at Home and Abroad: Immunity for British Soldier during Overseas Operations', *JustSecurity*, 5 October 2016, available at https://www.justsecurity.org/33377/human-rights-home-abroad-immunity-british-soldier-overseas-operations/.

about the Convention: does it apply to the state acting overseas? The question is of crucial significance; if the Convention does apply with extraterritorial effect, then states acting in times of armed conflict outside of their own boundaries and even outside of Europe may not only be required as a matter of law to comply with the Convention, but might also be held accountable before the Court for their failures to do so.

It is a general principle of treaty interpretation that treaties *ordinarily* do not have extraterritorial effect.[15] This is certainly suggested by the text of the Convention, which requires the Contracting Parties to give effect to the rights protected therein 'to everyone within their jurisdiction'.[16] Whilst being within the jurisdiction of the state is not necessarily the same as being within the territorial boundaries of the state, there is ordinarily a connection between the two. Thus, it can be assumed that the wording of Article 1 was intended to limit the obligations to the territory of the state in the ordinary course of events.[17] However, the Court's jurisprudence shows that the reach of the Convention is not *necessarily* territorially bounded; instead, it will apply extraterritorially in exceptional circumstances.

What those exceptional circumstances are is not entirely settled. For some time it had been thought that *Loizidou v Turkey* provided the answer.[18] In 1974, along with hundreds of thousands of other Greek-Cypriots, Titina Loizidou had been displaced from her home in Northern Cyprus following the Turkish invasion of the island. She tried repeatedly to return but was always prevented from doing so by Turkish authorities guarding the occupied north of the island. She lodged an application against Turkey invoking violation of Article 1 Protocol 1, which protects right to property. Turkey claimed that Loizidou had legally lost the right to her property under the Constitution of the Turkish Republic of Northern Cyprus (TRNC). Turkey maintained that the TRNC was a state that was not a Contracting Party to the ECHR and therefore the Court had no jurisdiction. However, the TRNC was (and remains) a self-declared state recognised only by Turkey and, citing the special nature of the ECHR as a treaty for the protection of rights and a constitutional instrument of European Public Order, the Court held that it should take this into account in determining whether Turkey had responsibility for protection of Convention rights in the territory. Although the Court noted that Article 1 of the Convention meant that it was primarily limited by territory, obligations under the Convention could arise where a state exercised effective control of an area outside of its national territory as a result of military action. This was

---

[15] Article 29, Vienna Convention on the Law of Treaties.

[16] Article 1, ECHR.

[17] Bates, *The Evolution of the European Convention on Human Rights* (Oxford University Press, 2010), 111.

[18] *Loizidou v Turkey* (merits), 18 December 1996, Reports of Judgments and Decisions 1996-VI.

the case here: not only had the Turkish troops' invasion led to the establishment of the TRNC and the loss of Loizidou's property, but so too had Turkish troops prevented her from returning to her property on numerous occasions. For the Court, the large number of Turkish troops undertaking active duties in northern Cyprus was such that the state exercised effective overall control and was, therefore, liable for violations of the Convention that took place there. *Loizidou*, thus, stood for the proposition that effective control of an area brought Convention obligations with it. Under *Loizidou* it seemed irrelevant where the territory over which the state had effective control was: it could be within or outside of the Council of Europe. The controversial case of *Banković* seemed to settle this.[19]

Banković related to the NATO-led bombing of Belgrade by a number of Contracting Parties during the Yugoslav war. In the course of the air strikes, a television station was targeted and a number of civilians were killed. Among other things, the applicants in this case claimed that the Contracting Parties in question had violated the Convention by failing to plan the operations in a manner that would minimise the risk of civilian casualties, and had failed to comply with the duty to investigate deaths that arises under Article 2. However, what was then Yugoslavia was not a Contracting Party to the Convention, and so the first and most important question was whether or not the Convention could be said to apply at all.

In answering this, the Court held that the Convention was primarily territorially limited and would apply extraterritorially only in exceptional situations. Where the location of the alleged violation was within the territories of any Contracting Party to the Convention this was said to be within the legal space – or *espace juridique* – of the ECHR, so that the Convention would apply there.[20] This was justified by the fact that the rights enjoyed by persons within the jurisdiction of a Contracting Party should not be reduced to naught because a different Contracting Party – already subject to those rights standards in the ordinary course of events – was operating upon them in that space.[21] The notion of an *espace juridique* was entirely novel, developed by the Court to try to conceptualise ways of ensuring that those who already enjoyed Convention rights would continue to enjoy them, even in the (rare) event of another European state 'taking over' some form of control there. However, the delimitation of that space also, of course, identified geographical space outside of the *espace juridique*: space in which the Convention did not ordinarily apply, and in relation to which something *extra*ordinary would need to happen to alter that.

---

[19] *Banković and Others v Belgium and Others* (dec.) [GC], no. 52207/99, ECHR 2001-XII.

[20] Ibid., para. 80.

[21] Ibid. In this the Court drew also on its expressed desire to avoid 'a regrettable vacuum in the system of human-rights protection' in *Cyprus v Turkey* [GC], no. 25781/94, ECHR 2001-IV, para. 78.

What was then Yugoslavia fell into that space outside of the *espace juridique* and so the Court was required to elucidate the situations in which the Convention might be said to apply there. According to the Court:

> In sum, the case-law of the Court demonstrates that its recognition of the exercise of extra-territorial jurisdiction by a Contracting State is exceptional: it has done so when the respondent State, through the effective control of the relevant territory and its inhabitants abroad as a consequence of military occupation or through the consent, invitation or acquiescence of the Government of that territory, exercises all or some of the public powers normally to be exercised by that Government.[22]

In this case there was no effective control because there had been no 'military occupation', but rather an air strike. This, combined with the fact that there was no danger of a vacuum of Convention-rights protection arising, meant that the Convention did not apply in this case.

Banković was heavily criticised in the literature[23] as it seemed for some to expose a kind of illogic at the heart of the Convention, namely that a state would not be bound by *international* human rights standards in a particular case simply because that state happened to be acting 'abroad'. On the one hand, that proposition seems to undermine the basic tenet that human rights are universal and enjoyed by all on the basis of humanity alone, but on the other hand it arguably refined that general *normative* principle into a workable set of *legal rules* about the applicability of a certain set of human rights standards, and their enforceability through the ECtHR on a particular territory. The real difficulty, of course, is with the apparent injustice of the outcome of such a position; the seeming lack of accountability for actions that are often heinous, including death and torture; and perhaps the (unpalatable) implication that whilst these violations were lamentable when they happened outside of the European public order,[24] these scenarios were not for the Strasbourg Court to remedy.[25] Were this to be the case it would, perhaps, not be entirely surprising.

We have already noted that the text of the Convention appears to limit its applicability by reference to the concept of 'jurisdiction'. This is a concept that has real content in international law; it is intended, among other things,

---

[22] *Banković and Others v Belgium and Others* (dec.) (above, n. 19), para. 71.

[23] See, for example, Milanovic, 'Al-Skeini and Al-Jedda in Strasbourg' (2012) 23 *European Journal of International Law* 121, O'Boyle, 'The European Convention on Human Rights and Extraterritorial Jurisdiction: Comment on "Life After Bankovic"' in Coomans and Kamminga (eds), *Extraterritorial Application of Human Rights Treaties* (Intersentia, 2004) 125, and Roxstrom, Gibney and Einarsen, 'The NATO Bombing Case (*Bankovic et al. v Belgium et al.*) and the Limits of Western Human Rights Protection' (2005) *Boston University Intl Law Journal* 23, 55.

[24] See the reference thereto in *Banković and Others v Belgium and Others* (dec.) (above, n. 19), para. 80.

[25] On this see further Milanovic, *Extraterritorial Application of Human Rights Treaties: Law, Principles, and Policy* (Oxford University Press, 2011), 85–86.

to clearly delimit where the authority of one legal system and its enforcement mechanisms ends and that of another begins.[26] Taken as a term of general international law, 'jurisdiction' here would mean in many ways just what the Court in *Banković* said it means: that the Convention applies outside the territory of the Contracting Party only where the state in question has either spatial or personal jurisdiction. Spatial jurisdiction would arise where the 'space' in which the actions complained of took place was under the effective control of the Contracting Party. Personal jurisdiction would arise where, at the time of the actions complained of, the victim was under the effective control of the Contracting Party. In *Banković* neither of these was the case; there was only an aerial campaign and the physical space in question was not under the effective control of the respondent states; neither were the victims under their effective control. Thus, the outcome from *Banković* arguably reflects these specific exceptions to the general rule that the Convention would not have extraterritorial effect, even whilst the articulation and application of a concept of *espace juridique* for the Convention might remain problematic but not particularly material to the outcome in the case per se. As a result, and notwithstanding the criticism of the outcome from the case, the approach taken in *Banković* might have suggested that the Court would develop and apply a relatively strict approach to the proposition that the Convention would only apply extraterritorially where either spatial or personal jurisdiction could be established. This is not only for the reasons of jurisprudential consistency but also (a) in deference to the legal systems of states where the actions complained of may have taken place, and the other parts of general international law that would apply in respect of armed conflict there, and (b) as an expression of self-restraint on the part of the ECtHR by extending its adjudicatory power beyond the Contracting Party *only* where that is clearly consistent with international legal conceptions of jurisdiction.

However, the reality is that the Court has taken what seems to be a much more constitutional approach to the question of extraterritoriality than the strict rules of general international law would seem to require. By this we mean that the Court appears to proceed on the implicit basis that *law follows power*, so that the Contracting Party should be *accountable* under the Convention for actions that appear to violate human rights, even where those actions take place abroad and without appearing to pay particular attention to whether the strict rules of personal and spatial jurisdiction are adhered to. Although this approach might be praised for an increased level of protection, at the same time it injects some uncertainty and unpredictability into the law under the Convention. In turn such a state of affairs gives some ground to the Contracting Parties to the Convention to claim illegitimacy of the Court's actions in the area of extraterritorial application of the Convention.

---

[26] For a comprehensive overview see Ryngaert, *Jurisdiction in International Law* (Oxford University Press, 2015).

This loose approach to territorial jurisdiction is evident in *Al-Skeini and Others v the United Kingdom*[27] which concerned five Iraqis who had been killed by UK troops in Basra, in northern Iraq, one of whom had died in a UK detention facility. Following *Banković* the domestic court had held that the UK could not be held accountable under the Human Rights Act 1998 (incorporating the ECHR) in respect of those who died and were not detained at the time by the UK because Iraq was outside of the *espace juridique* of the Convention and there was neither spatial nor personal jurisdiction in relation to them; in the judgment of Lord Bingham, *Banković* constituted a 'clear – and clearly restrictive – approach to Article 1 jurisdiction' that justified this way of addressing the question in the domestic court.[28]

In Strasbourg, the Court appeared to abandon the concept of *espace juridique*, at least as a 'hard limit' to the application of the Convention outside of the geographical space of the Convention's Contracting Parties. In a judgment that mentioned *espace juridique* only five times, two of which referred to its usage in the domestic Court, the Strasbourg Court held:

> The Convention is a constitutional instrument of European public order [...] It does not govern the actions of States not Parties to it, nor does it purport to be a means of requiring the Contracting States to impose Convention standards on other States.

> The Court has emphasised that, where the territory of one Convention State is occupied by the armed forces of another, the occupying State should in principle be held accountable under the Convention for breaches of human rights within the occupied territory, because to hold otherwise would be to deprive the population of that territory of the rights and freedoms hitherto enjoyed and would result in a 'vacuum' of protection within the 'Convention legal space' [...] However, the importance of establishing the occupying State's jurisdiction in such cases does not imply, *a contrario*, that jurisdiction under Article 1 of the Convention can never exist outside the territory covered by the Council of Europe Member States.[29]

With these two paragraphs, then, the Court effectively put an end to the *espace juridique* notion from *Banković*. It returned, in effect, to the position that whilst jurisdiction is primarily territorial under Article 1, the Convention will apply outside of the territory of a Contracting Party where it has effective control over a person or effective control over a territory *whether or not* that territory is within the so-called *espace juridique* of the Convention. According to the Court, the UK did have effective control over the relevant area of Iraq at the time that the five persons in question were killed:

---

[27] *Al-Skeini and Others v the United Kingdom* [GC], no. 55721/07, ECHR 2011.
[28] *Secretary of State for Defence v Al-Skeini & Others* [2007] UKHL 26, para. 131.
[29] *Al-Skeini and Others v United Kingdom* (above, n. 27), paras 141–142. See also *Al-Jedda v the United Kingdom* [GC], no. 27021/08, ECHR 2011.

[F]ollowing the removal from power of the Ba'ath regime and until the accession of the Interim Government, the United Kingdom (together with the United States) assumed in Iraq the exercise of some of the public powers normally to be exercised by a sovereign government. In particular, the United Kingdom assumed authority and responsibility for the maintenance of security in South East Iraq. In these exceptional circumstances, the Court considers that the United Kingdom, through its soldiers engaged in security operations in Basrah during the period in question, exercised authority and control over individuals killed in the course of such security operations, so as to establish a jurisdictional link between the deceased and the United Kingdom for the purposes of Article 1 of the Convention.[30]

After *Al-Skeini*, however, a question remained as to how effective control over either a person or an area would be established: how much control was sufficient to meet the apparent threshold requirement of 'effectiveness' for the purpose of applying the Convention, especially bearing in mind that extraterritorial application of the Convention is *exceptional* and that it remains primarily territorial in its application? This is particularly difficult to assess in situations where someone is not detained by the military forces of the state in question, or where the geographical area in which the alleged violation took place is not under the state's military control, but rather where there is what may seem like a more fleeting engagement between the state forces and the victim of the alleged violation. Just such a set of circumstances arose for consideration in the case of *Jaloud v the Netherlands*.

This case concerned a checkpoint in South East Iraq at which Dutch military officers were stationed. A car that had been ordered to stop refused to do so, and a Dutch lieutenant opened fire leading to the death of the applicant's son. The Dutch Royal Military Constabulary investigated whether any crime had been committed. It collected evidence, interviewed witnesses, and concluded that the use of force had been justified and no prosecution should follow. The applicant in *Jaloud* claimed that the investigation in question was not sufficient to satisfy the positive obligations relative to the right to life under Article 2 of the ECHR, but first had to establish that the Convention applied to the incident at all.

The Dutch troops in question were serving as part of a multi-national force and, at the time, were under UK command. However, the Court found that this alone was not sufficient to say that the acts in question could not be attributed to the Netherlands:

The fact of executing a decision or an order given by an authority of a foreign State is not in itself sufficient to relieve a Contracting State of the obligations which it has taken upon itself under the Convention. The respondent party is therefore not divested of its 'jurisdiction', within the meaning of the Article 1 of the Convention, solely by dint of having accepted the operational control

---

[30] Ibid., para. 149.

of [...] a United Kingdom officer [...] Although Netherlands troops were stationed in an area in south-eastern Iraq where SFIR forces were under the command of an officer from the United Kingdom, the Netherlands assumed responsibility for providing security in that area, to the exclusion of other participating States, and retained full command over its contingent there.[31]

In particular, the Court considered that the checkpoint in question was under Dutch control and found that this was sufficient to establish personal jurisdiction (i.e. effective control over the person) for the Netherlands over people passing through the checkpoint.

> The Court [...] notes that Mr Azhar Sabah Jaloud met his death when a vehicle in which he was a passenger was fired upon while passing through a checkpoint manned by personnel under the command and direct supervision of a Netherlands Royal Army officer. The checkpoint had been set up in the execution of SFIR's mission, under United Nations Security Council Resolution 1483 [...] to restore conditions of stability and security conducive to the creation of an effective administration in the country. The Court is satisfied that the respondent Party exercised its 'jurisdiction' within the limits of its SFIR mission and for the purpose of asserting authority and control over persons passing through the checkpoint. That being the case, the Court finds that the death of Mr Azhar Sabah Jaloud occurred within the 'jurisdiction' of the Netherlands.[32]

The Court went on to find that the duty to investigate under Article 2 had not been satisfied and, thus, that there was a violation of the Convention. Regardless of what might be considered to be the justice of the outcome of the case, *Jaloud* does raise a serious question about the rigour with which the Court is applying the concept of jurisdiction here. It is difficult to reconcile command control over a checkpoint with 'effective control' over a person, particularly in the light of a case like *Banković* where aerial bombardment of Belgrade did not establish personal jurisdiction over the persons then in the city. Whilst there are some important factual distinctions (e.g. the Dutch troops at the checkpoint had the power to order people to stop), these distinctions do not appear to be sufficiently material to properly distinguish the two cases from one another for the purposes of establishing jurisdiction. Instead, some are drawn to the conclusion that the Court here was essentially equating attribution with jurisdiction, i.e. proceeding on the basis that where an action could be attributed to the state, the state should be answerable for it under the Convention.[33]

---

[31] *Jaloud v the Netherlands* (above, n. 6), para. 147.

[32] Ibid., para. 152.

[33] For an argument to this effect, see Rooney, 'The Relationship between Jurisdiction and Attribution after *Jaloud v Netherlands*' (2015) 62 *Netherlands International Law Review* 407. This is certainly not accepted by all; see, for example, Milanovic, 'Jurisdiction, attribution and responsibility in *Jaloud*' EJIL: Talk, 11 December 2014, available at https://www.ejiltalk.org/jurisdiction-attribution-and-responsibility-in-jaloud/.

Should *Jaloud* reveal that the Court is, more or less, applying a proxy-attribution approach to the Convention's extraterritorial application one might argue that, leaving to one side the doctrinal difficulties with calling something 'personal jurisdiction' when it does not really comply with the requirements thereof, this results in a more *just* outcome. In other words, that states *should* be answerable for their compliance with human rights wherever they apply their power to individuals in a manner that implicates their rights. This is, essentially, a constitutional argument: that power should not be exercisable without attendant accountability mechanisms. However, even such an approach does not necessarily answer the key question here: why should the Convention be the law that is applied, and the Strasbourg Court the institution that should adjudicate on it?

There are at least two arguments *against* the expansion of extraterritoriality in this way. The first is pragmatic, and it is that by appearing to develop the extraterritorial application in an idiosyncratic and seemingly doctrinally incoherent way the Court adds further fuel to the fire in terms of allegations of illegitimacy. The second is that the Court may not be showing appropriate deference to international humanitarian law and might thus contribute to the fragmentation of international law.

As to the first of these – the claim of illegitimacy – we have already seen that arguments of illegitimate expansionism and evolution of the Convention through judicial innovation and activism are increasingly being made by Contracting Parties.[34] In relation to the specific matter of extraterritorial application of the Convention in situations of military activity, the UK is a particularly harsh critic of the Court. As already noted, the UK government has proposed 'presumptive derogation' in all cases of future military operations abroad,[35] and Prime Minister Theresa May committed to ensuring that she would 'never again – in any future conflict – let those activist, left-wing human rights lawyers harangue and harass the bravest of the brave – the men and women of Britain's Armed Forces'.[36] The implication from all of this, of course, is that being subject to the Convention during armed conflict interferes with military activity, and calls into question the integrity of service members through, for example, requiring investigations into 'historic' abuse allegations.[37]

Richard Ekins is a key critic of the Court's approach to extraterritoriality since *Banković*, and his arguments are indicative of the objections. As part of

---

[34] See analysis in Chapter 2.

[35] See above, n. 14.

[36] Prime Minister Theresa May, Speech to the Conservative Party Conference, Birmingham, 5 October 2016.

[37] See, for example, the Iraq Historic Allegations Team, available at https://www.gov.uk/government/groups/iraq-historic-allegations-team-ihat#mission; it notes that its 'work is a vital constituent part of the UK's obligation to conduct investigations into these allegations that are compliant with the European Court of Human Rights (ECHR) and the requirements of the International Criminal Court'.

a broader criticism of 'judicial imperialism',[38] Ekins, with others, characterises the Convention as a 'bridgehead [...] for the judiciary's incursion into military terrain',[39] and argues that this is rightly to be considered part of the Executive's role.[40] According to this analysis, *Banković* was clear authority for the fact that the Convention did not apply in Iraq at the time that the UK's military operations there commenced, but that in *Al-Skeini* the Court 'asserted a new interpretation that turned not primarily on territory but on vague ideas about control, public power, and the use of force'.[41] For Ekins, this is unquestionably undesirable, and the solution is not only to derogate but to change the Human Rights Act 1998 to limit its scope, perhaps even retrospectively.[42]

Such objections to the Court's developing extraterritoriality jurisprudence are objections to what many consider to be the 'creep' of the Court into military matters and overseas operations *and* to the very idea that human rights law has any role in regulating military activity of any description. As we already discussed in Debate 1, there is a school of thought that maintains that international humanitarian law is the appropriate corpus of law to apply to situations of armed conflict, and that it incorporates human rights standards in a manner that is appropriate to the specific stresses and strains of the conflict context. Whatever the source and thrust of these objections, they have fallen on fertile ground in parts of the UK establishment. We have already seen the suggestion of presumptively derogating from the Convention,[43] and tentative plans for a 'British Bill of Rights' to replace the Human Rights Act include a plan to ensure that the Bill of Rights is explicitly not subject to extraterritorial effect.[44] Whilst this would not limit the application of the ECHR by the Strasbourg Court, of course, it would create substantial hurdles to domestic litigation; the fact that it would be inconsistent with the Convention and may result in an adverse finding in Strasbourg is

---

[38] Ekins is a leading member of the Judicial Power Project, which claims that its 'focus ... is on the proper scope of the judicial power within the constitution' and that 'Judicial overreach increasingly threatens the rule of law and effective, democratic government'. Judicial Power Project, available at https://judicialpowerproject.org.uk/about/.

[39] Ekins, Morgan and Tugendhat, *Clearing the Fog of War: Saving our Armed Forces from Defeat by Judicial Diktat* (Policy Exchange, 2015), 9.

[40] Ibid.; see also Ekins, 'How to Address the Reach of European Human Rights Law', *Written Evidence to the Defence Sub-Committee*, 17 October 2016, available at http://data.parliament. uk/writtenevidence/committeeevidence.svc/evidencedocument/defence-subcommittee/ mod-support-for-former-and-serving-personnel-subject-to-judicial-processes/written/41201. pdf.

[41] Ibid., 5.

[42] Ibid., 15.

[43] See the text accompanying above, n. 14.

[44] Amos, 'British Bill of Rights Leak: A Comment on What We Know so Far' *The Human Rights Essay*, available at http://www.humanrightsessay.org.uk/Merris-Amos-british-bill-of-rights.html.

acknowledged but, according to Ekins, Parliament could simply refuse to change the law even in the face of such a finding:

> Parliament has not confirmed to the ECtHR's rulings in relation to prisoner voting. In principle, it would certainly be open to a sovereign Parliament to take a similar position again.

> The inevitable criticism that would be made [...] is that Parliament and the Government were placing the UK in breach of its international obligations. [...] The principled response would be to say that the UK is not willing to conform to rulings of the ECtHR that grossly misinterpret the ECHR and abandon the terms agreed by the member states.[45]

A further, more doctrinally interesting, objection might be levied to the development of the Court's jurisprudence on extraterritorial application of the Convention: that it constitutes the Court encroaching on the territory of general international law. The Convention is not, and was not, intended to create a system of judicially enforceable human rights for the world at large; rather, it was intended to protect rights within Europe and as against the states of Europe. Its mission is, in other words, essentially regional.[46] This does not mean that the rest of the world is without rights, of course; indeed, international human rights law applies, as – in situations of armed conflict – does international humanitarian law. Bearing this in mind, then, one could indeed argue that by developing extraterritoriality in the way it has done, and seemingly at least at times inconsistently with international legal principles of jurisdiction, the Court is extending itself into areas that are more properly regulated by other parts of international law. The fact that those parts of international law might not be as amenable to judicial adjudication and enforcement as is the Convention does not necessarily justify this encroachment; the Court has a specific jurisdiction and, just as national legal systems are expected to demonstrate respect for the legal systems of other countries and not apply themselves except in very limited situations to what happens in another state, so the ECtHR should show more restraint and respect to the other, more clearly applicable, bodies of public international law.

This argument is compellingly logical but of course it suffers from a serious flaw: that those other bodies of public international law may be incapable of holding a state to account for its actions in that other country and that individuals who have suffered grave violations of their rights might not have any forum or mechanism by which to attempt to make that state legally responsible. This is the justice-oriented attraction (doing the right thing) of the apparently constitutional approach to extraterritoriality that we see developed in the Court's case law from *Banković* to *Al-Skeini* and, particularly, *Jaloud*.

---

[45] Ekins, 'How to Address the Reach of European Human Rights Law' (above, n. 40), 21–22.
[46] *Banković and Others v Belgium and Others* (dec.) (above, n. 19).

Whether the utilitarian or outcome-oriented concern of justice, accountability or responsibility that this represents is sufficient to justify the Court's departure from settled principles of jurisdiction in international law is, however, a question on which severe disagreement continues to arise.

Debate 3
Should rights be suspended in times of emergency?

Not all situations of violence and insecurity meet the threshold of 'war' or 'armed conflict'. To this end, international human rights law often recognises the possibility of a state of emergency existing that would justify the 'relaxation' of human rights standards so that the state may do things in furtherance of 'security' in those situations that we would not ordinarily permit it to do.[47] The ECHR does this in Article 15:

1. In time of war or other public emergency threatening the life of the nation any High Contracting Party may take measures derogating from its obligations under this Convention to the extent strictly required by the exigencies of the situation, provided that such measures are not inconsistent with its other obligations under international law.
2. No derogation from Article 2, except in respect of deaths resulting from lawful acts of war, or from Articles 3, 4 (paragraph 1) and 7 shall be made under this provision.
3. Any High Contracting Party availing itself of this right of derogation shall keep the Secretary-General of the Council of Europe fully informed of the measures which it has taken and the reasons therefor. It shall also inform the Secretary-General of the Council of Europe when such measures have ceased to operate and the provisions of the Convention are again being fully executed.

Allowing states to derogate in times of emergency is part of the Faustian pact that underpins international human rights law: states accept international law's ability to regulate previously sovereign matters (namely the relationship between the state and those within its domestic jurisdiction), whilst the international system recognises that there are times when international supervision is relaxed (such as emergencies). However, the idea that security requires or justifies a reduction in rights relates to a controversy that far pre-dates international human rights law.[48] There are three primary areas of concern in this relation: whether a reduction in rights results in an enhancement of security,

---

[47] Article 4, International Covenant on Civil and Political Rights; Article 27(1), American Convention on Human Rights.
[48] For a useful overview of the broader political philosophical debates see, for example, Teson, 'Liberal Security' in Wilson (ed.), *Human Rights in the 'War in Terror'* (Cambridge University Press, 2005).

whether security measures introduced disproportionately and discriminatorily impact on some parts of the community more than others, and whether decisions about necessity and appropriateness of rights-restricting security measures should be subject to scrutiny by (national and international) courts.

At the heart of emergency derogation systems is the implicit claim that security crises require measures that would ordinarily be deemed unacceptably restrictive of rights in order to restore 'normalcy'. Some put this claim quite bluntly, asserting that there is a hydraulic relationship between security and 'liberty' (taken to mean rights, here) and even that an optimal point between them can be found, so that there is a clear relationship between the taking of security measures and the enhancement of rights enjoyment.[49] However, there is no evidence of such hydraulicism,[50] and in any case arguments of that kind tend to be short-term in their nature, failing to take proper account of the long-term costs of security measures such as reduced social cohesion and faith in the state, increased alienation and disenfranchisement, and potentially long-term insecurity.[51] Furthermore, and moving to the second concern, even if there were a relationship between security and rights of this kind, the reality is that very often the people whose rights are effectively reduced through such measures are not the people who perceive their security to have been enhanced. Security-enhancing measures are often imposed disproportionately on people from so-called suspect communities:[52] young men of colour in the UK, Muslim women in France, Kurds in Turkey, Chechens in Russia, journalists in Azerbaijan etc. The uneven societal impacts of such measures is a matter of real concern, not only because they may result in social disintegration and a sense of alienation from the state, but also because they may reflect discriminatory application of security measures, laws and policies.[53] This may, in turn, become normalised – seen as part of the everyday policing and governing of the state – so that the popular expectations of what the state can or should do are fundamentally adjusted.

If it is not clear that a reduction in rights protection (through derogation) necessarily increases security, and if it is the case that the application of security measures can result in discrimination and may not be effective in terms of security in the longer term, the question of whether derogation should be permitted clearly arises. Very few would argue that no adjustment or derogation should be permitted at all, either because there is a general (although not universal)

---

[49] See, for example, Posner and Vermeule, *Terror in the Balance: Security, Liberty and the Courts* (Oxford University Press, 2007).

[50] Ashworth, 'Security, Terrorism and the Value of Human Rights' in Goold and Lazarus (eds), *Security and Human Rights* (Hart Publishing, 2007).

[51] de Londras, 'Sustainable Security: A Proposal' in Akande et al. (eds), *Human Rights for Future Generations* (Oxford University Press, 2018), forthcoming.

[52] Hillyard, *Suspect Community: People's Experience of the Prevention of Terrorism Acts in Britain* (Pluto Press, 1993).

[53] Burgess and Maze, 'The Social Impact of EU Counterterrorism' in de Londras and Doody (eds), *The Impact, Legitimacy and Effectiveness of EU Counter-Terrorism* (Routledge, 2015).

understanding that security is required for the purposes of being able to exercise rights so that a short-term reduction in rights enjoyment might be justifiable for the purposes of restoring security and rights normalcy, or because of the pragmatic position that if the law does not allow states to temporarily adjust their human rights obligations they may simply act in the name of 'security' in violation of the law, so that it is better to have a system of effective supervision within which emergency measures can be taken than not to. The final proposition stands, however, only if there is appropriate and effective supervision of the law relating to derogation, i.e. if there are clear requirements that a state must comply with in order legitimately to derogate from the Convention.

Article 15 lays out three such requirements: (a) that the procedural requirements in Article 15(3) would be fulfilled, (b) that there would be a war or public emergency threatening the life of the nation (Article 15(1)), and (c) that the measures taken would go no further than is strictly required by the exigencies of the situation (Article 15(1)). There are, thus, procedural, threshold and substantive requirements.

The Procedural Requirement

The procedural requirement is quite straightforward: the Contracting Party that wishes to derogate must notify the Secretary General of the Council of Europe of the derogation, the measures taken and the reasons for the derogation. In truth, the notifications provided to comply with this procedural regulation tend to be quite cursory, which is perhaps to be expected as the notification requirement is essentially procedural and formal and there is no real scrutiny of the notification of the state of emergency – or of its cessation – on the part of the Secretary General. At the time of writing (January 2017) there were three active derogations under Article 15 (Ukraine, France and Turkey). Prior to then eight countries had entered derogations (Albania, Armenia, France, Georgia, Greece, Ireland, Turkey and the UK).

The Threshold Requirement

Article 15 permits of derogation only where there is a war or public emergency threatening the life of the nation. Thus, in cases where derogations have been at issue before the Court, the question of whether there existed a war or public emergency sufficient to permit derogation has arisen. Whilst the Court has laid down a broad definition of these concepts for the purposes of Article 15, it has been criticised for failing to subject states' claims that such a state of affairs exists to sufficiently rigorous examination.[54] Furthermore, the Court has appeared to 'relax' the definition of 'public emergency threatening the life of the nation' significantly in recent years.

---

[54] Greene, 'Separating Normalcy from Emergency: The Jurisprudence of Article 15 of the European Convention on Human Rights' (2011) 12 *German Law Journal* 1764.

In *Lawless v Ireland* the Court held that a public emergency sufficient to allow for derogation under Article 15 was to be understood as 'an exceptional situation of crisis or emergency which affects the whole population and constitutes a threat to the organised life of which the State is composed'.[55] In the *Greek Case* the Court added the requirement that the crisis or emergency would be 'actual or imminent'.[56] These two important early cases suggested that an emergency should be truly exceptional; that it should be said to exist only where the normal measures allowed under the Convention – including limitations to rights based on public safety and so on – were clearly inadequate.[57] However, in the intervening decades the apparently strict definition of emergency under Article 15 (in doctrinal terms, at least) has been substantially watered down, particularly in the important case of *A. and Others v the United Kingdom*.[58]

A. and Others v the United Kingdom involved a challenge to measures taken by the UK following the attacks on the United States of 11 September 2001. Although those attacks took place in the United States, the UK declared a public emergency and derogated from the Convention. It was the only Council of Europe state to do so, and in *A.* it was claimed that there was no public emergency threatening the life of the nation under Article 15 because (a) there was no actual or imminent emergency, (b) the alleged emergency was not temporary, and (c) the fact no other states in the Council of Europe had derogated from the Convention suggested that there was no public emergency.

The ECtHR, however, disagreed. Holding that '[t]he requirement of imminence cannot be interpreted so narrowly as to require a State to wait for disaster to strike before taking measures to deal with it',[59] and referring to how the 9/11 attacks had established the 'danger of a terrorist attack', the Court found that the UK was entitled to rely on the intelligence available to it at the time in order to determine that an attack was imminent and, thus, that the imminence requirement was fulfilled. Thus, the apparent requirement of 'imminence' appeared to have been approached with such flexibility as to allow any (presumably good faith) interpretation of intelligence pointing towards a possible attack to fulfil it. In so doing, the Court arguably undermined a limited definition of 'public emergency' in Article 15(1), and thus loosened one of the constraints designed to ensure that derogations could only exceptionally be resorted to by a Contracting Party.

That loosening was furthered when the Court turned to the question of temporariness. Article 15 does not mention that a public emergency threatening the life of the nation must be temporary, but such a requirement is implicit in the (legal) concept of emergency, which is designed to allow the state to take measures that would enable it to restore *normalcy*. Thus, emergency is clearly conceived as a state of affairs that is limited in time. However, the Court noted

---

[55] *Lawless v Ireland*, 7 April 1961, Series A no. 2, 27.

[56] *The Greek Case*, no. 3321/67, (1969) 12 YB 1, paras 112–113.

[57] Ibid., para. 113.

[58] *A. and Others v the United Kingdom* [GC], no. 3455/05, ECHR 2009.

[59] Ibid., para. 177.

that its case law had 'never, to date, explicitly incorporated the requirement that the emergency be temporary'.[60]

Thus, whilst the threshold requirement appears, at first glance, to constrain states' ability to declare an emergency and derogate under Article 15, the Court seems to have interpreted the concept of 'public emergency threatening the life of the nation' in such a way that it can be applied to a great number of situations, even ones that are liable to last for a considerable period of time – years, or perhaps decades.

This has been criticised by some as allowing for the concepts of emergency and normalcy to be 'collapsed' in a manner that gives states far too much leeway to derogate and introduce measures that we would not ordinarily consider to be appropriate or rights compliant.[61] However, it is arguable that there is some logic to the Court's approach. If the purpose of Article 15 is to allow states to act in order to counter 'threat[s] to the organised life of which the State is composed', then it must be capable of allowing effective state responses to contemporary threats. In contemporary Europe one of these is said to be a kind of persistent, disaggregated, transnational terroristic violence that can emerge suddenly, can persist without much centralised organisation, can be sustained with relatively modest resources, and cannot be 'reasoned' with as its apparent endpoint is not a negotiated settlement to a discrete dispute but rather a more substantial politico-social change across the entire continent (and beyond). The fact that this is not temporary, geographically constrained, or organised in a manner similar to a conventional army, for example, does not mean that it is not a public emergency that threatens the life of the nation; the alternative is to define it as normalcy and to limit the state to measures that are ordinarily permitted under the limitations built into the Convention rights and, the argument goes, a state should not be precluded from using the derogation if it considers these to be 'plainly inadequate'.

Indeed, although the Court has been at pains to make it clear that this decision – as to whether there is a public emergency as understood under Article 15 – is one that is properly subject to judicial supervision by the Strasbourg Court, it tends to afford a high level of respect (or we might call it 'deference') to the decision on this question that the state authorities make. In other words, the Strasbourg institutions almost never disagree with the state that there is in fact an emergency; in fact, it has done so only once, in the *Greek Case* in 1969.[62] The Court's approach is clear from its sentiment in *Brannigan and McBride v the United Kingdom*[63] to the effect that

> [I]t falls to each Contracting State, with its responsibility for 'the life of [its] nation', to determine whether that life is threatened by a 'public emergency' [...]. Contracting Parties do not enjoy an unlimited power of appreciation.[64]

---

[60] Ibid., para. 178.

[61] See Greene, 'Separating Normalcy from Emergency' (above, n. 54).

[62] *The Greek Case* (above, n. 56).

[63] *Brannigan and McBride v the United Kingdom*, 26 May 1993, Series A no. 258-B.

[64] Ibid., para. 43.

The Court has repeated this sentiment over the years, and for some commentators it is not at all clear that the Court subjects this important threshold decision to meaningful scrutiny,[65] so that the 'degree of scrutiny' it applies 'is hardly different from accepting the parties' own view of the situation'.[66] This, of course, is a matter of some concern, for as already noted the threshold criterion is one of the mechanisms by which the potential for abuse under Article 15 might be minimised.

If the Court does not apply a rigorous assessment at this stage, one might reasonably ask whether the threshold criterion can be effective in this task. However, the Court is not a fact-finding institution; it is supposed to interpret and apply law to pre-established facts. This limitation makes it institutionally challenging for the Court to apply the threshold criterion under Article 15 in a meaningful and rigorous way, simply because the existence of an emergency as defined by law is very much a matter of interpreting facts within a given set of circumstances in the state in question. Whilst it is not impossible for the Court to make such an assessment, it is difficult for it, since the national government and institutions thereof are most familiar with the factual situation, and with its impact 'on the ground'.

The Substantive Requirement

Given the difficulties that perhaps understandably arise in respect of determining the threshold question under Article 15, it might reasonably be expected that the Court would apply the substantive requirement under Article 15 with a closer degree of scrutiny, as indeed it does. The substantive requirement laid out in Article 15 has three parts, (a) that there would be no derogation from non-derogable rights listed in Article 15(2), (b) that any measures taken pursuant to a derogation would be consistent with the state's other obligations under international law (Article 15(1)), and (c) that such measures would go no further than 'the extent strictly required by the exigencies of the situation'.

The first of these substantive requirements is easily disposed of at this stage: Articles 3, 4(1) and 7 cannot be derogated from. Nor can Article 2, although as we have already seen Article 2 is not violated where a death results from 'lawful acts of war'. Any attempt to derogate from these Articles is, simply, a violation of Article 15 and thus impermissible.

The second substantive requirement enables the Court to consider whether a measure introduced pursuant to a derogation violates the state's other international obligations. If it does, then it also violates the Convention, not least

---

[65] See, for example, Gross and Ní Aoláin, 'From Discretion to Scrutiny: Revisiting the Margin of Appreciation Doctrine in the Context of Article 15 of the European Convention on Human Rights' (2001) 3 *Human Rights Quarterly* 625.

[66] Harris et al., *Harris, O'Boyle and Warbrick Law of the European Convention on Human Rights* (3rd edn, Oxford University Press, 2014), 835.

because Article 53 makes it clear that the Convention is intended to coexist with, and not limit, the rights and freedoms that are guaranteed under other international agreements that the state is a party to. Although one can imagine that this substantive requirement would be amenable to judgment by the Court, the reality is that it has rarely if ever had an impact in cases on whether there is a violation of Article 15. Instead of interpreting and assessing compliance with a state's other international obligations in Article 15 cases, the Court has tended to shy away from these questions. Whilst this might be explained by reference to a judicial respect for the authority of other international organisations in the interpretation and application of these texts (for example, the UN Human Rights Committee in applying the International Covenant on Civil and Political Rights), we have already seen that the Court has been quite willing to engage in substantive analysis of international law in other cases relating to war and insecurity but which do *not* invoke or involve Article 15 per se. It is, thus, perhaps somewhat curious that the Court is so 'hands off' in relation to this textual limitation on states' actions under Article 15.

This becomes less curious, however, when one considers the approach of the Court to the 'strictly required by the exigencies of the situation' limitation. In essence, this requires that *even where a state has derogated* it may only introduce measures that are necessary and proportionate to the emergency in question. Necessity here ('strictly required') is assessed by considering whether the ordinary law is insufficient to address the emergency,[67] giving considerable weight to the view of the Contracting Party as to both the need for extraordinary measures[68] and the unfeasibility of alternatives.[69] It means that the Court simply does not 'need' to consider if a particular interference violates other international obligations – it can still find it violating the ECHR.

Importantly, establishing that a measure was limited to that which was 'strictly required by the exigencies of the situation' does not require the state to establish that the approach taken to the derogation was the best, only, or most appropriate one that the state could have taken, although the question of whether a less restrictive alternative might have been adopted will be considered.[70] It does not even have to establish that the measure was effective in addressing the emergency.[71] In other words, it affords states a significant margin of appreciation in this relation. This means that the Court will not 'substitute its view as to what measures were most appropriate or expedient'[72] at the time of the derogation; it will simply consider whether the measures introduced went no further than was strictly required by the exigencies of the situation. This is, we suggest, reasonable in principle: as a general matter, it is not for courts to decide on what the state *should* do but only what it *may* do. The

---

[67] *Lawless v Ireland* (above, n. 55).
[68] *Ireland v the United Kingdom*, 18 January 1978, Series A no. 25.
[69] *Brannigan and McBride v United Kingdom* (above, n. 63).
[70] *Lawless v Ireland* (above, n. 55).
[71] *Ireland v United Kingdom* (above, n. 68).
[72] *Marshall v United Kingdom* (dec.), no. 41571/98, 10 July 2001.

former is a question of policy and the latter of law, although the two things are not easily separated in real terms and therefore the context of emergency and (in)security is a highly sensitive and complex one.[73] How, then, does the Court navigate the tricky terrain between them in assessing measures taken under Article 15?

The Court takes a highly contextualised approach to such analysis, recognising that what is proportionate in one situation may not be proportionate in another; rather, whether or not any measure is proportionate in any emergency depends on 'the rights affected by the derogation, the circumstances leading to, and the duration of, the emergency situation'.[74] The more severe the emergency, the more severe the measures that might be considered to be strictly required to address it,[75] although we must recall that both the existence and the severity of the emergency are determined by the Court giving a high degree of deference to the assessment of the respondent state. The question of duration is particularly important; although as we have already seen the Court does not insist that an emergency must be 'temporary' per se, it does note that where an emergency is of a long duration this will impact on the proportionality of the measures under consideration.[76] In other words, the longer the emergency goes on, the more the state is expected to return to something that resembles 'normalcy' in its attempts to address it. This is entirely consistent with the idea of allowing adjustment to our expectations of what interferences with rights might be considered permissible in an emergency: more repressive measures are supposed to be taken with the intention of returning the polity to a state of normalcy, i.e. with countering the emergency in question. Thus, a protracted emergency should not allow a protracted regime of rights restriction.

When considering whether a measure was 'strictly required by the exigencies of the situation' the Court will be attentive to whether there were safeguards in place to protect people who might be subjected to the derogating measures. This is particularly important where emergency measures are introduced to allow for protracted detention without trial, or variations to the trial process itself. In relation to the former, the role that safeguards play in the Court's analysis is readily discernible by comparing *Brannigan and McBride v the United Kingdom*[77] with *Aksoy v Turkey*.[78] Both concerned detention powers in situations of terroristic violence, but in *Brannigan and McBride* the Court noted that there was a right to see a solicitor within 48 hours of being detained

---

[73] For a range of views on the challenges for courts in adjudicating in times of emergency see, for example, Davis and de Londras (eds), *Critical Debates on Counter-Terrorism Judicial Review* (Cambridge University Press, 2014).

[74] *Brannigan and McBride v the United Kingdom* (above, n. 63), para. 43.

[75] *Ireland v United Kingdom* (above, n. 68).

[76] See generally *A. and Others v United Kingdom* (above, n. 58).

[77] *Brannigan and McBride v the United Kingdom* (above, n. 63).

[78] *Aksoy v Turkey*, 18 December 1996, Reports of Judgments and Decisions 1996-VI.

and that the writ of *habeas corpus* could be used to challenge detention in any given situation. The Court thus concluded that there were sufficient procedural safeguards in place to protect a detainee against arbitrary detention and mistreatment. In *Aksoy*, by contrast, the law allowed for detention of an individual without bringing them before a judge or other officer for up to 30 days, there was no access to lawyers, family or medics; and there was no way to challenge the lawfulness of detention. The detainee was, thus, liable to abuse and incommunicado detention, and the Court found (for the first time) that the measures introduced pursuant to the derogation went beyond the strict requirements of the situation.

As is clear from *Aksoy*, the Court can and sometimes does find that a state has gone beyond what Article 15 permits; however this is rare, and the approach taken to all Article 15-related analysis is one in which the assessment of the national governments is given great weight by the Court. Whilst there are good reasons for affording some margin of appreciation to these assessments, as already noted, there is much to be said for the contention that the Court gives so much weight to these assessments that it does not effectively enforce the substantive requirements of Article 15. If that is the case, then rights-bearers' ability to use these substantive requirements to limit state security action – which, as we know, is often extremely repressive and oppressive – is greatly reduced, and a broad question about the effectiveness of the Convention in times of emergency arises. The 'Faustian pact' of derogations relies, for its efficacy, both on good faith on the part of governments and rigour on the part of the international supervisory bodies, especially if domestic parliaments and courts have found it difficult to resist the temptation to 'rally around the flag' and enforce rights protection in the face of substantial security risks and state-assertions of necessity.

Debate 4
Does the Convention protect people from 'everyday insecurity'?

Thus far, we have concentrated on what we might call exceptional situations of insecurity; however, in reality insecurity is an everyday occurrence. All over Europe, domestic violence, sexual violence, police violence, corporal punishment and other forms of violent insecurity continue to pose substantial challenges. Such insecurity necessarily implicates rights; not only does one struggle fully to enjoy and exercise rights in situations of pervasive insecurity, but exposure to and failure of the state to prevent violence might, itself, constitute a human rights violation under the Convention. Whilst the jurisprudence of the Court ranges across corporal punishment,[79] conditions of detention (beyond

---

[79] See, for example, *Tyrer v the United Kingdom*, 25 April 1978, Series A no. 26; *A. and Others v United Kingdom* (above, n. 58); *Campbell and Cosans v the United Kingdom*, 25 February 1982, Series A no. 48; *Costello-Roberts v the United Kingdom*, 25 March 1993, Series A no. 247-C.

directly inflicted violence, per se)[80] and police violence,[81] we focus here on the ECtHR's approach to domestic violence as illustrative of the Convention's ability to protect against everyday insecurity.

The law has traditionally been slow and ineffective in addressing issues of domestic violence. Thought to take place in a 'private' domain in which the state ought not to 'interfere',[82] it was not until the UN Convention on the Elimination of all Forms of Discrimination against Women that international human rights law took a firm doctrinal stand against the maintenance of the so-called 'public-private divide'.[83] The ECHR might itself be read as a text that impliedly reinforces this divide; privacy and family life are protected from undue interference in Article 8, private property (including the home) is protected in Article 1 of Protocol 1, and whilst Articles 2 and 3 protect the rights to life and to be free from torture, inhuman and degrading treatment or punishment, that protection was originally conceived as being against state, as opposed to 'private', action.[84] However, over recent years the Court's jurisprudence has developed a substantial body of law on the state's obligation to protect people from domestic violence and to undertake effective investigations where a loss of life was not averted.

This is well illustrated by the case of *Bevacqua and S. v Bulgaria*.[85] The applicant in this case claimed that she was regularly beaten by her husband and that these beatings continued after she took their son, left her husband and filed for divorce. Before the finalisation of the divorce, a court order of shared custody was given in respect of the child, requiring continued contact between them, and she claimed that every time she pressed charges against him, her husband became more violent. Repeated requests for interim measures of protection were not promptly dealt with, and her then-ex-husband continued to assault her even after their divorce was finalised and she had secured custody of their son. At that time her request for a criminal prosecution was rejected, the authorities claiming that it was a 'private matter' between them. The Court held that the state had failed to fulfil its positive obligations under Article 8 (the right to private and family life), with particular attention to the rights of the child, but stressing that considering these allegations of abuse to be a 'private matter' was clearly incompatible with Article 8.

---

[80] See, for example, *Kalashnikov v Russia*, no. 47095/99, ECHR 2002-VI; *Dobri v Romania*, no. 25153/04, 14 December 2010; *Modarca v Moldova*, no. 14437/05, 10 May 2007.

[81] See, for example, *Leonidis v Greece*, no. 43326/05, 8 January 2009; *Iribarren Pinillos v Spain*, no. 36777/03, 8 January 2009.

[82] The public/private dichotomy has long been critiqued in feminist and feminist legal thought. For its classical criticism in international legal thought see Charlesworth and Chinkin, *The Boundaries of International Law: A Feminist Analysis* (Manchester University Press, 2000). See also Edwards, *Violence against Women under International Human Rights Law* (Cambridge University Press, 2011).

[83] Article 2, CEDAW.

[84] The ECHR was not unique in this. For a comprehensive overview see Thomas and Beasley, 'Domestic Violence as a Human Rights Issue' (1993) 15 *Human Rights Quarterly* 36.

[85] *Bevacqua and S. v Bulgaria*, no. 71127/01, 12 June 2008.

Even though *Bevacqua* resulted in a finding of violation, it did not focus clearly on the bodily rights of the primary victim of the abuse.[86] However, progress is being made in this respect under Article 2, which protects the right to life, including obliging the state to take steps to protect life including from the application of lethal force by non-state actors. Unfortunately, a very high number of women and children, as well as some men, die as a result of domestic violence every year, and in 2007 the Court established that the state could be liable in respect of this under Article 2. In *Kontrová v Slovakia*[87] the Court considered a case in which the applicant had filed a criminal complaint against her husband for beating her. Shortly thereafter, and accompanied by her husband, she attended at the police station where, with the assistance of an officer, she modified her complaint so that it constituted a minor offence in respect of which no further action was required by law. Less than two months later, her husband murdered their son and daughter. The Court held that Slovakia had violated Article 2; the original complaint meant that the police authorities were aware of the violent situation in the home and had domestic legal obligations to act on this, including to launch a criminal investigation. The fact that the applicant had subsequently modified her complaint, accompanied by her husband, did not mean that the state was relieved of its Article 2 obligation to take all reasonable steps to protect life.

This is not an unusual pattern in these cases: the state is aware of the threat that the assailant poses to family members and yet fails to take adequate steps to protect them. In *Branko Tomašić and Others v Croatia*,[88] court-ordered psychiatric treatment was not effectively administered to the assailant, who subsequently murdered his wife and baby on release from prison. In *Civek v Turkey*[89] the authorities were aware of the serious threat to life and of the deceased's harassment but failed to take reasonable steps to prevent her husband from murdering her. The key point here is not that the Court expects that states would be able to prevent all instances of fatal domestic abuse, but rather that it has made clear that Article 2 includes an obligation to take seriously the information available to state authorities and to act in order to protect life in situations of domestic and intimate-partner abuse.

A similar approach is discernible in the Article 3 jurisprudence, in respect of which it has been found that states have a procedural obligation to ensure effective investigation of allegations of abuse with a view to ensuring protection from such treatment. This was the case in, for example, *Valiulienė v Lithuania*[90] and *E.M. v Romania*.[91] In spite of this, however, it was always clearly

---

[86] Other cases focusing on Article 8 in this respect include *Hajduová v Slovakia*, no. 2660/03, 30 November 2010; *A. v Croatia*, no. 55164/08, 14 October 2010, and *Kalucza v Hungary*, no. 57693/10, 24 April 2012.

[87] *Kontrová v Slovakia*, no. 7510/04, 31 May 2007.

[88] *Branko Tomašić and Others v Croatia*, no. 46598/06, 15 January 2009.

[89] *Civek v Turkey*, no. 55354/11, 23 February 2016.

[90] *Valiulienė v Lithuania*, no. 33234/07, 26 March 2013.

[91] *E.M. v Romania*, no. 43994/05, 30 October 2012.

understood that domestic violence might engage the absolute prohibition on torture, inhuman and degrading treatment or punishment in Article 3. The important case of *Opuz v Turkey*[92] explores this.

The applicant and her mother had been subjected to years of violent abuse by the applicant's husband, and had made frequent complaints to the police. With the exception of one, these complaints had all been withdrawn, the women explaining that the husband had harassed them into doing so, including by threatening to kill them. Each time a complaint was withdrawn the police desisted from any investigation, deeming them 'family matters'. The husband subsequently stabbed his wife, the applicant, seven times, following which he was fined. In spite of both women claiming that their lives were in danger, he was released by the police following questioning. When they tried to move away, he shot his mother-in-law, killing her. He was convicted of murder and sentenced to life imprisonment; however, he was released pending appeal. His wife, the applicant, claimed that he continued to harass her.

As well as finding a violation of Article 2, the ECtHR importantly concluded that Turkey had violated Article 3 by its failure to protect the applicant. The mistreatment in this case reached the minimum level of severity to be considered inhuman and degrading treatment or punishment – the first time the Court had reached this conclusion in a domestic violence case – and the state had obligations to protect the applicant from such abuse. Instead, here, the authorities had not even used the measures available to them (limited as they were), and on the whole Turkey did not have an effective legal framework allowing for criminal proceedings in situations of this kind. Furthermore, and extremely importantly in the context of domestic violence, the Court proceeded to find a violation of Article 14 (the right to non-discrimination) in conjunction with Articles 2 and 3, holding that there was a climate of general passivity about domestic violence among the Turkish judiciary, in spite of the high incidence of such violence in the country, which in fact created an atmosphere conducive to domestic violence. The violence experienced by the applicant and her mother could, thus, be said to be gender-based discrimination resulting from authorities' failure properly to address domestic violence in the country.

Opuz, then, represented a landmark in the Court's treatment of domestic violence, recognising not only that domestic violence could engage Article 3 but also that a state's failure adequately to address domestic violence could constitute discrimination under Article 14. This continued with *Eremia v Moldova*,[93] in which the applicants (a woman and her two daughters) complained of the Moldovan authorities' failure to protect them from abuse from their husband and father, who happened also to be a police officer. The Court found violations of Article 3 and 8, and then drawing on *Opuz* also of Article

---

[92] *Opuz v Turkey*, no. 33401/02, ECHR 2009.
[93] *Eremia v the Republic of Moldova*, no. 3564/11, 28 May 2013.

14 combined with Article 3. As far as the Court was concerned, the authorities' failure to take action to protect the applicant amounted to repeatedly condoning her husband's treatment of her and reflected a discriminatory attitude to her as a woman. All of this was compounded by their unwillingness to act against a fellow police officer. Similar findings of discrimination in respect of domestic violence have since been made in *M.G. v Turkey* (Article 3 in conjunction with Article 14)[94] and *Halime Kiliç v Turkey* (Article 2 in conjunction with Article 14).[95]

In March 2017, this pattern was consolidated with the important cases of *Talpis v Italy*.[96] In this case, the applicant had been abused by her husband on several occasions, as had her children. The police had been called to the scene on the first occasion (when he beat the applicant and her daughter), and on the second occasion (when her husband attacked her with a knife and tried to force her to go with him and have sex with his friends) she sought assistance from a police patrol on the street, which fined him for carrying a prohibited weapon and suggested Ms Talpis go home. On that occasion she also engaged with an accident and emergency unit in a hospital, and then went to a women's shelter but after three months there she had to leave as they had insufficient space and resources to support her. For a short while she was then homeless but subsequently found a job and rented a flat. Her husband continued to subject her to psychological abuse by telephone during this time. In September 2012, Ms Talpis lodged a formal complaint against her husband and sought urgent protection for herself and her children. It was seven months before the police first questioned her, at which stage she mitigated the allegations and in August 2013 the file was closed. Around three months later Mr Talpis was found intoxicated on the street after the applicant had called the police concerning an argument with her husband. The police urged him to go home, and upon entering the apartment he attacked Ms Talpis and fatally stabbed his son. He also stabbed Ms Talpis in the chest. Her injuries were not fatal. Mr Talpis was subsequently convicted of murder and attempted murder, and sentenced to life imprisonment. Ms Talpis claimed that there had been a violation of her rights under Articles 2 and 3 in conjunction with Article 14. The Court found multiple violations in this case.

According to the judgment of the Court, the Italian authorities had failed to exercise the requisite diligence required to act in a timely and effective manner to protect the right to life of Ms Talpis and her son. This related not only to the failure to act promptly after the applicant's complaint in September of 2012 but also to the police failure to take any action to protect Ms Talpis and her children on the night of the stabbing, in spite of having engaged with her husband on a number of occasions that evening and the fact that the police knew, or should have known, that he posed a real threat to her. Similarly,

---

[94] *M.G. v Turkey*, no. 646/10, 22 March 2016.
[95] *Halime Kiliç v Turkey*, no. 63034/11, 28 June 2016.
[96] *Talpis v Italy*, no. 41237/14, 2 March 2017.

the unexplained and unjustifiable delay in acting on Ms Talpis' complaint in 2012 resulted in a violation of Article 3, particularly as she was a vulnerable person subjected to violence of sufficient severity to reach the threshold of ill-treatment under Article 3. Finally, the Court reiterated its position from *Opuz* that a state's failure to protect women against domestic violence violates the right to equal protection of the law. Here, the police failures to act to protect Ms Talpis and proceed with investigations in a timely manner was so serious as to effectively endorse the violence in question, constituting discrimination against her as a woman under Article 14. Interestingly, the Court also referred to reports of the UN Special Rapporteur on Violence against Women, the Committee for the Elimination of Discrimination against Women, and data from the National Bureau of Statistics to show that domestic violence is a serious and extensive problem in Italy, grounded in discrimination. The violence inflicted on Ms Talpis was, then, also said to be grounded on sex and thus to be a form of discrimination violating Article 14 in conjunction with Articles 2 and 3.[97]

This jurisprudence signals an important breakthrough in the Court's approach to domestic violence, recognising clearly the role that legislative, administrative and policing frameworks can play in implicitly condoning domestic violence (and thus implicitly acknowledging domestic violence as an out-working of structural inequality), whilst also identifying them as key elements in any attempt effectively to address domestic violence systemically and in individual cases. The Court's broader concentration on investigation, remedy and taking steps to protect persons from rights violation is consistent with its general approach to states' obligations in respect of everyday violence. The Convention, in short, requires states to recognise private violence as having a public dimension, to have in place appropriate legislative frameworks to address such violence, to take steps to protect people from violence, to investigate situations where violence occurs, and to ensure the availability of domestic remedies should it fail in so doing. Whilst none of this alone addresses the pervasive and structural prejudices and inequality of power that underpin so much everyday insecurity and violence, these developments in the Court's jurisprudence identify clearly the state's role in attempting to address and undo them, not merely as a matter of good will but as a matter of international legal obligation.

CONCLUSION

In situations of insecurity, rights matter. In many cases of systemic insecurity, war and emergency, states have not hesitated to interfere with human rights ostensibly in the name of restoring normalcy. The law accommodates this, and

---

[97] However, cf. the partly dissenting judgment of Judge Spano in this case, and the critique thereof in van Leeuwen, 'The Limits of Human Rights Law: Dissenting Androcentric Voices in Talpis v. Italy', *Strasbourg Observers*, 30 May 2017, available at https://strasbourgobservers.com/2017/05/30/the-limits-of-human-rights-law-dissenting-androcentric-voices-in-talpis-v-italy/.

Article 15 allows for reductions in rights protection in times of emergency; however, in order for that allowance to be exercised only when absolutely necessary a rigorous assessment of states' claims of insecurity and necessity is needed. We have seen in this chapter that such rigour is not always in evidence, even though it seems required to ensure the effective supervision of human rights compliance in times of emergency. However, those extraordinary situations are not the only times when insecurity needs to be addressed. Indeed, interpersonal violence is such a serious and widespread experience that insecurity might well be said to be a quotidian condition. In that context the question becomes whether the ECHR offers any potential to enhance personal security. As the jurisprudence on domestic and intimate violence shows, the Court is developing an approach that takes such insecurity seriously and places clear expectations on states to prevent and protect from these forms of normalised, but gravely serious, everyday insecurity.

FURTHER READING

Edwards, *Violence against Women under International Human Rights Law* (Cambridge University Press, 2011).

Ekins, Morgan and Tugendhat, *Clearing the Fog of War: Saving our Armed Forces from Defeat by Judicial Diktat* (Policy Exchange, 2015).

Greene, 'Separating Normalcy from Emergency: The Jurisprudence of Article 15 of the European Convention on Human Rights' (2011) 12 *German Law Journal* 1764.

Rooney, 'The Relationship between Jurisdiction and Attribution after *Jaloud v. Netherlands*' (2015) 62 *Netherlands International Law Review* 407.

CHAPTER 7

Socio-Economic Rights and the European Convention on Human Rights

So far throughout this book we have focused – as the European Convention on Human Rights (ECHR or Convention) does – on rights that might broadly be defined as 'civil and political'. However, these are not, of course, the only kinds of human rights that exist either in philosophy and ethics, or in law. More than a decade after the Convention was signed into law, international human rights law developed treaties focusing on both civil and political rights (the International Covenant on Civil and Political Rights) *and* socio-economic rights (the International Covenant on Economic, Social and Cultural Rights). Although there are important differences between these international covenants (and these are extensively canvassed elsewhere[1]), the basic principle of indivisibility and universality underpin them.[2] By this, we mean the principles in international human rights law that both categories of rights are supposed to be universally enjoyed by all human beings *and* are indivisible.

This notwithstanding, some continue to question the status of socio-economic rights. The precise contours of this debate do not need to be revisited here,[3] but the broader questions of the role of rights, of courts, and of human rights courts per se are relevant to Debate 1 in this chapter: should the ECHR be used to protect socio-economic rights? This is an important question, and depends to some extent on how far we think courts should 'stretch' classically conceived civil and political rights to address poor socio-economic conditions, as well as concerns that socio-economic matters are complex, polycentric issues with inescapable resource implications for states that should be approached with caution – if at all – by courts.

---

[1] For a comprehensive overview on the differences, and similarities, between the two see Gavison, 'On the relationships between civil and political rights, and social and economic rights' in Coicaud et al. (eds), *The Globalization of Human Rights* (United Nations University Press, 2003).

[2] See the Vienna Declaration and Programme of Action (1993).

[3] See, for example, O'Connell, *Vindicating Socio-Economic Rights* (Routledge, 2012), Chapter 1.

These questions have become especially urgent in recent years, since the Global Financial Crises of the late 2000s ushered in periods of 'austerity' that caused intense economic hardship and exacerbated structural socio-economic inequalities, particularly in European states most sharply impacted by these austerity programmes. The attempt to resist an approach to economic recovery that is centred on austerity and the reduction in welfare provision by the state has resulted in imaginative litigation in the ECtHR which we consider in Debate 2: can the ECHR be used to challenge austerity?

This leads us, then, to the third debate in this chapter, focused on Article 14 and the anti-discrimination norm in the Convention. Article 14 is, at first glance, a 'relatively insipid'[4] (or some might say 'parasitic' right[5]), by which we mean that it does not – on the face of it – create a stand-alone right to be free from discrimination (much less to equality) but rather affirms the right to non-discrimination in the enjoyment of *other* Convention rights. It has long been argued that this is inadequate to ground an effective jurisprudence of anti-discrimination under the Convention, but recent jurisprudence suggests some shift away from a strict construction of Article 14 in this limited way and towards something more attuned to the protection of a substantive conception of equality. In addition, Protocol 12 to the Convention has created a freestanding right to non-discrimination, although it is far from being universally ratified by all of the Contracting Parties to the Convention and rarely used by the European Court of Human Rights (ECtHR or Court). We thus close the Chapter by asking whether the right to non-discrimination in the ECHR can promote socio-economic equality.

Debate 1
Should the ECHR be used to protect socio-economic rights?

The ECHR primarily protects civil and political rights, with the exception of rights to education (Article 2, Protocol 1) and to the protection of property and possessions (Article 1, Protocol 1). However, there is a relationship between civil and political, and socio-economic, rights. Indeed, the Court recognised this relationship as early as *Airey v Ireland*[6] when it found that a failure to make civil legal aid available was a breach of Article 6 rights to due process. According to the Court, the Convention 'is designed to safeguard the individual in a real and practical way as regards those areas with which it deals',[7] and where that requires 'extend[ing] into the sphere of social or economic rights' so be it.[8] Indeed, the Court continues to make findings relevant to

---

[4] Fredman, 'Emerging from the Shadows: Substantive Equality and Article 14 of the European Convention on Human Rights' (2016) 16 *Human Rights Law Review* 273, 273.

[5] *Whaley v Lord Advocate* [2004] SC 78, para. 93

[6] *Airey v Ireland*, 9 October 1979, Series A no. 32.

[7] Ibid., para. 26.

[8] Ibid.

socio-economic rights in the field of access to justice, finding particularly that unreasonably high fees can result in people being unable to bring disputes before courts or tribunals.[9]

This brings us to an important point in the discussion of socio-economic rights under the Convention: that the Court has largely addressed them only inasmuch as they relate to the 'areas with which [the ECHR] deals', rather than on a stand-alone basis. This is perhaps not surprising. The potential for protecting socio-economic rights when they are clearly linked to the civil and political rights expressly protected within the Convention is substantial. For example, there is 'space' within a right to be free from inhuman and degrading treatment to establish a state's obligation to ensure a meaningful and adequate provision of medical care,[10] which bears close resemblance to the right to an adequate standard of healthcare as protected in socio-economic rights instruments and jurisprudence.[11] Similarly, the right to private and family life can be developed in a way that recognises an obligation to ensure that people can live in a way that accords with their cultural practices.[12] This too might then bear a resemblance in substantive and practical terms to the right to culturally appropriate housing protected under socio-economic rights instruments and international jurisprudence.[13] Thus, it is clear that there is *space* for some socio-economic right to be protected in a practical sense, particularly in relation to the positive obligations that have been developed in Convention jurisprudence in order to give full effect to the rights protected therein.[14] The question, however, that we consider here is whether such jurisprudential developments *ought to be* undertaken.

Perhaps the first argument against such development is that the text explicitly precludes the protection of such rights, largely on the basis that silence might be considered to indicate exclusion, and thus that protecting them – even in effect if not in form – is an unacceptable extension of the Convention beyond its intended meaning. Indeed, in Chapter 4 we saw that just such a criticism is levied by some states against evolutive interpretation of the Convention in other contexts. In relation to those debates we noted that such a criticism is sometimes rooted in an overly formalistic conception of 'original consent' as determining the extent of a state's international obligations, and furthermore that techniques of interpretation had been developed by the Court in order to establish the legitimacy of such evolutive interpretation, albeit that there may still be cases in which the Court might be said to

---

[9] See, for example, *Mehmet and Suna Yiğit v Turkey*, no. 52658/99, 17 July 2007.

[10] *D. v the United Kingdom*, 2 May 1997, Reports of Judgments and Decisions 1997-III.

[11] Article 25, Universal Declaration of Human Rights; Article 12, International Covenant on Economic, Social and Cultural Rights.

[12] See, for example, *Winterstein and Others v France*, no. 27013/07, 17 October 2013.

[13] Article 11, Universal Declaration of Human Rights.

[14] See Palmer, *Judicial Review, Socio-Economic Rights and the Human Rights Act* (Hart Publishing, 2007), Chapter 1.

go 'too far' by reference to the text, purpose, and understanding of the Convention.[15] Can such arguments also be made in respect of the development of socio-economic protection within Convention jurisprudence? On the face of it, the answer is yes; after all, if evolution is acceptable in some contexts, why not in others? However, the counter-argument would be to point to the purpose of the Convention as originally promulgated, and to note that whilst evolution of the Convention *in line with the original overall purpose of the treaty* is legitimate and justifiable, evolution *which extends the scope of the treaty beyond its original purpose* is not. In other words, that some limits to evolution must be accepted, and that those limits might be found in the purpose of the Treaty, as suggested by Article 31(1) of the Vienna Convention on the Law of Treaties:

> A treaty shall be interpreted in good faith in accordance with the ordinary meaning to be given to the terms of the treaty in their context and in the light of its object and purpose.

We already saw, in Chapter 1, that the Convention was developed and proposed as a mechanism for protecting the peoples of Europe from tyranny and oppression. Its purpose was, thus, to enable human flourishing primarily through protecting democracy, the rule of law, and participation in government. This is quite in line with the liberal internationalism that also underpinned the founding of the European Coal and Steel Association[16] around the same time: democracy, free markets, capital and civil liberties would be the lifeblood of developing and preserving peace and prosperity.

In that mindset, rights were primarily negative (protections *from* interference) rather than positive (entitlements *to* state action), and (quite in line with this) provision for material human necessities – food, shelter, medical care, for example – was primarily to be achieved through developing individual economic power and resources by freeing markets *not* through legally enforceable rights. Capital was the route to socio-economic security, not state protected and legally justiciable human rights. Whilst states might provide a welfare net that was not because *human rights* demanded it, but because the concept of statehood and the domestic social contract did; it was for the domestic government – and usually the Executive – to decide on the exact contours of that provision.

Within this framework, the concept of socio-economic rights protection per se is somewhat alien; it would certainly seem to fall outside of the purposes of the Convention understood in the round, and outside of the common constitutional and democratic conceptions of material provision as existed when the Convention was founded. In the original proposal for the rights to be

---

[15] See, for example, Hoffmann, 'The Universality of Human Rights' (2009) 125 *Law Quarterly Review* 416.
[16] The predecessor of the European Union.

protected within the Convention, the only thing that might be defined as a socio-economic right to be found related to property, and even then the proposed protection was for 'freedom from arbitrary deprivation of property'.[17] Even read in line with the original proposal for 'equality before the law',[18] it is difficult to read this as a proposal aimed at redistribution and tackling systemic inequalities. It is, rather, aimed primarily at ensuring that persons can protect what they already have; the least progressive way of conceptualising a right to property that one might imagine from the perspective of concern for providing the basic necessities for humans to survive, not least to thrive.

Importantly, both the approach to negative and positive rights, and the constitutional cultures of the state parties, are now quite different to how they were in the early 1950s. The Court has developed positive obligations designed to ensure the protection and enjoyment of rights, and not merely focused on whether states have unjustifiably interfered with protected rights (i.e. the negative enquiry).[19] In other words, positive obligations have been developed to ensure the fulfilment of protected rights, which in turn are now sometimes conceptualised as rights *to* and not merely rights *from*. Expanding the protection thus available under the Convention to address situations of material need, where the state's failure to provide basic necessities means that the person cannot enjoy the protected right, might be said to be a relatively modest jurisprudential leap if one accepts the development of positive obligations per se.

This is particularly so when we take into account the fact that state parties to the Convention increasingly protect some kind of economic or socio-economic rights by constitution or legislation, and indeed that this is part of constitutional culture in some post-Soviet states in particular which became members of the Council of Europe following the fall of the USSR. O'Cinnéide has convincingly shown that social constitutionalism is part of European legal heritage and culture(s).[20] If the Convention truly does reflect a 'common heritage of political traditions, ideals, freedom and the rule of law'[21] across the member states of the Council of Europe, and if those can evolve as the membership expands, perhaps one can argue that there is a justification from purpose for limited protection of socio-economic goods under the Convention. There is,

---

[17] European Movement, *European Convention on Human Rights*, ING/5/E/R (1949), proposed Article 1(k) as cited in Bates, *The Evolution of the European Convention on Human Rights* (Oxford University Press, 2010), 56.

[18] Ibid., proposed Article 1(i).

[19] Akandji-Kombe, *Positive Obligations under the European Convention on Human Rights* (Council of Europe, 2007); Mowbray, *The Development of Positive Obligations under the European Convention on Human Rights by the European Court of Human Rights* (Hart Publishing 2004); Dickson, 'Positive Obligations and the European Court of Human Rights' (2010) 61 *Northern Ireland Legal Quarterly* 203.

[20] O'Cinnéide, 'European Social Constitutionalism', available at https://ssrn.com/abstract=2921173.

[21] Preamble, ECHR.

in other words, at least an argument that the *purpose* of the Convention now may be more than simply to protect against tyranny and oppression, but in fact to support human flourishing through the protection of rights. Were such an argument to be considered compelling, the purpose of the Convention *now* might be said to include enabling people to make legal claims for socio-economic goods on the state where these are needed to give effect to the rights protected within the text of the Convention.

This argument potentially stumbles on the fact that the broader systems of rights protection of which the Convention is a part – the human rights system of the Council of Europe – has developed a parallel mechanism for the protection of socio-economic rights. In 1961 the European Social Charter was introduced to protect socio-economic rights within the Council of Europe system. A system of government reporting was established;[22] this was to be the main enforcement mechanism and there was no way to bring complaints of a breach of the Charter to the ECtHR (although of course the Court could, and increasingly does, refer to the Charter in its case law just as it does to other international instruments[23]). The two systems – Convention and Charter – are separate, with the Charter's enforcement and implementation being overseen primarily by a committee of experts now known as the European Committee on Social Rights. Since 1995, the reporting process has been complemented by a system of collective complaints,[24] seemingly motivated by a desire to include more actors in the process of assessing compliance with the Charter and, thereby, increasing the rigour and effectiveness of the enforcement machinery.[25] Unlike the Court, the Committee applying the Charter has been able to establish and attempt to enforce substantive socio-economic rights, such as the right to social assistance (protected by Article 13(1) of the Charter), even in the face of a state's claims that it enjoys a wide margin of appreciation in devising and applying conditions for accessing such assistance.[26] Whilst the

[22] Pursuant to Article 21 of the European Social Charter the Contracting Parties are obliged to send to the Secretary General of the Council of Europe a report at two-yearly intervals, concerning the application of such provisions of Part II of the Charter as they have accepted.

[23] *Demir and Baykara v Turkey* [GC], no. 34503/97, ECHR 2008, paras 45, 49, 50; *Konstantin Markin v Russia* [GC], no. 30078/06, ECHR 2012, para. 55.

[24] According to Article 1 of the Additional Protocol to the European Social Charter Providing for a System of Collective Complaints the Contracting Parties recognise the right of the following organisations to submit complaints alleging unsatisfactory application of the Charter: a) international organisations of employers and trade unions; b) other international nongovernmental organisations which have consultative status with the Council of Europe and have been put on a list established for this purpose by the Governmental Committee; c) representative national organisations of employers and trade unions within the jurisdiction of the Contracting Party against which they have lodged a complaint.

[25] See Churchill and Khaliq, 'Violations of Economic, Social and Cultural Rights: The Current Use and Future Potential of the Collective Complaints Mechanism of the European Social Charter' in Baderin and McCorquodale (eds), *Economic, Social and Cultural Rights in Action* (Oxford University Press, 2007), 200–201.

existence of the Charter and its associated enforcement mechanisms may not convincingly ground an argument that socio-economic rights are adequately protected by another process and thus do not *need* to be protected through the Convention, it does lend some weight to the argument that the Convention neither expressly *nor impliedly* protects those rights, and that extending its scope to offer such protection is illegitimate.

There are further, doctrinal concerns, with extending the Convention's protection to socio-economic rights. The first, expressed well by Warbrick some years ago, is that the fact such rights are not protected within the text of the Convention may mean that a 'political right not to have destitution thrust upon one by the state' may become conflated with the legal socio-economic right to social support in a way that 'might lead to setting the bar so low that the economic or social rights lose all its useful purchase'.[27] This is, in effect, an argument that the socio-economic right suffers or is somehow denuded by being reshaped into a civil and political right under the Convention; an argument that has doctrinal attraction but which might seem less attractive to practitioners, advocacy groups, and individuals and communities interested in finding *practical* ways to enforce their (political and legal) socio-economic claims and rights against the state.

A related doctrinal concern is that by using civil and political rights under the Convention to protect socio-economic rights in practical terms, the civil and political rights may suffer; they might become 'degraded'.

This is a complex claim that, when disaggregated, has many layers to it and certainly can be related to the broader, theoretical claim that is still sometimes made that socio-economic rights are *substantively different* to civil and political rights, are not (or should not be) justiciable, and drag courts into inappropriate areas of activity such as resource allocation.[28] We do not need to rehearse these broader arguments here, or indeed the many rebuttals to them, but they do provide an important backdrop as they reflect an intuition on the part of some that socio-economic rights are *less legally important* than civil and political rights. Moving on from that contextual note, let us examine some of the jurisprudence under Article 3 of the ECHR to explore the concern that socio-economic protection under this provision may be damaging to the norm.

Article 3 provides

> No one shall be subjected to torture or to inhuman or degrading treatment or punishment.

---

[26] See, for example, *European Roma Rights Centre v Bulgaria* Complaint No. 48/2008 (Decision 31 March 2009) (The Collective Complaints Committee on European Social Charter).

[27] Warbrick, 'Economic and Social Interests and the European Interests and the European Convention on Human Rights' in Baderin and McCorquodale, *Economic, Social and Cultural Rights in Action* (Oxford University Press, 2007), 256.

[28] For a comprehensive account of the arguments on social rights per se see, e.g., Gearty and Mantouvalou, *Debating Social Rights* (Hart Publishing, 2010).

The core underpinning jurisprudential claims in the Article 3 cases are that the negative right to be free from torture, inhuman and degrading treatment or punishment is absolute, that no proportionality analysis is provided, that there is no defence to claims of interference, and that violations of this right to be free form torture in particular carry a special stigma.[29] The Court thus treats these violations as particularly serious, as do the Contracting Parties and applicants to the Court. Partly as a result of this, the Court will only find that the right to torture has been violated where a minimum level of severity in ill-treatment has been reached, and findings of inhuman or degrading treatment or punishment are also sparingly made. However, Article 3 has proved to be fertile ground for the development of socio-economic protection in the Court, perhaps counter-intuitively given how difficult it is to meet the threshold requirement to establish a violation. However, the case law under Article 3 suggests that the Court has recourse to it in respect of socio-economic provision only in very severe circumstances.

This is well illustrated by *M.S.S. v Belgium and Greece*.[30] This case concerned the conditions of detention of asylum seekers in Greece – conditions that the Court had already expressed concern in relation to.[31] Belgium had sent the applicant back to Greece on the basis that, as this was the first EU country he entered, this was where his asylum application had to be processed. However, in Greece *M.S.S.* had been detained in appalling conditions, before living on the streets without receiving any social assistance or material support from the state. Noting that human dignity is a foundation of Convention rights, and refusing to accept that Greece's straitened economic conditions should be taken into account when considering whether the treatment of asylum seekers violated Article 3, the Court held that the lack of food, hygiene, a home and material resources which resulted in *M.S.S.* living in extreme poverty was a violation of Article 3. As a member of a vulnerable group (asylum seekers) the state's positive obligations to protect people from torture, inhuman and degrading treatment or punishment under Article 3 extended to providing him with a home. Belgium was also said to violate Article 3 by sending *M.S.S.* to Greece and thus exposing him to these inhumane living conditions. Depending on the circumstances, the Court held, a 'serious deprivation of basic human needs' may result in a breach of Article 3.[32]

---

[29] On Article 3 generally see, e.g., Mavronicola, 'What is an "absolute right"? Deciphering Absoluteness in the Context of Article 3 of the European Convention on Human Rights' (2012) 12 *Human Rights Law Review* 723.

[30] *M.S.S. v Belgium and Greece* [GC], no. 30696/09, ECHR 2011.

[31] See, for example, *S.D. v Greece*, no. 53541/07, 11 June 2009; *Tabesh v Greece*, no. 8256/07, 26 November 2009; *A.A. v Greece*, no. 12186/08, 22 July 2010, para. 160.

[32] *M.S.S. v Belgium and Greece* [GC], (above, n. 30), para. 252.

These circumstances are important. The Court made it clear that whether or not Article 3 had been violated was to be determined by reference to a six-part test:

1. Was the person in a condition of particular severity, which meant that she was unable to cater for his most basic needs?[33]
2. Was the person a member of a 'particularly underprivileged and vulnerable population group in need of special protection'?[34]
3. Was the person 'wholly dependent on State support [...] faced with official indifference in a situation of serious deprivation?'[35]
4. Did the state take action (at its own initiative) to relieve these conditions as appropriate to the state of vulnerability and insecurity of the person?[36]
5. Could the state have 'substantially alleviated his suffering' through prompt action?[37]
6. Did the state 'have due regard to the applicant's vulnerability'?[38]

This is clearly a demanding test. It does not amount to a 'right to a home' in a general sense – indeed, the Court expressly precluded giving any such meaning to Article 3 or to the judgment. Instead it means that the state's positive obligations to protect against torture, inhuman and degrading treatment or punishment – long established in the case law of the Court – meant that, in certain circumstances, Article 3 may require the provision of basic material necessities. Furthermore, the Court placed great emphasis on the concept of vulnerability, which it suggests herein relates to one's membership of a group, as opposed to a particular analysis of individual circumstances.[39] Asylum seekers are, prima facie, vulnerable, according to Judge Rozakis, and thus require an advanced level of protection that enables them to claim material provision under Article 3, although there was not unanimity among the judges on that point.[40]

In extreme cases such as *M.S.S.*, the protection of socio-economic rights does not degrade the protection against torture per se under Article 3. The threshold test applied is clearly a high one,[41] and as Thornton notes the extent

---

[33] Ibid., para. 254.
[34] Ibid., para. 251.
[35] Ibid., para. 253.
[36] Ibid., para. 259.
[37] Ibid., para. 262.
[38] Ibid., para. 263.
[39] Although see also *Sufi and Elmi v the United Kingdom*, nos 8319/07 and 11449/07, 28 June 2011, applying the vulnerability test from *M.S.S. v Belgium and Greece* [GC] (above, n. 30).
[40] See the opinion of Judge Sajó on this point. *M.S.S. v Belgium and Greece* [GC] (above, n. 30), Partly Concurring and Partly Dissenting Opinion of Judge Sajó.
[41] See also the admissibility decision in *Budina v Russia* (dec.), no. 45603/05, 18 June 2009.

of the lack of social supports that seems necessary to trigger an Article 3 obligation is such that *M.S.S.* cannot be said to provide for a right to social protection per se, or even to indicate especially clearly the usefulness of Article 3 as a vehicle for protection of socio-economic rights.[42] The threshold – namely, one of utter destitution resulting directly from state actions – is so high that most situations of hunger, homelessness and material need simply would not meet it notwithstanding the degradation often experienced in situations of extreme poverty.

Instead, what *M.S.S.* suggests – and it is not the only case to do so – is that the Convention might be used to require a state not to impose destitution or socio-economic devastation upon someone (including by deporting them to a state where their basic socio-economic needs, such as healthcare needs, would not be met[43]), but not to require the state to materially support persons as a matter of human rights law per se. If that truly is the extent of the protection for socio-economic wellbeing under the Convention, one might argue that it does not require too great a level of anxiety about undue expansionism into the field of socio-economic rights protection by the Court.

Debate 2

Can the ECHR protect socio-economic wellbeing in a time of austerity?

Realistically, many millions of people live in situations of socio-economic need without reaching the threshold of destitution. In Europe, as elsewhere, some dimensions of economic inequality with serious implications for the enjoyment of civil and political rights are structural. By this we mean that this economic inequality emerges not 'merely' from the individual circumstances of the person in question, but also from a socio-political inequality of power that marginalises certain groups and makes them more likely to experience economic disempowerment compared with other sectors of the population. The causes of such structural inequality are complex and often combine historical marginalisation with sexism, racism, disablism and other prejudices and biases that permeate society resulting in disadvantage in social services, lack of access to public services such as education or healthcare, and entrenched inequality in labour markets. Asylum seekers, children, women, older people, ill people, people with disabilities, and ethnic and religious minorities are among those most likely to experience structural inequality and, at the same time, least able to access political power in order to attempt to address it. For marginalised groups, then, litigation and the law are often important avenues towards

---

[42] Thornton, 'European Convention on Human Rights: A Socio-Economic Rights Charter?' in Egan, Thornton and Walsh (eds), *Ireland and the European Convention on Human Rights: 60 Years and Beyond* (Bloomsbury, 2014).

[43] See *D. v United Kingdom* (above, n. 10), *Sufi and Elmi v United Kingdom* (above, n. 39).

attempting to address material conditions of inequality that undermine them in attempting fully to enjoy and exercise their human rights in the civil and political sphere, even if courts may not always be well equipped – or judiciaries especially prepared – to intrude too far into what is sometimes seen as the primarily political domain of resource allocation and the distribution of socio-economic goods.

Deep-seated inequalities have not been eradicated within the Council of Europe and, indeed, have arguably been exacerbated in the past decade. The Global Financial Crises of the late 2000s ushered in a period of structured and severe 'austerity' across Europe, and particularly in countries (such as Greece, Portugal and Spain) that had been 'bailed out' by the International Monetary Fund, the European Central Bank, and the European Commission (i.e. 'the Troika'). These austerity programmes raised severe concerns in respect of socio-economic rights; they brought about serious decreases in welfare payments and social protection, often resulted in the dramatic reduction of available public health and educational facilities, and had especially serious negative implications for people and groups already economically disadvantaged primarily because the bail outs were conditional on substantial fiscal adjustments in the 'saved' countries; adjustments that, in the case of Greece, for example, were said to have brought about 'a welfare state retrenchment unprecedented in the post-war period'.[44] Austerity has had significant negative impacts on the enjoyment of social and economic rights, not only in countries that were 'bailed out' but also in other Council of Europe states that have introduced reductions in social protection (or 'welfare') in order to 'balance the books'.[45]

One may argue that the ECHR offers an important avenue to try to address the socio-political structures that underpin inequality. A key barrier, of course, is the fact that the Convention does not protect socio-economic rights per se, as we have already outlined in Debate 1. Notwithstanding that, in some cases ECHR litigation has successfully been used in the attempt to construct rights-based resistance to austerity. Similarly to the Article 3 cases considered above, however, it would appear that a particularly high threshold of socio-economic deprivation must be met in order for the Court to intervene. This is well illustrated by *Nencheva and Others v Bulgaria*.[46]

The applicants' children were profoundly disabled and resided in a state institution. However, austerity measures imposed by the government following a recession in Bulgaria resulted in a situation where the institution could not provide sufficient food, lighting, sanitation or medical treatment to these children, who subsequently died. In this case, the municipal authorities and those working within the institution in question had attempted to secure

---

[44] Koukiadaki and Kretsos, 'Opening Pandora's Box: The Sovereign Debt Crisis and Labour Market Regulation in Greece' (2012) 41 *Industrial Law Journal* 276, 276–277.

[45] On the impact of the Global Financial Crises on rights generally see, for example, Council of Europe, *Safeguarding Human Rights in Times of Economic Crisis* (Council of Europe, 2013).

[46] *Nencheva and Others v Bulgaria*, no. 48609/06, 18 June 2013.

further resources from the central state authorities, but were granted only very limited additional funds. The applicants claimed that the failure properly to resource the institution resulted in a violation of Article 2 in this case, i.e. the right to life. The Court held that it did, but in so doing it repeatedly noted the exceptional circumstances at play here: the state authorities were aware of the 'real and imminent risk' of death,[47] and failed adequately to respond in order to protect the children's right to life. This has clear parallels with cases where the failure to respond to known situations of domestic and intimate violence resulted in the death of children,[48] and is thus a significant acknowledgement that protecting the right to life can be about ensuring adequate material resources to prevent death, but only where the circumstances are truly exceptional. The threshold, again, is thus very high, and the consequences of failing to meet it devastating.

Relevant too is the fact that these children were in the direct care of the state.[49] Compare this to situations where the state reduces salary or social security payments, potentially leading to a failure to access food, shelter, electricity, healthcare and so on for the people in receipt thereof. In these cases, much of the case law has focused on Article 1 of Protocol 1: the right to the peaceful enjoyment of possessions. In *Koufaki and Adedy v Greece*,[50] deemed inadmissible in 2013, the Court noted that the reduction by 20 per cent in the remuneration, benefits and pensions of public servants did not result in the applicants being incapable of subsisting, and thus did not disproportionately interfere with property rights; in a time of economic hardship such a reduction in the remuneration of public servants could be justified. This does not mean that austerity measures can never be found to violate Article 1 of Protocol 1. In *N.K.M. v Hungary*, for example, the Court found a violation where the government introduced a backdated tax of 98 per cent on severance pay for civil servants beyond a certain threshold. Notwithstanding the fact that the Court usually allows a wide margin of appreciation in matters of taxation, the applicant had completed 30 years as a civil servant, was deemed to have 'already earned' her severance pay, and was now being asked to endure what the Court considered to be an excessive burden of addressing Hungary's poor economic situation.[51] Tulkens has argued that this case is particularly significant; for her it indicates that the Court is increasingly realising the interdependence of socio-economic and civil and political rights.[52] However,

---

[47] Ibid., para. 121.

[48] *Opuz v Turkey*, no. 33401/02, ECHR 2009.

[49] Similar findings have been made in relation to the state's obligation to ensure the provision of food, shelter, sanitation, medical treatment etc. for those in state detention. See, for example, *Ananyev and Others v Russia*, nos 42525/07 and 60800/08, 10 January 2012.

[50] *Koufaki and Adedy v Greece*, nos 57665/12 and 57657/12, 7 May 2013.

[51] *N.K.M. v Hungary*, no. 66529/11, 14 May 2013.

[52] Tulkens, 'The European Convention on Human Rights and the Economic Crisis: the Issue of Poverty', *EUI AEL; 2013/08; Distinguished Lectures of the Academy.*

protecting someone from a negative interference with already-owned property is materially different, from the perspective of alleviating economic hardship, from compelling the state to distribute its resources in a manner that addresses socio-economic inequality.[53] *N.K.M.* is, thus, a case that illustrates the usefulness, but also the limitations, of 'classical' protections against negative interferences with property for attempting to address the societal impacts of austerity.

Thus, whilst the Convention is useful in resisting austerity in situations of extreme hardship, it does not seem especially likely that it can or will fundamentally reshape or determine the imposition of austere fiscal and economic measures in times of recession in a rights-compliant manner. Instead, other processes designed specifically to protect socio-economic rights may have to be relied upon. In the Council of Europe context, of course, this points us towards the Charter of Social Rights already considered in Debate 1. A short detour to the Committee's approach to austerity measures introduced as part of the negotiated 'bail out' of Greece by the IMF, ECB and European Commission illustrates the potential for these mechanisms more fully to appreciate and address the socio-economic impact of austerity.[54]

General Federation of Employees of the National Electric Power Corporation (GENOP-DEI) and Confederation of Greek Civil Servants' Trade Unions (ADEDY) v Greece[55] concerned a cut to the minimum wage for workers under the age of 25. The claim was that this cut breached the right to fair remuneration in Article 4(1) of the Charter, which provides:

> With a view to ensuring the effective exercise of the right to a fair remuneration, the Parties undertake: to recognise the right of workers to a remuneration such as will give them and their families a decent standard of living.

The Committee found that the acceptability of the reduction in the minimum wage for young people must be assessed by reference to proportionality, with particular attention to whether there was an objective justification and whether the measure was proportionate to achieving that. Here the extent of the reduction in the minimum wage was disproportionate to the objective (of getting younger people into the labour market at a time of economic crisis) and, regardless of the fact that such a reduction was required by the bail-out conditions, violated the Charter rights of younger people. Let us imagine the potential outcome if the measure had been challenged before the ECtHR instead:

---

[53] So too does it differ from requirements to transfer property in times of socio-political transition, as illustrated in, for example, *Jahn and Others v Germany* [GC], nos 46720/99, 72203/01 and 72552/01, ECHR 2005-VI.

[54] See also *Federation of Employed Pensioners of Greece (IKA-ETAM) v Greece*, Complaint 76/2011.

[55] *General Federation of Employees of the National Electric Power Corporation (GENOP-DEI) and Confederation of Greek Civil Servants' Trade Unions (ADEDY) v Greece*, Complaint 66/2011.

it did not relate to already earned monies and so Article 1, Protocol 1 likely would not have been violated,[56] and it did not impose destitution on younger people so that Articles 2 and 3 would likely not be considered to have been violated, not least because the Court would likely have demonstrated deference to the means in which the state party was attempting to address an extremely poor national economic situation. The Charter and the Committee supervising it could, thus, recognise, address and attempt to remedy the rights-related implications of the imposed measures in a way that the Court applying the Convention likely would have struggled to do.

This raises important questions about the effectiveness of the Convention, which connect inevitably with the matter of 'purpose' already considered in Debate 1 and, indeed, in Chapter 1 of this book. Taking human rights in the round, it is unquestionable, as Salomon has put it, that 'the governance of the [global financial] crises in the European Union has led to massive violations of human rights'.[57] Although those rights are primarily socio-economic in nature, their violation, of course, has implications for civil and political rights: for the ability to support one's children and thus avoid state intervention and keep one's family together (enjoying Article 8 rights), for the ability to access education (enjoying Article 2 Protocol 1 rights), for the ability to access appropriate medical care and thus avoid death (enjoying Article 2 rights), and so on. The divide between civil and political and social and economic rights might be artificial in real terms, but it is nevertheless reflected in international human rights law instruments. Within that framework the ECtHR's mandate is to protect civil and political rights as outlined in the Convention. As a result, socio-economic rights can be protected only when there is a clear connection to the enjoyment of those rights. Thus, whilst the Court and Convention can be used to try to prevent some rights violations flowing from austerity measures, they seem ill-equipped effectively to address austerity and its exacerbation of socio-economic inequality per se.

Whether this points to the ineffectiveness of the Convention system relates to one's perspective on its purpose. If it is, still, a mechanism for protecting against tyranny and oppression (understood within a capitalist paradigm that does not recognise extreme economic hardship and structural inequality as a form of oppression) then this is no indictment of the Convention system per se. However, if the purpose *of human rights* is to enable human flourishing as the lifeblood of democracy and the rule of law, which in turn are core conditions for peace, prosperity and stability across the region, one may well come to a contrary conclusion.

---

[56] Although cf. the Court's case law on pensions: *Lakićvić and Others v Montenegro and Serbia*, nos 27458/06, 37205/06, 37207/06 and 33604/07, 13 December 2011; *Gaygusuz v Austria*, 16 September 1996, Reports of Judgments and Decisions 1996-IV; *Wieczorek v Poland*, no. 18176/05, 8 December 2009.

[57] Salomon, 'Of Austerity, Human Rights and International Institutions' (2015) 21 *European Law Journal* 521, 522.

Debate 3

Can the right to non-discrimination promote socio-economic equality?

In many ways, the debates that we have outlined already in this chapter point to a broader contestation not only about the Convention but about human rights law generally, which was hinted at in the preceding paragraph: *what is human rights law for?* Conventionally, it was considered as a means of limiting state power in order to protect those within states' jurisdiction from repression, oppression and violation of classical civil liberties. Whilst the broader literature on and international legal instruments of human rights law have moved on from that relatively limited, but nevertheless important, conception of the purpose of human rights law to at least some extent, the ECHR remains a classically constructed civil and political rights instrument reflecting this conception of the purposes of human rights law per se. Bearing that in mind, it is perhaps unsurprising that the original Convention text did not include any right to equality or even any general, standalone right to non-discrimination, but rather merely provided in Article 14 for what McCrudden calls the non-discriminatory 'distribution of the other human rights protected by the ECHR'.[58] Article 14 states:

> The enjoyment of the rights and freedoms set forth in this Convention shall be secured without discrimination on any ground such as sex, race, colour, language, religion, political or other opinion, national or social origin, association with a national minority, property, birth or other status.

Whilst the list of grounds is somewhat outmoded, the Court has stressed that it is not exhaustive ('such as … ' and 'other status'), but is rather illustrative.[59] The Court has thus used Article 14 to consider discrimination claims in relation to sexual orientation,[60] health,[61] age,[62] 'illegitimacy',[63] disability[64] and more.

Article 14 creates a right to non-discrimination in the enjoyment of other Convention rights and *not* a right to non-discrimination per se. Recognising this, Protocol 12 was introduced in 2000. This provides:

> The enjoyment of any right set forth by law shall be secured without discrimination on any ground such as sex, race, colour, language, religion, political or other opinion, national or social origin, association with a national minority, property, birth or other status. No one shall be discriminated against by any public authority.

---

[58] McCrudden, 'Equality and Non-Discrimination' in Feldman (ed.), *English Public Law* (Oxford University Press, 2004), para. 11.86.
[59] *Salgueiro da Silva Mouta v Portugal*, no. 33290/96, ECHR 1999-IX.
[60] Ibid.
[61] *Kiyutin v Russia*, no. 2700/10, ECHR 2011.
[62] *Schwizgebel v Switzerland*, no. 25762/07, ECHR 2010.
[63] *Inze v Austria*, 28 October 1987, Series A no. 126.
[64] *Glor v Switzerland*, no. 13444/04, ECHR 2009, para. 80.

However, Protocol 12 has not been ratified by all of the member states; indeed, at the time of writing (May 2017) nine Contracting Parties (Bulgaria, Denmark, France, Lithuania, Monaco, Poland, Sweden, Switzerland and the United Kingdom) had not even signed it, and only 20 had ratified it.

The Debate with which we close this chapter, then, is as to whether the right to non-discrimination as protected in the ECHR can promote socio-economic equality.

It is important at the outset to acknowledge the general shortcomings of non-discrimination as a vehicle to achieving equality. It is widely recognised in much of the equality and non-discrimination literature that *a right not to be differently treated* is not the same as *a right to be equally treated*, particularly as non-discrimination requires nothing more than treating similar cases alike, whereas equality may require more. Non-discrimination thus accords far more with what is termed 'formal equality' than it does 'substantive equality'. Formal equality concerns itself with consistency of treatment; as Barnard and Hepple put it, it 'embodies a notion of procedural justice which does not guarantee any particular outcome'.[65] Whilst formal equality might be helpful to ensure that, for example, women and men are paid the same salaries for comparable work, it does nothing to address inequalities of opportunity that may mean that women are far more likely to be in lower paid work types than men, or the capacity of 'the market' to pay people for their work at a rate that is too low for one to live on. In other words, formal equality works *within* existing economic, political, legal and social structures, but cannot address the inequalities that those structures produce, reflect and perpetuate. Substantive equality, on the other hand, recognises and attempts to address these structures and has, Fredman argues, four key aims: redistribution, recognition, participation and transformation.[66] The two, then, are clearly vastly different things.

If the right to non-discrimination within the Convention – either in Article 14 or in the standalone Protocol 12 form – reflects this formal conception of equality then it seems unlikely to be able to promote socio-economic equality *even if* the Convention protects socio-economic rights which, as we have already seen, it might be said to do only in a very limited sense (if at all). The earlier jurisprudence on Article 14 certainly suggests its interpretation and application as an instrument of formal equality, resulting in what O'Connell calls the 'failure of the Strasbourg Court to promote a substantive conception of equality which would address questions of systematic disadvantage and oppression'.[67] Indeed, whilst this criticism is directed at the cases in which

---

[65] Barnard and Hepple, 'Substantive Equality' (2000) 59 *Cambridge Law Journal* 562, 563.

[66] Fredman, 'Substantive Equality Revisited' (2016) 14 *International Journal of Constitutional Law* 712; see also Fredman, 'Providing Equality; Substantive Equality and the Positive Duty to Provide Resources' (2005) 21 *South African Journal on Human Rights* 163, 167.

[67] O'Connell, 'Cinderella comes to Ball: Article 14 and the right to non-discrimination in the ECHR' (2009) 29 *Legal Studies* 211, 212.

Article 14 was used by the Court, it is important to note that there were many cases in which Article 14 was pleaded but where the Court made its decision solely on the basis of other Articles,[68] such as *Sander v the United Kingdom*[69] in which a violation of Article 6 was found in respect of racist comments by jury members, but in which Article 14 is hardly discussed at all.[70]

Given the structure of Article 14, it is clear that any attempt to establish impermissible discrimination must first satisfy the Court that the behaviour complained of falls into the 'ambit' of another Convention right. In many cases, the Court has given scant, if any, attention to the ambit requirement, albeit largely by dealing with the complaint under another Article altogether. For example, in gay rights cases the Court has primarily considered the claims under Article 8 alone, and not as discrimination under Article 14 taken in conjunction with Article 8.[71] Although this might be said to sidestep the prima facie restrictiveness of the ambit requirement, it remains challenging to address socio-economic inequality by using this approach, not least because the Court is largely limited to considering socio-economic matters within the context of expressly protected civil and political rights. However, the Court has shown significant creativity in bringing socio-economic matters within the ambit of rights, even finding that welfare payments can fall within the ambit of Article 1 of Protocol 1 notwithstanding its general position that money is not property.[72] It has also been proactive in the context of employment, finding, for example, that an employment ban might have an impact on the right to enjoyment of private life under Article 8 because it removes the capacity to make a living.[73]

Importantly, there is no requirement that the 'primary' right be violated in order for the Court to find that Article 14 has been violated;[74] in other words, even if the right to property is not violated, it might be discriminatorily applied in a manner that violates Article 14. This principle of autonomy is critical to the non-discrimination case law of the Court,[75] not least because it allows for

---

[68] For analysis see Harvey and Livingstone, 'Protecting the Marginalised: The role of the ECHR' (2001) 51 *Northern Ireland Legal Quarterly* 445.

[69] *Sander v the United Kingdom*, no. 34129/96, ECHR 2000-V.

[70] For critique see Dembour, 'Still Silencing the Racism Suffered by Migrants... The Limits of Current Developments under Article 14 ECHR' (2009) 11 *European Journal of Migration and Law* 221.

[71] See, for example, *Lustig-Prean and Beckett v the United Kingdom*, nos 31417/96 and 32377/96, 27 September 1999.

[72] *Gaygusuz v Austria* (above, n. 56); *Luczak v Poland*, no. 77782/01, 27 November 2007 (but cf. *Stec and Others v the United Kingdom* [GC], nos 65731/01 and 65900/01, ECHR 2006-VI).

[73] *Sidabras and Džiautas v Lithuania*, nos 55480/00 and 59330/00, ECHR 2004-VIII.

[74] This was not always the case; earlier case law required a breach of the original right (making an Article 14 analysis somewhat unnecessary); see Fredman, 'Emerging from the Shadows', (above, n. 4).

[75] *Case 'Relating to Certain Aspects of the Laws on the Use of Languages in Education in Belgium' (merits)*, 23 July 1968, Series A no. 6.

the Court to bring socio-economic matters within the 'ambit' of a Convention right for the purposes of Article 14 with relatively little attendant risk of allegations of illegitimacy.[76]

Finding that alleged discrimination falls within the ambit of the rights protected by the Convention is only the first step of the test of discriminatory treatment used by the Court. After finding that the treatment complained of falls within the ambit of a Convention right, the Court considers whether there is indeed a difference in treatment, and then whether there is an objective and reasonable justification for such difference. For some time, the Court took a relatively conservative approach to this latter question, focusing largely on whether differences in treatment could be justified through the application of a proportionality test:[77] a classically 'formal' approach to equality. However, in recent years some scholars have discerned important shifts in the Court's approach, even to the extent that, Fredman argues, 'recent jurisprudence [...] contains many glimmers of substantive equality'.[78] Fredman finds this not only in what she called the 'elasticity of grounds' (i.e. the Court's willingness to recognise non-articulated grounds of discrimination considered above), but also in the gradual move away from focusing exclusively on a formal assessment of whether treatment was 'equal'. In *Thlimmenos* the Court found that excluding all those with criminal convictions from admission to the profession of accountant discriminated against those, like the applicants, whose criminal convictions related to conscientious objection (in this case to military service, ground in religious belief). The Court thus accepted that discrimination could arise where 'States without an objective and reasonable justification fail to treat differently persons whose situations are significantly different'.[79] In *D.H. v Czech Republic* the Court then established the important principle that indirect discrimination could violate Article 14, so that 'a difference in treatment may take the form of disproportionately prejudicial effects of a general policy or measure which, though couched in neutral terms, discriminates against a group',[80] even if that was not its intent.[81]

Whilst Article 14, then, has its limitations – not least its 'ambit' requirement – it clearly has the capacity to be deployed in a manner that tackles serious socio-economic inequalities *where they relate to the exercise of Convention rights*.

On the face of it Protocol 12's protection against discrimination should offer a greater scope for transformative change. Like Article 14 it lists indicative

---

[76] On ambit and its connection to autonomy see Baker, 'The Enjoyment of Rights and Freedoms: A New Conception of the "Ambit" under Article 14 ECHR' (2006) 69 *Modern Law Review* 714.

[77] *Belgian Linguistic Case* (above, n. 75); *Abdulaziz, Cabales and Balkandali v the United Kingdom*, 28 May 1985, Series A no. 94.

[78] Fredman, 'Emerging from the Shadows' (above, n. 4), 274.

[79] *Thlimmenos v Greece* [GC], no. 34369/97, ECHR 2000-IV, para. 44.

[80] *D.H. and Others v the Czech Republic* [GC], no. 57325/00, ECHR 2007-IV, para. 184.

[81] *Oršuš and Others v Croatia* [GC], no. 15766/03, ECHR 2010, para. 150.

and non-exhaustive grounds, and it can be deployed in respect of any right 'set forth by law' including socio-economic rights protected in domestic law. However, thus far Protocol 12 has attracted ratification from less than half of the Contracting Parties and has not been widely used. Indeed, there are fewer than 10 judgments in which Protocol 12 features.

The first case in which it was used was a Grand Chamber judgment in *Sejdić and Finci v Bosnia and Herzegovina*.[82] Part of this judgment was concerned with the fact that in Bosnia only people who declared themselves as Bosniacs, Croats and Serbs can run for the presidency; the applicants were none of these. As the right to free elections in Article 3 of Protocol 1 does not cover presidential elections, Article 14 was inapplicable, but Bosnia and Herzegovina had ratified Protocol 12. The Court found a violation of Article 1 of Protocol 12 since the applicants who were of Roma and Jewish origin respectively could not run for these posts. In doing so, the Court held that the meaning of discrimination under Protocol 12 was the same as under Article 14, so that justification for differences in treatment were possible. However, in this case no sufficiently robust justification for the difference in treatment between the applicants existed. Accordingly, the right to non-discrimination had been violated.

The majority of cases the Court dealt with in relation to Protocol 12 are the follow-up cases from *Sejdić and Finci*,[83] and the fact that Protocol 12 is not considered where the application can be decided under Article 14[84] (combined with the relatively low number of ratifications) means that the case law is scarce. However, even as the case law under Protocol 12 expands, this will simply expand the Court's approach to discrimination under Article 14 to all legally protected rights, and not only Convention rights. Thus, the capacity of the Convention to progress socio-economic equality in Europe will depend on the extent to which the germs of substantive equality discernible in more recent jurisprudence are developed in the future.

Even then, however, the success of the Convention in advancing socio-economic equality in Europe will inevitably be limited by the rights to which the Contracting Parties afford protection in law. Article 14 will continue to be 'parasitic' on the Convention rights, Article 1 of Protocol 12 on rights protected in law by the states. Arguably, this is the only feasible way to achieve a balance between the clear connection between socio-economic inequality, human flourishing, and ability to access and enjoy civil and political rights on the one hand, and the textual and historical limitations of the ECHR on the other.

---

[82] *Sejdić and Finci v Bosnia and Herzegovina* [GC], nos 27996/06 and 34836/06, ECHR 2009.

[83] See *Pilav v Bosnia and Herzegovina*, no. 41939/07, 9 June 2016; *Zornić v Bosnia and Herzegovina*, no. 3681/06, 15 July 2014.

[84] *Sejdić and Finci v Bosnia and Herzegovina* (above, n. 82), para. 51.

CONCLUSION

The classical division between socio-economic rights and civil and political rights is artificial. The relationships between these bodies of rights are complex but clear, and it is through recognising these relationships that the ECtHR has managed to develop a jurisprudence that is concerned with conditions of material wellbeing. However, the Court is unquestionably limited to some extent by the text of the Convention, which is largely concerned with civil and political rights, whilst the Social Charter and its Committee have a clearer focus on socio-economic rights. These limitations have meant that the Court has exercised caution in addressing socio-economic wellbeing, tending, for example, to require extreme deprivation before intervening. The inadequacy of this from the perspective of socio-economic rights per se is clear, but it is arguable that developing the Convention further would so far exceed the apparent intended scope of the Convention as to wander into the territory of illegitimacy.

FURTHER READING

Fredman, 'Emerging from the Shadows: Substantive Equality and Article 14 of the European Convention on Human Rights' (2016) 16 *Human Rights Law Review* 273.

Mowbray, *The Development of Positive Obligations under the European Convention on Human Rights by the European Court of Human Rights* (Hart Publishing, 2004).

Salomon, 'Of Austerity, Human Rights and International Institutions' (2015) 21 *European Law Journal* 521.

Thornton, 'European Convention on Human Rights: A Socio-Economic Rights Charter?' in Egan, Thornton and Walsh (eds), *Ireland and the European Convention on Human Rights: 60 Years and Beyond* (Bloomsbury, 2014).

CHAPTER 8

Implementing the Convention: The Execution of ECtHR Judgments

Throughout this book so far we have undertaken a number of debates about particular approaches to interpretation and application of the European Convention on Human Rights (ECHR or Convention). However, we have largely left unconsidered whether the Convention really 'works' as a framework for the protection of rights; whether it is *effective*. This question is complex. It relates to a whole host of different sub-issues, including the extent to which national parliaments take account of the Convention, whether it is integrated into policy-making processes and so on. In this chapter, we look critically at the implementation of the jurisprudence of the European Court of Human Rights (ECtHR or Court), engaging in a number of debates that are fundamentally concerned with what the 'real world' impact of the decisions of the ECtHR is within the Contracting Parties.

This requires engagement with a number of different issues. First, we must consider the capacity of the Court to order remedies in situations where a breach of the Convention is found. To that end, Debate 1 asks what remedies the Court can order. This is more than a simple doctrinal or formal question. As will become clear within our consideration of that debate, over the years the Court has evolved its remedial capacities from merely ordering just satisfaction (the payment of monies to successful applicants) and leaving the task of dealing with the reasons of such violations to the states' discretion, to sometimes clearly stating the actions that are expected from respondent states.

This active approach to the development of remedies in the Court goes fundamentally to the question of whether, and if so how, the Court can effectively address rights violations by the Contracting Parties, and indeed how far the Court should go in developing mechanisms to make its own judgments more effective. There is a clear international *legal* obligation on a respondent state to execute the judgment of the Court and implement the remedies as ordered (Article 46). However, in Debate 2 we go beyond this purely doctrinal legal obligation to explore broader and more contentious questions of states' resistance to execution of ECtHR judgments.

167

What are the arguments put by states when they are not inclined to abide by the legal obligation in Article 46, and how might these arguments be addressed?

Moving beyond the strictly doctrinal question of whether states are legally obliged to execute the judgments of the Court is important for two reasons. The first, which we consider in Debate 2, is that it is increasingly clear that the 'mere' fact of legal obligation is not sufficient, at this time, to compel some states to remedial action. Instead, at least some Contracting Parties to the Convention resist execution on the basis of, for example, resource constraints, alleged incompatibility with domestic law, or arguments of the democratic illegitimacy of the ECtHR when considered alongside domestic political and legal institutions. Developing convincing arguments in response to such recalcitrance is clearly fundamental to the future effectiveness of the Convention. The second reason why it is important to develop arguments in favour of the implementation of the Court's judgments that go beyond bald statements of legal obligation is reflected in Debate 3.

In this debate, we consider whether non-respondent states should give effect to ECtHR judgments. Although non-respondent states are not legally 'bound' by the ECtHR's judgments, the effective implementation of the Convention is best achieved through the Contracting Parties taking steps to ensure compliance with the Convention before the point is reached where litigation in Strasbourg is required. It is thus important to consider whether, and if so why, states *ought to* give effect to these judgments, even if they are not strictly obliged to do so.

Debate 1

What remedies can the Court order?

At the start of its operation, the ECtHR issued only declaratory judgments, meaning that if the Court had found a violation of the Convention it would not prescribe the exact measures that the Contracting Parties should undertake in order to ensure compliance with the Convention. Although the judgments of the Court are binding on the Contracting Parties under Article 46, this approach meant that the Court would avoid interfering with (or being accused of interfering with) the sovereignty of the Contracting Parties by dictating the mode of execution of a particular judgment. The Committee of Ministers would then decide whether the measures adopted by the respondent state were sufficient to implement the judgment. In recent years, the Court has become more prescriptive about the measures a respondent state needs to undertake to comply with the Convention. Before we consider the evolution of the Court's attitude to remedies, we first look into what remedies are available to the Court.

These remedies are known as individual and general measures, and it is assumed that the states will react to an adverse judgment by instigating such measures to address the violation that has been identified. Usually the Court does not actually specify these measures beyond financial remedy (i.e. just satisfaction), but leaves it to the states and Committee of Ministers to work out the means of execution. In *Marckx v Belgium* (see Chapter 4), for example, the Court stated that 'the Court's judgment is essentially declaratory and leaves to the State the choice of the means to be utilised in its domestic legal system for performance of its obligation'.[1] Moreover, the Court considered inadmissible attempts by previously successful applicants to claim a violation of the Convention for non-implementation of a previous judgment. Over recent years, however, the Court has begun to specify the measures to be taken in at least some cases.

Individual measures normally include just satisfaction that has to be paid to the applicant to cover her pecuniary and/or non-pecuniary damages. Just satisfaction is governed by Article 41 of the Convention, which states that if the Court finds that there has been a violation of the ECHR, and if the internal law of the Contracting Party concerned allows only partial reparation to be made, the Court shall, if necessary, afford just satisfaction to the injured party. Thus, Article 41 seems to require that the national law of the Contracting Party would not sufficiently provide for compensation, and, second, that compensation would be necessary before just satisfaction could be awarded.

The Court originally stuck firmly to the principle that both of these requirements would have to be fulfilled, and often the Court would deliver a separate judgment on the matter. In more recent cases, however, the ECtHR tends simply to include its analysis of the award of just satisfaction in the final paragraphs of the operative part of the judgment.[2] Indeed, the award of just satisfaction has become more or less standard, with very little attention being given to the apparent requirements of Article 41.[3]

This raises a serious question about whether it is appropriate for the Court to award such compensation almost automatically and without carefully considering the constraints enshrined in Article 41. This debate is of importance beyond the seemingly simple question of adherence to Article 41; the ECtHR was not created to replace national mechanisms for compensation but to be subsidiary to them, so that its function should be about articulating and applying the Convention standards, rather than awarding monetary compensation per se. This is not least because the Convention will be most effective if an adverse finding in Strasbourg results in a change to state practice, and not merely the payment of monetary compensation, as states have sometimes argued is the extent of their remedial obligation.[4]

---

[1] *Marckx v Belgium*, 13 June 1979, Series A no. 31, para. 58.

[2] See, as one example of many, *Ananyev v Russia*, no. 20292/04, 30 July 2009, para. 64.

[3] Compare, for example, the Court's handling of just satisfaction in *De Wilde, Ooms and Versyp v Belgium* (Article 50), 10 March 1972, Series A no. 14 and *Manerov v Russia*, no. 49848/10, 5 January 2016.

[4] See Dzehtsiarou and Greene, 'Legitimacy and the Future of the European Court of Human Rights: Critical Perspectives from Academia and Practitioners' (2011) 12 *German Law Journal* 1707, 1709.

This is not to suggest that the payment of monetary compensation is unimportant; for many, access to the ECtHR may be their last chance of recognition of rights violation and the payment of appropriate compensation following a lack of success in the domestic legal system. Moreover, routine findings of violations and awards of just satisfaction may create an extra incentive for the Contracting Party to initiate some fundamental reforms in order to avoid repeatedly being brought to Strasbourg. Since the Court has relatively few tools of implementation in its arsenal, just satisfaction in the form of monetary compensation may, in some cases, act as a sufficient incentive for implementation of the judgment and better compliance with the Convention. To some extent, this is likely to depend on the context in which the state is engaging with the Court: should the state not be minded, or able, to pay compensation or to engage constructively with the Convention system, 'simple' monetary awards against it are unlikely to nudge it towards rights adherence. Instead, the state may simply refuse to pay, and thus not to execute the judgment. Indeed, this is what Russia did in the case of *OAO Neftyanaya Kompaniya Yukos v Russia*,[5] and what Turkey did in the case of *Cyprus v Turkey*;[6] both highly sensitive decisions in their domestic political contexts.

Having said that, just satisfaction is in fact the least contentious of the remedies the Court might order in a case of violation of the ECHR. In the vast majority of cases, the Contracting Parties pay just satisfaction within three months of the judgment becoming final. Another aspect of individual measures – namely the precise actions that are required from the State in a particular case – is much more contested.

We have already noted that only slightly over a decade ago the judgments of the Court stopped being purely declaratory. Although the Court still delivers declaratory judgments in most cases, there are some instances in which it articulates the measures it expects the respondent state to take in order effectively to execute its judgments.[7] One of the first judgments in which the Court took

---

[5] *OAO Neftyanaya Kompaniya Yukos v Russia*, no. 14902/04, 20 September 2011. The Constitutional Court of Russia declared this case unexecutable. See Judgment of 19 January 2017 No. 1-П/2017 in the case concerning the resolution of the question of the possibility to execute in accordance with the Constitution of the Russian Federation the Judgment of the European Court of Human Rights of 31 July 2014 in the case of OAO Neftyanaya Kompaniya Yukos v Russia in connection with the request of the Ministry of Justice of the Russian Federation. A courtesy translation is available on the website of the Russian Constitutional Court, available at http://www.ksrf.ru/en/Decision/Judgments/Documents/2017_January_19_1-P.pdf.

[6] *Cyprus v Turkey (just satisfaction)* [GC], no. 25781/94, ECHR 2014. The response of Turkey: 'Turkey won't pay Cyprus despite decision in Strasbourg', *Deutsche Welle*, 13 May 2014, available at http://www.dw.com/en/turkey-wont-pay-cyprus-despite-decision-in-strasbourg/a-17631966.

[7] On the prevalence and effect of specifying such measures see Mowbray, 'An Examination of the European Court of Human Rights' Indication of Remedial Measures' (2017) 17 *Human Rights Law Review* 451.

this approach was *Assanidze v Georgia*. In this case, Georgian authorities had illegally detained the applicant in violation of Article 5 of the Convention, in respect of which the Court held:

> As regards the measures which the Georgian State must take, subject to supervision by the Committee of Ministers, in order to put an end to the violation that has been found, the Court reiterates that its judgments are essentially declaratory in nature and that, in general, it is primarily for the State concerned to choose the means to be used in its domestic legal order in order to discharge its legal obligation under Article 46 of the Convention, provided that such means are compatible with the conclusions set out in the Court's judgment. This discretion as to the manner of execution of a judgment reflects the freedom of choice attached to the primary obligation of the Contracting States under the Convention to secure the rights and freedoms guaranteed. However, by its very nature, the violation found in the instant case does not leave any real choice as to the measures required to remedy it.[8]

The case of *Oleksandr Volkov v Ukraine* is an example of an even more directive approach to individual measures by the Court. The case concerned the irregular dismissal of a member of the Supreme Court of Ukraine, in respect of whom the Court held that it

> cannot accept that the applicant should be left in a state of uncertainty as regards the way in which his rights should be restored. The Court considers that by its very nature the situation found to exist in the instant case does not leave any real choice as to the individual measures required to remedy the violations of the applicant's Convention rights. Having regard to the very exceptional circumstances of the case and the urgent need to put an end to the violations of Articles 6 and 8 of the Convention, the Court holds that the respondent State shall secure the applicant's reinstatement to the post of judge of the Supreme Court at the earliest possible date.[9]

Both of these cases illustrate the Court's development – on its own initiative – of a far more assertive role in, and more directed approach to, remedies for violation of the Convention. Whilst this might be attributed to a concern with the number of clear violations coming before the Court, and unenthusiastic or incomplete execution of judgments, there are clear questions about the legitimacy and potential impacts of the Court having developed individual measures of this kind. One might question the Court's authority in this relation; there is no clear textual mandate within the Convention for instructing states to take such measures and, as a subsidiary international court, it might be considered that its role is to identify violations and then leave it to domestic authorities to determine *how* (although not *whether*) to address them through execution

---

[8] *Assanidze v Georgia* [GC], no. 71503/01, ECHR 2004-II, para. 202.
[9] *Oleksandr Volkov v Ukraine*, no. 21722/11, ECHR 2013, para. 208.

of the ECtHR's judgment. On the other hand, one might argue that remedial innovation of this kind is a logical development of the Court's jurisdiction
over individual complaints, which was originally optional but has now developed into a cornerstone of the Convention system. Without the potential to
direct individual measures to remedy the identified rights violations in a particular case, one might question the usefulness of the Court per se. Furthermore, the Court had earlier been criticised for its lack of willingness to identify
specific remedies, which some considered to be an impediment to the effective
execution of its judgments.[10] The Court, thus, began to develop its more specific remedial approach, moving away (in large part) from providing primarily
declaratory relief.[11]

General measures 'adopted [...] [to] prevent [...] new violations similar to
that or those found or [to] put [...] an end to continuing violations'[12] require
substantial and sometimes systemic change in domestic law, and are perhaps
unsurprisingly, thus, sometimes met with considerable controversy. In some
cases, the Court *only* required general measures for execution of the judgment.
For instance, in the case of *Hirst (no. 2)* (see Chapter 2) the Court found
that the blanket disenfranchisement of prisoners in the UK violates the Convention[13] and that a change of law on prisoner disenfranchisement (a general
measure) is required for UK law to comply with the Convention.

For some, the development and deployment of explicit references to general
measures in the Court's judgments in recent years illustrates its increasing willingness to be 'active' (or some might say 'activist') in response to structural
problems in human rights protection in a particular country. Indeed, the development of pilot judgments also suggests that the Court is trying to find ways to
address broader human rights challenges in the Contracting Parties.

Rule 61 of the Rules of Court provides that the Court may initiate a
pilot-judgment procedure and adopt a pilot judgment where the facts of an
application reveal the existence of a structural or systemic problem or other
similar dysfunction in the Contracting Party which has given rise or may give
rise to similar applications. Rule 61 also establishes that the Court should, in its
pilot judgment, identify both the nature of the structural or systemic problem
or other dysfunction as established, and the type of remedial measures which
the Contracting Party concerned is required to take at the domestic level to
address it. The Court can also set a deadline for the implementation of its proposed reforms. This development, initiated by the Court, is important but does

---

[10] European Commission for Democracy Through Law (Venice Commission), *Opinion on the
Implementation of the Judgments of the European Court of Human Rights*, Op. No. 209/2002
(Dec. 2002).
[11] See the analysis of this in Helfer, 'Redesigning the European Court of Human Rights:
Embeddedness as a Deep Structural Principle of the European Human Rights Regime' (2008)
19 *European Journal of International Law* 125.
[12] Appendix 4 (Item 4.4), Rules of the Committee of Ministers for the Supervision of the Execution of Judgments and of the Terms of Friendly Settlements, Rule 6, Section 2.
[13] *Hirst v the United Kingdom (no. 2)* [GC], no. 74025/01, ECHR 2005-IX.

not completely strip the Contracting Parties of the power to frame its internal policies. In pilot judgments, the Court does not specify in a detailed way the shape that the proposed reform should take, and the respondent state retains considerable discretion. The development of pilot judgments was a significant step towards the Court's attempt to ensure 'embeddedness' of the Convention in domestic systems,[14] but it is not without its risks. An obvious danger of the pilot judgment procedure is that the Contracting Parties might not be willing actively to engage with it; that the Court would outline a clear remedy but find its judgment unexecuted, potentially calling its authority and effectiveness into question. In truth, the pilot judgment procedure has been something of a mixed bag in terms of success.

In *Burdov v Russia (no. 2)* the Court considered an issue of non-execution of the enforceable judgments of national courts. Such non-execution violates Article 6 of the Convention: the right to fair trial. The Court found that this was a widespread problem, not limited to the case before it, and indicated general measures that Russia should take to address it. In particular, the Court held that

> the respondent State must introduce a remedy which secures genuinely effective redress for the violations of the Convention on account of the State authorities' prolonged failure to comply with judicial decisions delivered against the State or its entities. Such a remedy must conform to the Convention principles as laid down notably in the present judgment and be available within six months from the date on which the present judgment becomes final.[15]

Russia requested the extension of the six-month term for execution, and after about 12 months introduced a new law that provided a domestic remedy for failure to execute the final judgments of domestic courts.[16] The ECtHR has prima facie accepted that this remedy is effective.[17] The pilot procedure here, thus, helped to address both systemic rights violations in domestic law *and* workload management for the Court, illustrating the potential usefulness of pilot judgments where they are executed by the respondent state. In contrast, however, we might consider the pilot judgment in *Greens and M.T. v the United Kingdom*.[18] This followed the non-execution of the decision in *Hirst (no. 2)* (on prisoner voting), and involved the Court prescribing general measures to the UK in the following terms:

> [T]he respondent State must introduce legislative proposals [...] within six months of the date on which the present judgment becomes final, with a view to the enactment of an electoral law to achieve compliance with the Court's judgment in *Hirst* according to any time-scale determined by the Committee of Ministers.[19]

---

[14] See further Helfer, 'Redesigning the European Court of Human Rights' (above, n. 11).

[15] *Burdov v Russia (no. 2)*, no. 33509/04, ECHR 2009, para. 141.

[16] Federal Act 68-Ø from 30 April 2010 'On compensation for a violation of the right of trial in reasonable time or right for a judicial act to be executed in reasonable time'.

[17] *Nagovitsyn and Nalgiyev v Russia*, no. 27451/09 and 60650/09, 23 September 2010.

[18] *Greens and M.T. v the United Kingdom*, nos 60041/08 and 60054/08, ECHR 2010.

[19] Ibid., para. 115.

Although technically the government did introduce legislative proposals that would allow some prisoners to vote, these proposals were rejected by an overwhelming majority of the Parliament[20] and there has been no change to domestic law on disenfranchisement. Here, then, the pilot judgment did not successfully nudge systemic change to address the violation already addressed in *Hirst (no. 2)*, which still has not been executed by the UK. Very recently, and almost 12 years after the judgments in *Hirst (no. 2)* became final, the UK Government announced plans to allow some prisoners to vote, but these plans had not yet been realised at the time of writing (December 2017).[21]

It is reasonable to ask here whether the pilot judgment truly made any significant difference to rights-related remedy in either of these cases. The truth is that the majority of judgments of the Court are routinely executed; in general terms only those judgments that are politically sensitive or require major resource (re)allocation in order to ensure their execution become problematic. The pilot in *Burdov (no. 2)* is neither of those: it does not require major financial investment, is mostly technical in nature, is aimed at improving procedural protection of human rights on the national level, and did not come into conflict with any major domestic political wrangling on the issue. Simply put, there were neither economic, political nor 'principled' reasons for the state to resist execution. This stands in clear contrast to *Hirst (no. 2)* and its pilot counterpart *Greens and M.T.* The issue of prisoner voting is extremely politically sensitive in the United Kingdom, as is the issue of so-called 'judicial power' and the legitimacy (or otherwise) of the ECtHR 'telling Westminster what to do' where the parliament has already taken a firm position on the matter. Indeed, so trenchant had the then-Prime Minister been when *Hirst (no. 2)* was handed down that it was Parliament, and not the ECtHR, that should decide who would get to vote in the United Kingdom that 'backing down' in implementing the Court's judgment might well have had undesired political costs in the domestic sphere.[22]

This reflects the concern that execution of pilot judgments (or indeed any judgments of the Court) may have as much to do with domestic political conditions as with the form of the judgment and the measures directed within

---

[20] The Backbench Parliamentary Debates, 'Prisoners' Right to Vote', available at http://www.publications.parliament.uk/pa/cm201011/cmhansrd/cm110210/debtext/110210-0002.htm.

[21] Siddique, 'Government Reportedly Planning to Allow Some UK Prisoners to Vote', *The Guardian*, 29 October 2017, available at https://www.theguardian.com/society/2017/oct/29/government-planning-to-allow-some-prisoners-to-vote-european-court-human-rights.

[22] For more on political dimensions of non-execution see de Londras and Dzehtsiarou, 'Mission Impossible? Addressing Non-execution through Infringement Proceedings in the European Court of Human Rights' (2014) 66 *International and Comparative Law Quarterly* 467.

it.[23] A judgment of the ECtHR might be particularly politically sensitive if the domestic parliament can block execution (for example by voting against legislative change required for execution), if it concerns unpopular minorities without the political power to exert sufficient pressure on the institutions of the state to create significant political costs for non-execution, or if the government operates in an environment in which the ECtHR is perceived to be actively and illegitimately interfering with the sovereignty of the respondent state. As an issue, prisoner enfranchisement in the UK displays all of these symptoms of political sensitivity: it requires legislative change, it concerns the rights of prisoners who have limited popular sympathy and political power, and it is being considered in an environment increasingly uncomfortable with 'judicial power' and the Court (as discussed in Chapter 2).

Pilot judgments represent a relatively recent strategy on the part of the Court to be more prescriptive about general measures. That is not to say that declaratory findings of human rights violation are not useful per se; a merely declaratory finding should be sufficient to prompt political and legal reform in order to address the underpinning issue from which the rights violation might be said to flow. Combined with just satisfaction (where awarded) it can fulfil the two classical functions of remedy in public law: to 'redress the wrong done to the plaintiff [... while ...] ensuring that future public action complies with the requirements of the law'.[24] However, the transformative potential of declarations of violation is very much dependent on its reception within the politico-legal context to which it is directed. Given the very wide range of domestic legal and political systems to which the ECtHR is now 'speaking' with the increased Council of Europe membership of 47 states, it is perhaps not surprising that it has supplemented declaratory relief and its ability to order just satisfaction with other approaches, including pilot judgments.

Debate 2

Must respondent states execute judgments of the ECtHR?

Article 46 of the ECHR is very clear: the decisions of the Court are binding on the respondent states. As a result, there is an international legal obligation to execute these judgments. We have already seen, in Debate 1, that the Court can order a range of remedies, some of which may be less challenging for a state to execute than others. However, notwithstanding the fact that execution may involve different challenges and different techniques depending on the form of remedy that is ordered, the Article 46 obligation to execute continues to apply. It does not discriminate between the different remedial forms.

---

[23] Although specifying general measures in the operative part of the judgment does seem to enhance execution, the sample numbers are relatively small compared to the general number of cases before the Court. See further Mowbray, 'An Examination' (above, n. 7).

[24] Sathanapally, *Beyond Disagreement: Open Remedies in Human Rights Adjudication* (Oxford University Press, 2012), 11.

Thus, the simple question of whether a respondent state *must* execute the judgments of the Court is amenable to a straightforward answer as a matter of international law: 'yes'. Without equivocation, then, we can and should say that execution of ECtHR judgments is very simply a requirement of the Rule of Law; adherence to an existing legal obligation.[25] However, notwithstanding this straightforward doctrinal answer, one might imagine a number of arguments against suggesting that respondent states must *always* execute the judgments against them that are handed down by the Court. We can divide these into arguments of principle, arguments of the constitution, and arguments of practicality. We first outline some of the contours of each of these arguments, before suggesting an argument for execution in spite of them.

Arguments of Principle

In almost all states in the Council of Europe, we can say that domestic law has been made 'lawfully' by the democratically elected parliament whose role is to reflect the will of the People. There will, then, sometimes be situations in which being required to change that law following a decision of a 'foreign' court may cause tensions, notwithstanding the fact that doing so is a requirement of the Rule of Law.[26] If we leave to one side, for a moment, the *legal* argument of obligation, we can ask whether the proposition that a domestic parliament might resist execution and, through so doing, enter into a kind of dialogue with Strasbourg may not be not entirely outrageous in principle, particularly if the individual remedies (if any) that are ordered by the Court are given effect to, but the general measures (such as legal change) are not. After all, if the implementation of the Convention is a matter for all of the institutions of the state and not *only* the courts (as it is), then why is it that the courts may enter into a dialogue of contestation (as considered in Chapter 2 and further in Debate 3 below), but the other institutions of the state may not?

One answer to this provocative question may be that parliamentarians are likely to be swayed by popular opinion and a need to satisfy electoral wiles in a way that the courts are not, and – if rights are about human dignity and not about bestowing upon people privileges that 'the majority' decides they should have – mere politics ought not to have the same dialogical status as courts. This argument has an instinctive attraction in most European states, but is a little more difficult to sustain within the constitutional tradition of the United Kingdom where, indeed, the constitution – including constitutional rights – *is* political, and where Parliament is recognised as having a role (if not the ultimate role) in determining its content.[27] The argument may also be somewhat

---

[25] See, for example, Donald, 'Tackling Non-Implementation in the Strasbourg System: The Art of the Possible?' *EJIL: Talk*, available at https://www.ejiltalk.org/author/adonald/.

[26] See also Article 27, Vienna Convention on the Law of Treaties.

[27] For the classical argument see Griffith, 'The Political Constitution' (1979) 42 *Modern Law Review* 1.

more difficult to sustain in states where the judiciary is compromised, either by a lack of judicial independence or by the design of judicial institutions in a way that privileges the views, policies and politics of the ruling party.[28] In recent years, there have been attempts to reshape the constitutional courts in Hungary and Poland, for example, to ensure that the government's desired outcome is likely to be shared by the majority of judges, and the courts of Turkey have been purged of approximately 4,000 so-called traitors following the coup against President Erdoğan in 2016.

It is, thus, by no means clear that either the parliaments or the courts of the member states of the Council of Europe uniformly have the accountability, independence, and respect for the rule of law that such an argument is predicated on. However, where the institutions in question *do* have those traits (at least to the extent possible in any polity), there are likely to be questions on which reasonable people might reasonably disagree[29] and, in relation to these, the simple argument of legal obligation under Article 46 may not be sufficient to satisfy the dissenter who considers the decision of the domestic institutions to have a greater claim to authority, given its roots in a democratic, deliberative and reflective exercise, than that of the ECtHR.

Arguments of the Constitution

However strong arguments might be about parliamentary will overriding the decisions of the ECtHR, arguments about the primacy of domestic constitutional provisions have a potentially more compelling nature. Situations where domestic constitutional law and international law are in conflict with one another are particularly complex, but again domestic law may well have something to say about the relationship. A wide variety of approaches can be identified across Europe.[30]

The first is one that recognises the effective primacy of the international legal norm over the domestic constitutional norm. In such situations, a finding of incompatibility between the domestic constitutional provision and the international obligation will lead to a change in the domestic constitution, which in turn will be effected by the appropriate mechanism according to domestic law.

---

[28] For a recent analysis of judicial independence across Europe see Consultative Council of European Judges, *Challenges for Judicial Independence and Impartiality in the Member States of the Council of Europe* SG/Inf(2015)3rev.

[29] Waldron, 'The Core of the Case Against Judicial Review' (2006) 115 *Yale Law Journal* 1346.

[30] For a useful, although incomplete account, see Keller and Stone-Sweet (eds), *A Europe of Rights: The Impact of the ECHR on National Legal Systems* (Oxford University Press, 2008). See also Martinico and Pollicino (eds), *The Interaction between Europe's Legal Systems* (Edward Elgar, 2012); Motoc and Ziemele (eds), *The Impact of the ECHR on Democratic Change in Central and Eastern Europe Judicial Perspectives* (Cambridge University Press, 2016).

For example, Article 11 of the Slovak Constitution provides that international treaties on human rights and basic liberties that were ratified by the Slovak Republic and promulgated in a manner determined by law take precedence over its own laws, provided that they secure a greater extent of constitutional rights and liberties than domestic law does.[31]

The second approach is to recognise the domestic constitution as a 'block' on internationalism, so that the authority of an international provision is recognised as 'trumping' domestic law *inasmuch as it does not conflict with the Constitution*. Usually, this principle is developed and applied by the domestic courts themselves. In Italy, the ECHR is placed between the Constitution and the national statutes: below the former but above the latter.[32] Attaching a super-legislative status to the ECHR means that the Constitutional Court needs at least to take into account the case law of the ECtHR. Yet the Italian Constitutional Court has limited the impact of the Strasbourg case law by suggesting that Italian judges should give effect to 'consolidated law' or 'pilot judgments'.[33] In Germany, the Constitution has primacy over the ECHR.[34]

The third approach is to provide that a domestic court may specifically deem the decision of an international court to be incapable of execution because it conflicts with the domestic constitution. Thus far, the Russian Federation is the only state in the Council of Europe in which such an approach is taken explicitly; we discussed this in Chapter 2, and the development has attracted much concern, such as this from the Venice Commission:

> States have to remove possible tensions and contradictions between rulings of the ECtHR and their national systems, including – if possible – via means of dialogue. This is a tool which has proven its effectiveness in many instances, in several Council of Europe member States. The Russian Federation should have recourse to dialogue, instead of resorting to unilateral measures, which are at variance with the Vienna Convention on the law of treaties which stipulates that a state has to interpret the treaty 'in good faith' (Art. 31).[35]

The fourth approach is expressly to incorporate the international standard at a sub-constitutional level, so that incompatibility with the Convention can result in, for example, a domestic court 'interpreting up' a statute, but does not

---

[31] See also Article 10 of the Constitution of the Czech Republic.

[32] Judgments Nos 348 and 349 (24 October 2007) (It).

[33] Judgment No. 49 (26 March 2015) (It).

[34] This is laid down in *Görgülü* 2 BvR 1481/04 (14 October 2004) BVerfGE 111, 307 (Ger); see further Dzehtsiarou and Mavronicola, 'Relation of Constitutional Courts/Supreme Courts to the ECtHR' in *Max Planck Encyclopedia of Comparative Constitutional Law* (Oxford University Press, 2017).

[35] European Commission for Democracy Through Law (Venice Commission). *Interim Opinion on the amendments to the Federal Constitutional Law on the Constitutional Court of the Russian Federation adopted by the Venice Commission at its 106th Plenary Session* (CDL-AD(2016)005-e), para. 100.

disturb the constitutional standard in question. This is the approach taken in Ireland, for example, under the ECHR Act 2003. In such a system, the incompatibility between the Convention and the Constitution may lead to constitutional change *where politics determines that it should*, but domestic law does not require such a change to be introduced.

The fifth approach is to give the ECHR – or the domestic statute implementing it – a constitutional status, so that it can only be changed in accordance with the requirements for amending constitutional statutes in the domestic legal system. This is what happened in Austria, where the ECHR has constitutional status and conflicts between the *Bundes-Verfassungsgesetz* (which is the primary constitutional text) are satisfied by application of *lex posteriori derogat legi priori* principle (i.e. that a later law repeals an earlier law).[36] In the UK the Human Rights Act 1998 has the status of a constitutional statute, so that the doctrine of implied repeal does not apply to it as it does to most statutes in the United Kingdom.[37] Whilst this does not give the ECHR the status of domestic constitutional law, it brings it obliquely into the constitutional realm through the obligation of the courts to account for ECtHR jurisprudence (under section 2), the power to interpret domestic statutes as far as possible in line with the Convention (under section 3), and the inclusion of much of the Convention text as a Schedule to the Act.

All of these approaches reflect the complexity of the relationship between a domestic constitutional provision and the Convention. Whilst a domestic statute is an expression of democratic will refracted through parliamentary processes, a Constitution is something more: it is a mechanism for restraining political and democratic will, a superior law usually entrenched in some way, often an expression of domestic values, and not uncommonly a key mechanism in the creation of domestic constitutional culture. It is, thus, difficult when that domestic constitutional culture is at odds with a transnational legal order of which the state is a part (through membership) but which may not always accord with what governments sometimes describe as 'national values'. These contentious questions are often, but not always, associated with issues relating to societal norms, such as the definition of marriage. However, where a domestic constitution is understood as according the right to marry to opposite-sex couples only, for example, or as precluding the legalisation of abortion, one might argue that incompatibility with an international standard ought not be sufficient to force a change in that constitutional order, but that such change should emerge from domestic, organic processes of constitutional evolution.

Whilst that argument has a certain intellectual attraction to it, on a practical level it is clear that international litigation is often a key lever for domestic

[36] On the ECHR in Austria see Thurnherr, 'Austria and Switzerland' in Keller and Stone-Sweet (eds), *A Europe of Rights: The Impact of the ECHR on National Legal Systems* (Oxford University Press, 2008).
[37] *Thoburn v Sunderland CC* [2002] 4 All ER 156; *R. (HS2 Action Alliance Ltd) v Secretary of State for Transport* [2014] UKSC 3.

activists and advocates who wish to bring about a shift in national constitutional provisions and constitutional cultures and values. The processes of constitutional change are not always accessible to marginalised groups and individuals, and sometimes an international 'nudge' is required to force an issue onto the agenda or, indeed, to compel the constitutional change itself. If this is acceptable in the case of ordinary legislation, one might argue that the acceptability of the same principle in relation to the Constitution ought to be conceded, and that it is only an unjustified veneration of the constitutional text as communicating some sense of common identity and values from which these marginalised individuals are often excluded that holds one back from taking such a position.

Arguments of Practicality

In some cases, non-execution is justified by the Contracting Parties on the basis of practicality. This argument, once more, holds no truck from a legal doctrinal perspective, but is nevertheless interesting, sometimes made by states, and thus worth considering. It can emerge in a number of different ways.

First, and perhaps most obviously, where the ECtHR requires general measures it simply may not be possible to undertake the legal change that this entails. If it requires fresh legislation, a parliamentary majority might not be secured. Where the legal change is constitutional this may be even more complex. Although constitutional change is brought about by legislation in many states (such as Bulgaria (for most constitutional provisions)), it is not uncommon for legislation changing the constitution to require a 'super majority', as is the case in the Czech Republic. Even a government with a simple majority may not be able to secure a super majority, and the upper house in bicameral systems may not be controlled by the federal government. It may operate without a whip,[38] have unelected and non-party affiliation structures,[39] or represent states/cantons/länder and not be susceptible to control by the national governing parties, for example.[40] Some states even require an election to amend the Constitution. In Belgium, the law proposing constitutional change must be published, following which there is a general election, and only following that can the proposed amendments to the Constitution be introduced (with a two-thirds majority in both Houses of parliament), with the election acting as a *quasi*-referendum on the proposed change. In Denmark, a proposed change must be approved by parliament, following which a general election must be held. The new parliament elected in that general election must then approve the proposed amendment again and there must then be a

---

[38] For example, there is no formal 'whip' in the UK's House of Lords.
[39] For example, the Irish Senate is almost all unelected and is not organised in party-political terms.
[40] For example, in Germany.

referendum of the People. Where constitutional change requires a referendum (as it does also in Ireland and Switzerland, for example) the referendum, even if put to the People, simply may not pass. It may well be the case that the People determine that *regardless of what the ECtHR says* they want to maintain a constitutional position that is at odds with the Convention. If the ultimate decision maker on constitutional change is the People, then the most a government can realistically do by means of execution is to put the proposal to the People and argue for its adoption. It cannot guarantee that the required legal change will be effected. Thus, the very nature of bringing about constitutional change may be a real practical barrier to execution.

Even if complex legal change is not required, resource constraints may make execution of an ECtHR judgment difficult to achieve. In some cases the general measures to be implemented – for example to greatly accelerate criminal justice processes in order to tackle undue delay resulting in Article 6 violations – might only be achieved at an enormous cost, and there is an argument that allocating budget and prioritising between different areas of required investment is a matter that is best decided upon by governments themselves. This is, one might argue, particularly the case in situations of extremely limited resources, austerity, mass unemployment and high levels of poverty (including among children); conditions that prevail today in some European states. It is sometimes supposed that only socio-economic rights are costly to implement, but civil and political rights are also resource-intensive; consider the price, for example, of improving the physical infrastructure of a state's prisons, of establishing voting processes in extremely remote locations, of providing free legal aid to all indigent criminal defendants. These are not cost-free rights. States' resources are not boundless, but their distribution always requires policy decisions by political institutions. In other words, prioritisation always operates when decisions about expenditure are being made, so one might argue that it is no effective defence to say 'we could not afford to execute the judgment', or 'we preferred to invest our resources elsewhere'; indeed, the Court has made it clear that financial constraints cannot justify a failure to protect Convention rights.[41] That argument, which at first seems one of simple practicality, relates as closely to concepts of sovereignty as do arguments of principle and the constitution. At their heart, they are all arguments that come from a basic claim: *the ECtHR should not be able to tell us what to do.*

The Argument for Execution

In spite of all of these arguments against execution, the simple legal reality is that states do have an obligation to execute judgments against them under Article 46. Indeed, there is also a broader international law obligation to do so; Article 26 of the Vienna Convention on the Law of Treaties requires states

---

[41] See, for example, *Azinas v Cyprus*, no. 56679/00, 20 June 2002, para. 41.

to respect the international treaties it has ratified, and Article 27 provides that provisions of domestic law cannot be relied upon to justify a failure to perform a treaty. The argument for executing judgments under Article 46(1), then, is one of legal obligation. That legal obligation relates to the broader project of creating an international rule of law: of recognising international legal obligations as legally binding (thus endorsing international law's status *qua* law), and of recognising the decisions of international courts as binding in the same way as those of domestic courts (thus recognising an international rule of law that cannot be subverted by simple will).

Of course, this is not to say that the decisions of international courts are *the same* as the decisions of domestic courts. In many significant ways they are different, and indeed domestic legal systems often have in-built mechanisms to reject the decisions of courts, not as to the outcome in a particular case but as to the broader legal framework. Thus, for example, if the Irish Supreme Court finds that a provision of the Constitution has a meaning that the government does not consider workable or favourable, the Government can propose a change to the Constitution to the People and thus attempt to change the baseline legal norm.[42] The People, then, have the ultimate say. But in the meantime the decision of the Supreme Court would be complied with; it is the authoritative legal instrument until a more authoritative one (in this case emanating from the People) comes into existence.

In other systems, it is Parliament that would decide on whether to change the Constitution, but the same general point stands: domestic legal systems tend to have processes that allow for ensuring the Court does not have 'the final say', so to speak, on the broader legal standard.[43] At first blush, this is not as clearly present in the ECHR: whilst States can propose and initiate changes to the Convention text that may lead to the amendment of the Convention in due course, this is complex and requires widespread agreement – and ratification – from the other Contracting Parties. However, states *do* have ways to engage with the Court to try to revisit the baseline legal standard: through judicial dialogue, through imaginative arguments before the Court, through 'signalling' disagreement with the Court's approach by means of Parliamentary debates and so on. The Court has ways of listening: through European consensus, through evolutive interpretation, and through the margin of appreciation, for example. Thus, whilst the system is different to that often found in domestic legal systems, this kind of response from the states is possible and, sometimes, successful. Thus, the Rule of Law demands compliance with judgments

---

[42] For more see de Londras and Gwynn Morgan, 'Constitutional Amendment in Ireland' in Contiades (ed.), *Engineering Constitutional Change: A Comparative Perspective on Europe, Canada and the USA* (Routledge, 2012).

[43] For a broader discussion see de Londras, 'In Defence of Judicial Innovation and Constitutional Evolution' in Cahillane, Gallen and Hickey (eds), *Judges, Politics and the Irish Constitution* (Manchester University Press, 2017).

of the Court in respect of the particular case, but that does not mean the system has no space within it for contestation and refinement of the standards in question.

This points to an important distinction in considering the question of non-execution; the distinction between *whether* to execute and *how* to execute. Whilst there is no question *in law* about whether a state must execute, there may be a question *in fact* about how the state has gone about this process of execution. Thus, the discourse that takes place between the Committee of Ministers and the state, and the possibility to seek clarification on what a judgment requires from the Court (under Article 46(3) and potentially 46(4)) are important mechanisms for figuring out whether the state's purported actions to execute the judgment suffice, whilst still ensuring that a state – even one that wants to mount a challenge to or is unhappy with the legal interpretation applied by the Court in the case – is positively engaged with the process of execution.

That engagement – that willingness to execute even if the state does not agree with the judgment as an expression of 'diffuse support'[44] for the Court – is of fundamental importance. Not only does it underpin the status of the Convention as law, and the Rule of Law in Europe, but it also protects the system against contagious non-execution, where states begin to claim not only that they can contest how to execute, but that they can decline to execute at all. As Nils Muižnieks wrote, 'A future where each Council of Europe member state reorganises its internal constitutional hierarchy so that the Convention can be trumped is a danger to the rule of law in that state and in all other states.'[45] This reinforces the fact that the Council of Europe is a community of states, and that the Convention and the protection of rights thereunder is a collective enterprise. The action of one state, particularly a 'norm entrepreneur',[46] in undermining the Convention through a refusal to execute has potentially deleterious impacts on the entire system by encouraging or implicitly endorsing a similar approach in others.[47] Thus, there is a moral responsibility on states to engage positively and constructively with execution for the

---

[44] See, for example, Lupu, 'International Judicial Legitimacy: Lessons from National Courts' (2013) 14 *Theoretical Inquiries in Law* 437.

[45] Muižnieks, 'Non-implementation of the European Court of Human Rights' Judgments: Our Shared Responsibility', 23 August 2016, available at https://www.ein.org.uk/blog/non-implementation-courts-judgments-ours-shared-responsibility.

[46] Norm entrepreneurs can be understood as those 'with the skills and resource to undertake a project or to make things happen' (Herro, 'Norm Entrepreneurs Advocating the Responsibility to Protect, and Peacekeeping Reform Proposals' in Curran et al. (eds), *Perspectives on Peacekeeping an Atrocity Prevention* (Springer, 2015), 41). In this context, they are states with the ability to change the behaviours of others through their leadership, behaviour and representations.

[47] See, for example, Bates, 'The Continued Failure to Implement *Hirst v. UK EJIL: Talk,* available at https://www.ejiltalk.org/the-continued-failure-to-implement-hirst-v-uk/.

good of the system as a whole, and in order to ensure that the post-war European project(s) continue to be effective in protecting rights and freedoms across the continent.

We know, however, that this moral and legal duty to execute judgments does not always translate into action, and thus a question as to whether states can be compelled to execute judgments arises. At the moment, the Committee of Ministers mostly uses diplomatic pressure on Contracting Parties that have not executed judgments against them; an approach that is sometimes ineffective. The Committee also, however, has the legal power to initiate infringement proceedings under Article 46(4). This provision, added by Protocol 14, has never been used. It provides:

> If the Committee of Ministers considers that a High Contracting Party refuses to abide by a final judgment in a case to which it is a party, it may, after serving formal notice on that Party and by decision adopted by a majority vote of two-thirds of the representatives entitled to sit on the committee, refer to the Court the question whether that Party has failed to fulfil its obligation under [Article 46(1)].

Whether the infringement proceeding under Article 46(4) is likely to be useful is the subject of substantial debate. On the one hand, the Parliamentary Assembly of the Council of Europe, human rights activists and some commentators encourage the Committee of Ministers to use infringement proceedings against states on which other forms of pressure have been ineffective.[48] On the other side of this debate are those who think that utilisation of Article 46(4) will have limited practical effect on improving the enforcement of the Court's judgments.[49]

Article 46(4) provides that if the Committee of Ministers considers that a Contracting Party refuses to abide by a final judgment in a case to which it is a party, it may, after serving formal notice on that Party and by decision adopted by a majority vote of two-thirds of the representatives entitled to sit on the Committee, refer to the Court the question whether that Party has failed to fulfil its obligation to implement the judgment. If the ECtHR finds that the state has failed to execute the judgment, this constitutes a further violation of the Convention (this time of Article 46(1): the obligation to execute).

The idea behind Article 46(4) was to give the Committee of Ministers an enforcement tool that would be more effective than diplomatic actions such as resolutions and discussions with the state, but less detrimental to the Council of Europe than suspending a state's membership. However, real questions about its utility arise. First, it is not clear that the basic requirements for triggering Article 46(4) could be met: achieving a two-thirds vote in the Committee of

---

[48] de Vries, 'Implementation of Judgments of the European Court of Human Rights' (PACE, Report, 9 September 2015, Doc 13864), available at www.assembly.coe.int/nw/xml/XRef/X2H-Xref-ViewPDF.asp?FileID=22005&lang=en; Donald, Tackling Non-Implementation' (above, n. 25).

[49] de Londras and Dzehtsiarou, 'Mission Impossible?' (above, n. 22).

Ministers would be extremely challenging. The Committee is a political body that is formed of the ministers of foreign affairs from the Contracting Parties, many of which have failed fully to execute judgments against them. Picking out one country for Article 46(4) proceedings may lead to accusations of scape-goating, and to nervousness among other states likely to find themselves the subject of similar votes in the future. That said, it is true that some states are more trenchant in their non-execution, especially in cases relating to political dissent and the like, and might fairly be identified for infringement proceed-ings. Since the introduction of this procedure in 2010 the Committee of Min-isters has initiated it only once: in relation to Azerbaijan in the case of Ilgar Mammadov.[50] This request is still pending before the ECtHR at the time of writing (in December 2017) and its outcome and impact are uncertain.

The second practical challenge is that by using this procedure the Com-mittee of Ministers would implicitly be accepting that it has failed in super-vising the execution of a particular judgment. Lambert-Abdelgawad has well observed that international institutions do not readily make manifest their fail-ures in such a way,[51] and this may suggest that the majority of attempts to trigger Article 46(4) simply would not be successful for lack of political will-ingness in the Committee of Ministers itself.

However, perhaps the greatest contestation on the question of infringement proceedings relates to what, if anything, they would achieve if the practical challenges of triggering Article 46(4) could be overcome. Infringement pro-ceedings have to be heard in the Grand Chamber, meaning that there would be substantial delay in hearing a case once the Committee of Ministers had decided to refer it. During that time there would be limited incentive for an already-recalcitrant state to make any progress on execution of the judgment in question, leaving rights unenforced during that time and meaning that, even if the respondent state had been willing to do *something* (albeit something inad-equate to constitute full execution in the view of the Committee of Ministers), it would do *nothing* from the point of initiating Article 46(4) of the ECHR proceedings to the time when the Court delivers its decision on the infringe-ment proceeding.

More pressingly, however, it is not clear whether a finding of further infringe-ment under Article 46(4) would really achieve anything from a practical per-spective. The reality is that an Article 46(4) procedure effectively tells us what we already know: that a state has failed to respect a judgment of the Court. One might argue that if a state cared enough about its international reputation

[50] *Ilgar Mammadov v Azerbaijan*, no. 15172/13, 22 May 2014. See also 'Committee of Ministers Launches Infringement Proceedings against Azerbaijan', *Council of Europe Newsroom,* 5 December 2017, available at https://www.coe.int/en/web/portal/-/coun-cil-of-europe-s-committee-of-ministers-launches-infringement-proceedings-against-azerbaijan.
[51] Lambert-Abdelgawad, 'The Court as a Part of the Council of Europe: the Parliamentary Assembly and the Committee of Ministers' in Føllesdal, Peters and Ulfstein (eds), *Constitut-ing Europe: The European Court of Human Rights in a National, European and Global Context* (Cambridge University Press, 2013).

to remedy violations of the Convention when they were identified, they would already have executed the judgment in question. If not, it is difficult to tell what difference a further judgment from the Court would make to the willingness to execute. Certainly, an adverse finding in an Article 46(4) proceeding may create greater and refreshed international pressure for execution of the original judgment, but the impact of that pressure cannot easily be foreseen. Much is likely to depend on how other political powers – neighbours, allies and fellow Council of Europe members – use that pressure created by the international court, and how domestic courts and domestic political structures also respond to it in fresh litigation that might be taken at the domestic level. The potential usefulness of Article 46(4) may, then, lie in reigniting effective political pressure on the respondent state to execute the original judgment against it.

Debate 3
Should non-respondent states give effect to ECtHR judgments?

Judgments of the ECtHR do not have *erga omnes* effect. In other words, they are legally binding on the respondent states *only*. The Court's judgments commonly include both a determination of the dispute before it *and* often statements on the meaning of the Convention and its provisions. Such statements are, of course, of relevance beyond the particular facts of the case before the Court; it is the ECtHR that has the role of developing an autonomous and determinative interpretation of the Convention, so that its findings on the meaning and effect of the ECHR may be of broader effect. It is of the essence of the Convention that the national authorities would give effect to the Convention, with cases to the Court having been foreseen as, in effect, exceptional, where the national authorities have not succeeded in implementing the Convention. That is an important part of the principle of subsidiarity that underpins the Court's jurisdiction.[52] This suggests that there is a logical expectation of the Convention *as interpreted by the Court* being applied and implemented at national level. It is not a legal obligation but a logical consequence of the functioning of the system. This implementation is the role of all parts of the state: the executive is expected to plan policy by reference to its Convention obligations, the legislature to attempt to legislate only in compliance with the Convention, public authorities to apply and implement the law and bureaucracy of the state consistent with Convention rights, and courts to take account of the Convention and case law of the ECtHR to the extent permissible by domestic law.

---

[52] See Spielmann, 'Judgments of the European Court of Human Rights Effects and Implementation'. Keynote Speech', available at www.echr.coe.int/Documents/ Speech_20130920_Spielmann_Gottingen_ENG.pdf, 5; Spano, 'Universality or Diversity of Human Rights?' (2014) 14 *Human Rights Law Review* 487.

It is on domestic courts and their role in implementing the Convention that we concentrate here. Consideration of this requires a preliminary appreciation of the different approaches to the role of international law in domestic legal systems across the Council of Europe. It is sometimes said that the relationship between municipal and international law can be roughly categorised as either monist or dualist, with monist systems treating international law as having domestic effect upon ratification, and dualist systems requiring explicit imple-mentation (usually by legislation) before an international legal instrument can be relied on as binding authority in domestic law. However, as we have already seen, across the Council of Europe there is a wide variety of approaches even within these two broad schools.

Even if the Convention has domestic legal effect, however, the domestic impact of judgments from Strasbourg against other Contracting Parties is a matter of some contention, not least because there is no international legal obligation for the national authorities to execute those judgments. In essence, then, the approach to such judgments will depend largely on judicial approaches towards them. In some states, such as Lithuania and Croatia, these judgments are treated as effectively binding; in others, such as the UK and Ireland, they are explicitly non-binding, although they are to be taken into account when considering Convention-related cases. Where domestic law has made the juris-prudence of the ECtHR binding on its courts then there is little to debate; the principled decision on the role of these judgments has been taken *as a matter of domestic law* and that domestic law is simply applied. However, where domestic law allows for the domestic court to take account of *but not be bound by* these judgments, debates about what this does – and should – mean may ensue. This is the case in the United Kingdom.

Section 2 of the Human Rights Act 1998 requires domestic courts to take account of Strasbourg jurisprudence; almost identical wording is used in the ECHR Act 2003 in Ireland. On the face of it, this means that such decisions ought to be treated just as other persuasive sources are: parties may rely on them to try to convince the court to take one approach or another to a ques-tion, and judges may use them in reaching decisions. In all circumstances, the use of so-called 'foreign law' for the purposes of domestic law interpretation and adjudication is contentious.[53] For some, this is entirely illegitimate: domes-tic law should be decided on the basis of domestic precedents alone. However, an absolute aversion to the use of such sources as persuasive precedent is an extreme and seldom-expressed position. Caution about reliance on such sources largely emanates from a concern for judicial legitimacy. For some schol-ars, courts are *always* treading on sensitive ground: they do not have domestic democratic legitimacy that might come from direct election from the people,

---

[53] On the broader debates on this see, for example, Fredman, 'Foreign Fads of Fashions? The Role of Comparativism in Human Rights Law' (2015) 64 *International and Comparative Law Quarterly* 631.

and they may well make decisions that upend the acts of parliament or the government, the members of which *are* directly elected. This is not the place to engage in this much wider debate about the limits and legitimacy of the judicial role, but it is worth noting at this stage that the debate about the role of ECtHR judgments in domestic law is related to that larger and very longstanding academic and judicial debate about the role of 'foreign' law per se.

It does, however, have a somewhat different character in the particular context of the interpretation and application of the Convention and, where relevant, its implementing provisions in domestic law. It is beyond dispute that the ECtHR has the ultimate role of interpreting and applying the Convention.[54] As a matter of international law the ECHR means what the Court says it means. It is, thus, relatively uncontroversial to suggest that where a domestic court is assessing what the Convention per se might mean, and where there is a decision on this from Strasbourg, the domestic court might *ordinarily* follow that decision and then consider its implications for the questions of domestic law that arise.

This is not to suggest that the Strasburg Court and its domestic counterparts have no necessary or productive relationship in the context of the development and implementation of the Convention; quite to the contrary, in fact. The ECtHR is connected to domestic courts and their work as considered in Chapter 2. What we mean by this is that all of these courts have a role in developing and implementing the corpus of European human rights law that forms part of the so-called European Public Order. In respect of the relationship between domestic courts and the ECtHR, this means that there is an important role for (informal) cooperation and collaboration, and indeed at times for contestation and disagreement, on the meaning of the Convention. Such discourse and quiet collaboration does not undermine the authority of the Strasbourg Court: its decision in a particular case remains binding as against the parties, and the respondent state must still execute it. In this way, such *judicial* contestation is markedly and importantly different to the *political* contestation that underpins much of the non-execution we have considered in Debate 1 of this chapter.

Within a framework of this kind, there must – one might argue – be some space for contestation, so that domestic courts might consider themselves able to express disagreement with the decision of the Strasbourg Court about the meaning of any particular provision. In situations where the judgments were not handed down against the state in question, there is no reason in international law why the domestic court might decide to treat the cases in question as not being binding upon them.

The value of this collaborative engagement on the meaning of the Convention – an engagement that includes not only 'taking account of' the Strasbourg

---

[54] Pursuant to Article 32 ECHR the jurisdiction of the Court shall extend to all matters concerning the interpretation and application of the Convention and the Protocols.

jurisprudence but also cross-court engagement, judicial training, and fora that facilitate extra-curial judicial interactions – is not only that the involvement of domestic courts and judges with Strasbourg institutions may bring to light some practical or doctrinal complications with the ECtHR approach that were not otherwise apparent (which is in itself important), but also that the domestic courts and judiciaries might develop a sense of co-ownership over, and co-authorship of, the Convention and its jurisprudence. After all, only a very small proportion of the cases that concern the Convention ever gets to the Court, and fewer still get past the admissibility stage. Most Convention matters are addressed domestically, either through legislation, practice or judicial decisions. The effectiveness of the Convention as part of a system for the protection of human rights calls for engagement between domestic and European judiciaries in order to better embed the Convention and ensure that its principles and rights are protected even without a case having to be taken to the Court.

The controversy, of course, arises when we distil that general principle (that collaboration between domestic judiciaries and the Court is to be welcomed) into rules of law that might determine how that collaboration would work in practical terms when a case raising a Convention issue comes before the domestic courts. What weight ought the domestic courts to give to the jurisprudence of the ECtHR that, as we have already noted, is not binding on them as a matter of international law? The simple answer to this question is that it is a matter for domestic law to decide.

In the UK, the early approach under the Human Rights Act 1998 – which was largely similar in Ireland under the 2003 Act – was to treat Strasbourg jurisprudence as if it were *effectively* binding, subject to very limited circumstances (the mirror effect). This approach remains controversial, even though the judicial approach to ECHR jurisprudence has certainly moved on significantly; so much so that, as Masterman puts it, the 'mirror' has been crack'd.[55]

In spite of this, however, it remains politically popular to claim, in the UK context, that British courts should decide matters of British law; not 'foreign' judges. This criticism, which comes down to a critique of domestic courts applying ECtHR jurisprudence in their consideration and interpretation of domestic law, has popular appeal and political power; however, it ultimately misunderstands the *status quo*. First, as already noted, the decisions of the ECtHR rarely stand in isolation: not only are they subject to (and sometimes emergent from) dialogue between the Court and domestic courts, but they also frequently involve the Court taking domestic law into account in order to consider, for example, whether there is any European consensus on the legal question before it. Thus, whilst they ultimately emanate from the ECtHR, they are products, often, of the intermingling of the legal traditions across the Continent, which

---

[55] Masterman, 'The Mirror Crack'd', *UK Constitutional Law Blog*, 13 February 2013, available at https://ukconstitutionallaw.org/2013/02/13/roger-masterman-the-mirror-crackd/.

emerges from the make-up of the Court, and its Registry, the arguments put to the bench and the practice of undertaking comparative law research in the Court. Second, this argument fundamentally misunderstands Strasbourg decisions as being binding on non-respondent states. Neither the Convention nor the Human Rights Act 1998 *requires* domestic institutions to treat ECtHR decisions as having *erga omnes* effect. Instead, it was UK courts – particularly in the case of *Ullah*[56] – that interpreted a UK Act of Parliament (the Human Rights Act 1998) as effectively requiring these decisions to be treated as *quasi*-binding, albeit subject to some exceptions. Thus, *if* these judgments are binding on domestic courts (as we do not think they are) then that is *because* this is the interpretation given to a domestic statute by the domestic court itself. Furthermore, and importantly, even if domestic courts *do* treat or characterise the ECtHR judgments as 'binding' this approach might be adjusted through domestic law, in a manner that fits with the domestic constitutional arrangements in place in any given state. To remain with the UK example for consistency of analysis, it is open to Parliament to take a range of steps to resist the outcome of an individual case in which the Strasbourg jurisprudence was treated thus (for example, not to change the law following a Declaration of Incompatibility under section 4 of the Human Rights Act 1998, or to amend a law that has been interpreted 'up' to Convention compliance by the domestic court), and indeed to make clearer to domestic courts that statute does not require such an approach (for example, by amendment of the Human Rights Act 1998). Where state authorities or politicians persist in presenting the so-called bindingness of Strasbourg jurisprudence as a problem with the Convention per se, then, they are either inadvertently or purposefully passing off what is a *domestic* legal arrangement as the product of a misrepresentation of what *international* legal arrangements require.

This is, however, likely to become somewhat more complex if the ECtHR begins to hand down advisory opinions, as Protocol 16 anticipated. Protocol 16, also known as the Protocol of Dialogue, will enter into force after 10 ratifications. It was opened for ratification in 2013 and at the time of writing (May 2017) it was signed by 11 parties and ratified by 7. Once ratified, this will allow the highest courts and tribunals of a Contracting Party to request the ECtHR to give advisory opinions on questions of principle relating to the interpretation or application of the rights and freedoms defined in the Convention. It is envisaged that ratifying states will grant some of their higher courts competence to request advisory opinions from the ECtHR, and that if one of these courts faces a question of ECHR interpretation which is not clear from the jurisprudence they would request an advisory opinion from Strasbourg. The request would first be considered by a panel of five judges in the ECtHR, and if accepted the Grand Chamber would be convened to deliver an advisory opinion as requested.

---

[56] *R. v Special Adjudicator (ex parte Ullah)* [2004] UKHL 26.

As Protocol 16 is not yet in force, it is not clear how precise and unambiguous these opinions might be. Interestingly, Article 47 of the Convention currently contains a provision allowing the Court to give advisory opinions but these opinions cannot deal with the content or scope of the rights enshrined in the Convention. Given this limited mandate, the Court has only given two advisory opinions, both relating to election of judges, and both relatively technical.[57] In contrast to this limited jurisdiction under Article 47, the proposed new advisory opinion mechanism is intended to intensify the dialogue between the highest national courts and the ECtHR; in principle, such dialogue should be welcome as it ensures embeddedness of the ECHR in the national states and develops jurisprudence of the ECtHR in a non-confrontational fashion which is impossible in contentious cases. Having said that, one might question whether advisory opinions are capable of enhancing dialogue. Both procedural and substantive concerns can be raised here.

The procedural concern relates to the questionable utility of advisory opinions in a practical sense. In order to get such an opinion, the highest national court would have to adjourn the case in which an opinion is sought and wait until the ECtHR delivers its judgment. That judgment will have to be handed down by the Grand Chamber consisting of 17 judges, meaning that there will likely be a considerable delay before the hearing takes place. Should the case in the domestic court relate to criminal proceedings, the delay might be such as to even call into question compliance with the defendant's Article 5 and Article 6 rights. One can readily imagine that a process for expediting the requests for advisory opinions would be devised in the ECtHR in order to address this delay, but of course this would have a knock-on effect on the Grand Chamber's broader work and cause further delays in hearing the cases referred or relinquished to the Grand Chamber already. There is, thus, a real concern about the impact of advisory opinions on the workload of the Grand Chamber. Whilst the Court can usually manage its workload by rejecting applications for referral to the Grand Chamber and, in this case, not accepting requests for advisory opinions, this seems counterproductive. If the advisory opinion procedure is designed to enhance dialogue, one cannot imagine that the Court would refuse many requests. Indeed, should the Court refuse the request for an advisory opinion and find the case in question before it through an individual complaint following an autonomous interpretation of the Convention by the national court, one can imagine a cooling of dialogue and relations were the ECtHR to find that the national court – which had asked for, and been refused, an interpretation by Strasbourg – had erred in its application of the Convention.

---

[57] Advisory Opinion on Certain Legal Questions Concerning the Lists of Candidates Submitted with a View to the Election of Judges to the European Court of Human Rights (No. 1), 12 February 2008; Advisory Opinion on Certain Legal Questions Concerning the Lists of Candidates Submitted with a View to the Election of Judges to the European Court of Human Rights (No. 2), 22 January 2010.

The substantive concern about advisory opinions relates to their likely effects on the judgments of national courts. Although these advisory opinions would not be legally binding on the national courts that requested them, we might reasonably expect that a national court that requested such an opinion would be unlikely to reject the interpretation therein expressed, but much might depend on how the advisory opinions are written (whether at a level of generality or very precisely), whether a culture of judicial dialogue develops around these advisory opinions, and whether national courts actually develop a practice of requesting them at all. The success of the whole enterprise, then, will be very much dependent on how it is embraced, used, and engaged with by the domestic authorities, in this case the domestic courts.[58]

CONCLUSION

In many ways, these debates about the likely usefulness of the advisory opinion mechanism are microcosms of the debates about the effectiveness of the Convention that we have canvassed throughout this book. At the end of the day, the ECHR is a joint and collective enterprise by the Contracting Parties and the bodies of the Council of Europe. Its success relies not only on the approaches and interpretations of the Court, but also on the reception of the Convention in domestic systems, the willingness of states to enforce expectations of compliance with one another, and the extent to which the Convention, as enforced by the ECtHR, can and does strike a balance between the needs for effective rights protection, predictability and foreseeability of law, dialogue with national authorities, and evolution to govern novel and complex questions of contemporary governance. At times this has required innovation, either in the interpretation of the Convention or in the (remedial and procedural) tools available to the Court, but that innovation has brought criticism from states and other actors concerned that the Convention is being taken 'too far' by the Court. Resolving those tensions, whilst still protecting individual rights, is the core of the challenge faced by the Convention and, in essence, lies at the heart of almost all of the debates we have considered throughout this book.

FURTHER READING

de Londras and Dzehtsiarou, 'Mission Impossible? Addressing Non-execution through Infringement Proceedings in the European Court of Human Rights' (2014) 66 *International and Comparative Law Quarterly* 467.

Dzehtsiarou and Mavronicola, 'Relation of Constitutional Courts/Supreme Courts to the ECtHR' in *Max Planck Encyclopedia of Comparative Constitutional Law* (Oxford University Press, 2017).

---

[58] Dzehtsiarou and O'Meara, 'Advisory Jurisdiction and the European Court of Human Rights: A Magic Bullet for Dialogue and Docket-Control?' (2014) 34 *Legal Studies* 444.

Dzehtsiarou and O'Meara, 'Advisory Jurisdiction and the European Court of Human Rights: A Magic Bullet for Dialogue and Docket-Control?' (2014) 34 *Legal Studies* 444.

Helfer, 'Redesigning the European Court of Human Rights: Embeddedness as a Deep Structural Principle of the European Human Rights Regime' (2008) 19 *European Journal of International Law* 125.

Mowbray, 'An Examination of the European Court of Human Rights' Indication of Remedial Measures' (2017) 17 *Human Rights Law Review* 451.

Printed by Printforce, the Netherlands